My BIPOLAR JOURNEY

Harry Sadd

Copyright © 2019 by Harry Sadd
All rights reserved. No part of this book may be reproduced, scanned, or distributed in any printed or electronic form without permission.
First Edition: April 2019
Printed in the United States of America
ISBN: 1645500608
ISBN: 9781645500605

TABLE OF CONTENTS

Bipolar 1
Memories Of Childhood 4
Bears 13
Chapter 2 16
Of Cubs And Camp 27
Springtime 43
Hospital 53
Summer Frolics 54
Fade To Autumn 65
White Winters 76
Christmas 87
A Ten O'clock Scholar 98
The Play's The Thing 113
The Lake 124
Work And Play 138
Painter 155
Knights 169
O Come Let Us Adore Him ! 171
The Ten Commandments 172
St. Mary Magdelene 177
Stand And Be Counted 180
Family 182
Let It Snow 184
Holy Week 186
Motor Home 188

Painting	192
Tax Time	193
Tax Time 99	195
Landlord	198
The Decline And Fall Of Afordable Housing	200
On Her Blindness	205
Colonscopy	211
A Muffin For Breakfast	215
A New Cell	224
Enduring	235
A Ray Of Hope	255
Assault	262
Afterwards	279

BIPOLAR

In 1997 my eldest son was diagnosed with bipolar and admitted to Ledger House for treatment. At the interview with the doctor I was asked if anyone in the family had bipolar. It was at this point that I realized that it was me. I was bipolar. The years slipped by and I remembered the agony of being in River view mental hospital. At the time we were more concerned for our son than for me. As we struggled with his illness it was all we could do to keep our family afloat. It was a long time before we had any semblance of normality crept back into our lives. Even after we got home he would go out at night, at the strangest hours, and seemed to need no rest. By the time the fall term had arrived he was back to normal and passed grade 12 without any problem. Now we could relax and off he went to university. Alas it was not to be! He went manic again either through not taking his medication or just because he liked the high. He lived in a halfway house and tried to make ends meet. By this time he was on permanent disability so we did not have to contribute to his upkeep. He struggled through university going one year then being manic and missing the next. Finally, after ten years, he graduated and his mother and I were so proud of him. They kept changing his medication and by trial and error they finally got it right. There was no thought of him using his university degree but rather he settled on being a bridge director. Now, by the grace of God, he has achieved a measure of stability.

MENTAL PRISONS

My son and I played bridge to while the time,
And daffodils arose from frozen ground to climb.
Sweet scented hyacinth did bloom and spread,
Their fragrance then upon his curly head.

Through childhood's teary scrapes and joys we came,
Delighting in God's world we shared the same
Desires and read those books so rare and strange
Which on new places brought our minds to range.

The boy became a man so full of light,
My heart was singing with his promise bright.
But deep below the placid surface clear
Black currents of great power did appear.

Through night of blasted fear he roamed alone,
While helpless we who loved stood by the phone,
To hope and pray that one day will occur
A window clear within his sepulcher.

For three long years we fought so hard,
To keep the demon wraith outside our yard,
Till dank breath from fetid Mordor dim,
Stole from our son the light, upon a whim.

Now visions filled with fear torment his brain,
While we stand helpless, as they wind the chain,
Around his soul with drugs that twist and bend,
This once keen mind in knots that choke and rend.

Within the vale, sorrows dark delusion,
Comes Lucifer, lord of all illusion,
Drapes his beleaguered mind with lies,
Snares the soul with tempter's twisted ties.

    Now what of me. I remember the first time I went manic. It was March and the wind that howled seemed to flay may soul. I went from bad to worse. I slept little and felt that it was normal to get by on two or three hours sleep. I went from Nakusp to Victoria and the whole trip is a blur to this day. Once there I looked up my friend Denis and surprised him with my forthrightness. Next I went to our church and sang hymns or just nonsense I know not what until the priest came and took me to his study. There I casually admitted to having sex with his son. To say that he was shocked would be the understatement, but he had grown up in England and knew about boys. Above all this hung the seal of the confessional. I stayed the night and wound up going out to frighten some other friends of mine. In the morning they took me away to Riverview.

Now I was confined to a cell with nothing but a mattress in it. They had taken away all my possessions and I cried to the night but no one heard me. How long I was in this prison I know not. Eventually I was given my clothes back and returned to the open ward. They seemed anxious to talk about my disease but no one confronted the major issue. I was gay. I tried to run away and was brought back and eventually my mother came to me. Boy was I relived. Now I could get out of this horrid place. When I mentioned it to her she could not take me for I was committed involuntary, which meant that only the doctor could release me. I stamped off say I was going to kill myself. She hurriedly grabbed and nurse and found me calmed down.

Now it was back to the inside of that hated building, but the worst was yet to come. I had seen patients wheeled out of electro shock therapy flopping like a fish. The doctor insisted that I go through this process. There was no way out. Eventually I gave in and received several treatments though I don't recall how many. In May sometime I was released and determined not to ever go there again. In retrospect it was the worst thing that I could do. I was sent out into the world with no medication and a distinct lack of interest in finding out anything to do with bipolar. Flailing around in a morass of emotion I nevertheless continued on. One disaster followed upon another and in August I was summoned to the office of motor vehicles to have my license surrendered or to say otherwise. Upon opening my file he looked up at me and said, "You seem to have a very heavy foot." As that was what had happened I could not refute it. I said that I had bought a new car and that it would not go so fast. Please could I have my license. He agreed and I breathed a sigh of relief.

MEMORIES OF CHILDHOOD

I was five when we moved from Lumby to West Arrow Park where my father had taken a job hauling logs for Lloyd Gibson. In the gloom of a winter's evening we approached the cable ferry that connected East and West Arrow Park. We eased the converted army six by six onto the ramp while the dark stream gurgled under the bows. With the chains in place to prevent any untoward slide into the river, the motor whined, hauling in the cable that guided us to the other shore a quarter of a mile away. It was the first of many trips I would take on the cable ferries that connected the isolated communities with the outside world. As we neared the other shore the motor slowed, the ramps were lowered onto the landing, the chains were unshackled and off we went. Up the narrow winding road we crawled climbing under the shadow of Saddleback, the mountain that dominates the area. It must have been an omen of things to come for I have spent nearly all of my life trying to time my arrival so as to catch a ferry. If you missed one of these trips you had only to wait half an hour before the next trip while the ferries I catch today frequently leave you stranded for a couple of hours.

As the last light of a snowy winters day faded we arrived at the small house that would be our home for only a few months. I remember the snow crunching under our boots, cool and crisp, sparkling in the light of the trucks headlights. We unloaded a few boxes containing immediate necessities and entered the house. While mom held the flashlight dad lit the gas lamp and soon the glow from the mantles lit the room. Next came the fire to be started in an old tin heater. They were oval with a round lid, hinged at one side, with triangular vents at the bottom that allowed the air to enter freely and by which means the rate of burning could be controlled. Soon there was a huffing and puffing as the kindling crackled inside spreading the warmth throughout the room. It reached a roaring crescendo when suddenly the lid shot up into the air and a vast cloud of smoke entered the chamber. With a quick oath dad grabbed the poker and replaced the lid. The fire, having asserted it's independence from frail humanity, subsided to a dull roar which was assisted by closing the damper a little. It was my first encounter with these puffing dragons that would warm many of the houses we lived in.

With the gas lamp hissing quietly from it's hook in the ceiling mom lit the kitchen stove and began to cook supper. Half an hour later we gathered round the kitchen table to eat our hastily prepared meal and begin the process of moving in. In those days we stored our goods in an assortment of suitcases, steamer trunks and wooden butter boxes. It didn't take long to unpack all our worldly possessions as money was scarce and we were not encumbered with the electronic gadgets that families today find indispensable. Thus fed and unpacked we were hustled off to bed to snuggle under eiderdown comforters in a chilly bedroom.

In the morning we awoke early and got up after dad had lit the fires. After breakfast of hot "mush", our epithet for porridge, we pressed our noses up against the chilly window panes to get our first good look of our new surroundings. The air had cleared and the sun was just rising over the eastern mountains catching the new fallen snow which reflected the light like multifaceted diamonds. The fence posts that lined the road were topped with droopy caps of snow like pure white toques. The only marks on this pristine landscape were the tire treads where dad had driven the truck down the drive on his way to work. At the end of the drive the milkman had left two glass bottles whose contents had frozen forcing the milk out of the bottles, the caps perching precariously on top.

Eagerly we clambered into our snow suits to explore this winter paradise. Traipsing through the foot high snow we left trails of varying patterns wherever our explorations lead us. Falling in the snow we made angels by waving our arms and legs leaving imprints of ourselves to decorate the winter world. At last, tired and cold, we forsook our play to tramp into the house and shed our outer garments now covered with snow. Woolly mitts were shaken out and placed by the heater to dry while we took refuge in hot chocolate to warm our frozen hands and feet. Oh to be a child when winter clad 's our land !

As we had no relatives closer than England we made up for them by adopting our parents friends. Thus it was that Uncle Lloyd and Aunty Vi entered into our lives to become relatives in a way that our distant kin folk never could. It was only a short walk to their house and we would often go there to play in the horse barn creating make believe worlds from the comfort of the hay. When we were cold we could come into the warm kitchen where Aunty Vi would ply us with cookies and hot chocolate. In the barn we created a special place which we called "the bears den" where we could shelter from parents prying eyes and play at being kings or pirates, angels we were not ! One day we were awakened from sleep early in the morning by a knock on the door. Dad answered and soon came to inquire where we had stashed the left boots of the logging crew.

"Oh", we said. "They're in the bears den" After more coaxing we were persuaded to divulge the exact location of the missing footwear. We were never allowed to forget this incident and were often reminded of it long after we were grown.

Neither of our parents were churchgoers but they were more than content to let those who had firm beliefs take over the role of religious instruction. The result was that we went to United Church Sunday school, Roman Catholic camp and Anglican choir. Uncle Lloyd and Aunty Vi were staunch United Church members so we went to the little church in the village on Sundays while mom and dad stayed home to catch up on their reading. One Saturday it had snowed all day and we were delighted when Uncle Lloyd arrived on Sunday morning to take us to church in a horse drawn sleigh. We sat behind the box tucked up in blankets with Aunty Vi while Uncle Lloyd sat atop and handled the horse who pulled us at a fair clip along the icy roads. Except for the jangle of the harness there was no noise, not a single solitary mechanical sound interrupted our journey through the winter scene. It was like riding in one of those old fashioned Christmas cards. Tall firs and cedars lined the road covered in cloaks of snow like sentinel soldiers. The smaller birch and alder trimmed their nakedness with billowy dresses that clung to their branches as if to keep them warm. Icicles reflected the suns rays, gleaming brightly in a gallant attempt to ward off Jack Frost's bitter touch. As the forest slipped by we were transported to another world where, at any moment, we might see Peter and Sasha out in search of the wolf. The snow thrown up from the horses hooves swirled around us causing us to wrap the blankets tightly round while our cheeks now turned rosy red. We arrived at church flushed with excitement and sang our hymns of praise to God who made this world and all the wonders in it. Cheerfully we said good-byes after service and headed back into the mystery and silence of the kingdom of snow.

In the spring of the year we moved to the other side of the river and lost that close contact with the Gibsons though they were ever there to help when help was needed or to celebrate the milestones of our journey through life. My memories of the small house on the other side are few as we did not stay long. I remember getting up early to pick mushrooms which we fried for breakfast. Shortly after we moved in dad got us a puppy which thrilled my brother and I. We would play for hours with Smokey as we named him. But puppies, like life, are transitory and we lived close to the main road that ran from Nakusp in the north to Edgewood in the South. One morning we went out to play with Smokey and tried in vain to call him back as he chased the truck. There was a loud yelp and Smokey was thrown to the side of the road. We found him with his head on one side but he wouldn't move. With tears streaming down our faces we went to fetch dad who could surely help. It was not to be. We buried Smokey down by the river but we never forgot him. It was my first introduction to death and left a lasting impression and the knowledge that all life is transitory.

We remained in the house by the river until school began when we moved to Nakusp. The rented house was only a block from school and I could walk alone to the building that housed grades one to eight. Grade one was taught by a gray haired old spinster of the old fashioned school who taught the whole class by rote. I soon grew bored of going over lessons I had picked up the first time through so one day I decided to stay home and play with my brother. He was a year younger and didn't have to worry about such mundane matters, besides, I was too excited to go as I was going to a birthday party after school. We played in the vacant lot kitty cornered from our house. At two thirty my mother suddenly appeared to inquire why I wasn't in school.

"I didn't want to go." wasn't the right answer. I was given a choice. I could stay home form the birthday party or I could be spanked. With tears welling up in my eyes I opted to be spanked ; missing the party would have been unthinkable. I tried not to holler too loudly as mothers wooden spoon smacked my bare behind. Soon I was on my way to the party, a gift clutched tightly in my hands and an inclination to remain standing.

In October we were on the move again. It was tremendously exciting! We packed all our belongings and boarded the S.S. Minto, the old paddle wheeler that plied the Columbia from Arrowhead to Castlegar. The boat arrived about four in the afternoon and by five we were aboard and getting ready to eat in the dining room. They were elegant those old C.P.R. boats. There were linen napkins and table cloths, silver place settings that gleamed in the dim light while waiters hovered around to ensure you had all that you needed, all for a dollar a plate.

In the morning my brother and I were up early to watch the men cast off the gangplank. The whistle sounded and the large paddle at the rear began to turn. Slowly the old ship backed away from the dock, then slowly turned. The paddles stopped, the bows swung up the lake then the wheel recommenced in the opposite direction driving the Minto towards our new home at St. Leon. We were pulled away from this spectacle to eat but were soon nestled in two chairs aft watching the paddle wheel turn, endlessly throwing up drops of water that sparkled in the early autumn sunshine. At one time there were four of these beauties supplying the communities along the river but the Kettle valley railway meant that the main route from the Kootaneys to the coast no longer ran through the Arrow Lakes. We were slowly becoming a backwater country whose time had passed and where the pace of life would slow while the rest of the country roared ahead.

We stopped at Shorehome, the residence of the Herridges, long time member of parliament for the Kootaneys, then crossed the lake to Pinkston and finally we glided past Cape Horn and into the little harbour at St. Leon. When the Minto was retired in 1956 the little communities that had survived by transporting their goods to market on the boat withered. When the High Arrow dam was built in 1968 what was left was obliterated. Only the memory of these places remains stored in the memories of an older generation now rapidly dwindling.

St. Leon was dominated by the hotel that stood on the shore on the south side of the creek. It had once been a busy, thriving place, but now, in the autumn of 1952, it had faded, the exterior worn and weathered. We had a small place on the north side of the creek that was reached by a narrow road that passed over the bridge further upstream and wound its way back to the beach. Next door lived the Cusicks, our partners in this logging venture, and it was here that we would begin our life long association that would dominate my childhood memories. They had two boys, one five years older than me and the other half a year younger. Marty and Bruce were able to spend most of their time playing while we had to take our lessons by correspondence. In spite of this longing for the freedom of the little boys I enjoyed my schooling and began my lifelong pursuit of books. There were no televisions and even the radio reception was poor so there was little else to do of a long winter evening than to sit close to the fire and read. I remember my mother reading history and geography to me. One story was about a class that travelled in a flying boat all over the world. We travelled along the Amazon and visited the jungles then took off for the pampas of Argentina. It was marvellous stuff! I was reading a book about the early life of an Iroquois boy and mother helped me with words like "wigwam' and "wampum". No longer was I constrained by the slower members of my class and I could soar along at my own pace. In the six months that we lived here I completed grade one and had a good start on second grade.

Life here was simple and primitive. The house consisted of three rooms, a kitchen, living room dining room combination and two small bedrooms. There was an outhouse at the back and no running water or electricity. There were also no telephones so life went on quietly. Only the cry of the birds or the occasional logging truck broke the silence. Water was fetched by the bucketful from the nearby creek and heated on the kitchen stove while coal oil and gas lamps provided light. The gas lamps were similar to today's camping lanterns only they had two mantles and were filled with white gas and pumped by hand to obtain the necessary pressure. The mantles were flexible when new and were tied around the throat of the lamp with string. Pump up the bottom, turn on the gas and Presto ! Light! A nice bright light that hissed gently as the gas burned. Once the mantels had been burned they became fragile and one gentle touch was all that was required to dissolve them completely. They were very tempting targets for small fingers and we were yelled at more than once for poking the gauzy filaments.

A standard feature of all the houses we lived in was the wood pile with it's attendant chopping block. Dad would come home from work and heft the heavy double bitted axe, splitting the large blocks of tamarack and fir. I would marvel at the way the wood came so neatly apart at the centre but soon I was too busy hauling the wood to watch. Once the wood box inside the house had been filled the balance was stacked against the house where mom could easily reach it when her supply ran low. Everything had to be done by hand. We hauled water, boiled water and did loads of wash in galvanized tubs with a scrub brush and washboard. The tubs also served as bathtubs for the bath we took twice a week. They were round, about two feet high with a diameter of perhaps three or three and a half feet and my brother and I could sit inside together. Our parents were less fortunate having to wind themselves in and wash by degrees. Since there were no shops, all our food was delivered by the Minto on her twice weekly visitations, everything we ate had to be cooked at the kitchen stove. Mother managed to juggle cooking, looking after a baby and my younger brother, teaching school and cleaning in that era of no home appliances.

Shortly after we arrive it was Halloween and we had all been invited over to the hotel where the Gates family had a party. I remember the tall dining room blazing with light, actually lit by electricity provided by a portable generator. Various foods were set out on the table and my mouth watered as I gazed on the delectable treats. After this feast the greatest treat of all, a fireworks display. I had never seen such a show before and the glow of the sparklers and the explosion of the Roman candles burst onto my mind burning the images indelibly into my memory. Last of all came a number of large Catherine wheels that spun gloriously around lighting the grounds and reflecting off the still surface of the lake. It wasn't a large display but it is the one I remember most vividly today though I have seen many a great display since then. It was the beginning of many eventful Halloweens that would appear as the years wore on.

The next day we all trooped down to the ferry landing to meet dad's oldest brother, Uncle Nor, who was arriving on the Minto. He came off the boat looking much as I imagined he would and there was a great reunion. Uncle Nor had not seen his brother since 1946 when I was a babe in arms; my brother and sister he had never seen. I remember them talking long into the night as I drifted of to sleep the conversation humming in my ears. How we all managed in that small house I will never know but manage we did. It was great to have a real uncle with us, his presence connecting us with our roots back in England. I remember sitting on his boots while he bounced us up and down.

One exciting day dad came in and announced that I might go to Nakusp with him and Uncle Nor in the launch. The morning dawned cool and clear and we set out for the dock to get the boat ready. While we were doing this an even more astounding event took place, a float plane landed noisily and taxied up to the dock. The adults talked and shared local gossip while I admired the aircraft. Shortly thereafter dad came to me and asked if I would like to fly in the plane to Nakusp. Would I !! It was a dream come true! Soon I was in the passengers seat strapped down and ready for take off. The engine revved up and soon we were skimming along the surface of the lake, then suddenly we were in the air. The engine noise died down and we gained altitude. It was a lovely view looking down on the cliffs and shores while boats on the lake were reduced to mere toys. It was only a thirteen mile trip and all too soon it was over. Now the hard part began.

    I had to wait a couple of hours for the slower launch to arrive. It seemed like forever as I paced the wharf looking out upon the lake and the mountains that towered seven thousand feet above me. Finally they arrive and I was able to get something to eat. Our shopping done we began our return trip. We had just rounded the point of land that formed the harbour and the craggy cliffs of Cape Horn were in view when the motor died. To an impatient six year old it seemed we drifted for hours while dad and Uncle Nor tinkered with motor. Finally we were on our way again but it was dark by the time we arrived and I was one tired lad.

BEARS

With the coming of autumn came the bears. While black bears are usually shy and reticent we had one who continued to haunt the gully behind our house where we dumped our garbage. Bears scavenge at this time of year and the weather was mild so it had obviously decided to hang around and fatten up. One day my brother arrived next door at the Cusicks and told Marion in awed tones.

"Marion. There's a bear outside."

She thought that he was pretending and said." That's all right you run along and play with the bears."

"But Marion there really is a bear outside." he said the tears welling up in his large brown eyes.

She went out and not ten feet from the house stood a large bear tearing at the bark from an old stump. There was no one around but Marion and my mother as the rest of the men were back in the bush some five miles away where the logging site was. We were kept inside and eventually the bear ambled off but for a few days we were warned not to go far outside and not to enter the bush behind the house. One day the bear reappeared but this time one of the loggers was around and he shot it.

Bears are fine in the wild but when they start to live behind your house they become unwelcome guests, particularly if you have young children. In the manner of children's memories I remember clearly the name of the man who shot the bear, Jack Lang. I'm not sure why his name has remained with me to this day because I didn't know him well and we never saw him after we left St. Leon.

After Uncle Nor left life returned to normal with the three of us building hidey places where we could shelter from the prying eyes of adults. I'm convinced that deep down in the core of our being there is a fundamental desire for fire. When we were children fire was a necessity ; it warmed our houses, cooked our food and gave us light. Even today when I take city children on hikes they are fascinated by an open fire stirring the embers and playing with smoking brands. We were even more intrigued and, having the opportunity, took advantage of it. Matches were abundant and were used constantly by our parents to light cigarettes, fires and gas lamps. We managed to purloin some matches and took them to our hidey hole where we had an old pot in which we lit the flaming ends. Fortunately it was too wet at that time of year to be a fire hazard and I only remember the thrill of obtaining a light from one of the long wooden matches. Inevitably we were discovered. We were given a lecture about the dangers of uncontrolled fires and spanked for stealing the matches.

It was a very mild winter and what little snow that fell was wet and sloshy and didn't stay long. In the middle of December the Cusicks moved up to the logging camp and we were without our soulmate. The camp where the logs were cut was five miles up the mountain and I remember visiting and marvelling at the quantity of snow. Bruce and Ted were so lucky to have feet of the stuff while we languished below with a mere pittance. It was on one of those visits that I encountered steam toys. Teddy had a steam engine that you filled with water then lit an alcohol burner and placed it under the boiler. Pretty soon the water was gurgling and giggling then the piston began to move turning the flywheel which you could connect to other gadgets. It was indeed an altogether marvellous toy.

At Christmas came a wonderful surprise. When the Minto docked one small Labrador puppy disembarked and entered into our lives. She was black with a white slash underneath, a docked tail and an appetite second to none. We loved her and she helped to fill the void where Smokey had been and eased the loneliness and isolation of our lives. I'm not sure whether the bear had anything to do with her arrival but her barking would have frightened any animal.

Now that we were the only family left on the shore dad would often arrive in the truck with no one to help him trip the stakes. That was how I came to learn the tricky art of knocking the pins from the stakes that held the towering load of logs. A logging truck has four pieces of iron appropriately called "bunks" that cradle the logs while they are on the truck. By means of a cable and pin arrangement it is possible to trip either set of bunks. I'd have a hammer and stand at the cab end of the truck with my heart pounding while dad took the peeve and counted to three. On the count of three we would hit the pins hard and the stakes on the opposite side that were holding the logs on the truck came down. The logs rolled off the truck and entered the water with a thunderous crash. It was a little nerve wracking to stand directly under all those logs and when the pins were punched I moved back quickly. I could not understand at the time why my father took the rear end where the logs were smaller. Now I realize that if a log was going to swing it would be the lighter end that would come towards us. After I had recovered from the thrill of the moment we would stand back and watch the logs roll down the skid way and into the lake. Often all the logs didn't roll off and dad would have to take his peeve and manually persuade the recalcitrant timber to enter the water. All in all it was an experience calculated to speed up the heart rate of one small boy. I'm afraid that today there would be three union bosses complaining of unfair labor practices while the department of Social Services was hauling me into custody and charging my father with endangering his son. Life was simpler then, everyone pitched in to help and we needed everyone's hands.

In February or March of 1953 the resort hotel at Halcyon Hot Springs burned down. It was one of many hot springs that bubble out of the ground at temperatures near the boiling point. Dad spent a couple of weeks there as caretaker but we were nearing the end of our stay. He had cancer and was much sicker than anyone realized. In April we packed all our belongings once more and waited for the arrival of the Minto. We often wanted to get across the creek to go to the Hotel on the other side and I usually took the short cut by walking on a log that spanned the creek near the house. This saved me at least half a mile and I had done it so often I could do it in my sleep. Just before the boat arrived I took one more passage; and fell in ! My parents were not amused as all the clothes were packed and I had to be changed on the beach

CHAPTER 2

Everything was changed. Mom and dad were not there anymore because dad had to have an operation in Vancouver. It was not until much later that I learned that he had cancer and that he very nearly died. All we knew was that we stayed with Merve and Marion while our parents were away. Well that was nothing new. We had often stayed with friends before so this was just another of those interludes, besides, Marion was great fun and we loved her. Bruce, Marty and I were able to play together all the time now without the bother of visiting. We were given boundaries within which we were allowed the freedom to explore as we desired. The house was situated on the lake about two miles south of Nakusp and was reached by the main highway, a narrow, windy gravel road, that wound on down the lake. We were forbidden to go onto the road or down to the lake without supervision but the grass is always greener on the other side. After we had explored all of our side of the road we just had to cross it. Teddy caught us and we were hauled back to be smacked with a wooden spoon. It didn't make Teddy our favourite friend.

The biggest change was school. Now I was flung back into the regular classroom setting where I had not progressed far enough to keep up with the grade two students. I was dumped back to grade one where I stagnated for the rest of the term. It was a bitter pill to have my exploration of the world of books confined to Dick and Jane when more challenging works had been my staple fare. Boredom has it's consequences and I began to resort to other areas to amuse myself. We were provided with scissors for an art project and I levered in the fine cutting edge. The teacher droned on and I began to be tempted. The boy in front of me had suspenders and it would be tempting to see how these things worked on a really challenging assignment. I cut

Wayne's suspenders. He began to cry and when the teacher came to investigate she was angry. She tore off my suspenders and gave them to Wayne which then reduced me to tears. The years have come and gone but whenever we meet again I am reminded about them, like Rudyard Kipling I am told "Don't forget the suspenders, best beloved."

We received letters from mom, who was always a good writer, but I remember little of what passed between Marion and mom in what was a difficult time. I remember the day when I was told that mom had bought a house just up the hill from Cusick's and I was allowed to cross the road and climb the steep path that lead to the house. Crescent Bay road wound its way around the side of the mountain providing access to the homes and farms. It angled left from the highway just south of the bridge that crossed Nakusp creek. For half a mile it wound going gently up until it reached the point where the trail to Cusick's ended, then it took a hairpin turn snaking back across the steep banks before finally reaching a small plateau half a mile further up. As you can see by the pattern we were not inclined to go by the road when trails cut through turns shaving miles off a journey at the cost of climbing almost vertically up the slopes. I reached the road puffing and out of breath and completed the climb around the bend of the road. To my right a road ran off to the nearby farm and directly in front of me was our driveway now overgrown with weeds. The property we were to live in was bounded by the curve in the road and the house had not been lived in for some time. I waded through bracken ferns five feet tall until I stood gazing at the old log house.

I plowed my way through the thimble berries, their hard woody stems tearing at my hands and arms. Soon I was standing on a small patch of lawn looking up at the huge birch trees that stood sentinel watch over the house. The logs from which it was constructed were brown and dusty from age and the dust raised by the cars. The eaves were huge jutting out five or six feet on the ends and swooping low on the sides to enclose two verandas. There was a small patch of lawn in front of the house with a stream running through the middle. The roof of the back veranda nearly touched the bank and, cut into that bank, was a flight of stones steps that lead to the woodshed. The rest of the back yard was a wilderness of bracken and thimble berry with one trail leading to the garbage dump. Houses had their own spots to dump refuse in those days and as the contents were mainly tin cans there were seldom any problems. The West side veranda had a creaky wooden deck that overlooked the lake below and the mountains across the lake. All together it was a charming spot. The house was built entirely of logs with leaded glass windows across the two western corners of the building. One southern window in the kitchen and a smaller one on the eastern side, an even smaller window in the galley, one on the north side for the bathroom and two higher up on the ends where bedrooms snuggled in the attic. I rambled around the house peering in the windows but failed entirely to pierce the Stygian gloom.

 The old house would not easily yield all her secrets. Having satisfied my curiosity and sensing that I could go no further I began poking around the woodshed. It was empty. I began picking raspberries from canes that grew on the top of a rotting pile of shingles when I noticed something crawling up my leg. One bite then another convinced me that I was in the wrong place and I ran back down the trail as fast as I could brushing off the ants whose nest I had disturbed, and whose bites were now itching abominably.

 Fridays were times of pure magic for that was when we all piled into the old Ford Prefect and headed out for town to watch a movie. The shows were held in the Legion hall, where for a dime, a child could watch two hours of pure entertainment. There were news clips followed by an assortment of cartoons and a travel log of distant lands.. Sometimes the travel films were better than the main show but when the previews arrived you knew the introductions were over. The main event was about to begin. There were cowboy films where the Indians were always the bad guys and the hero managed to escape in the nick of time. Luciele Ball and Desi Arnez paraded their hilarious antics on the big screen while an assortment of war films and comedies were common fare. When we were older a proper movie theatre was built and it cost a whole quarter to see a movie. You were guaranteed to get your moneys worth. If the feature film was only an hour and a quarter long the balance of two hours would be filled. It's a far cry from today when I took my two boys to the movie and it cost twenty dollars for an hour and a quarter ! Sic transit gloria mundi.

At long last mom and dad arrived back in Nakusp and we moved into our new home. We piled out of the car which was parked on a flat section next to the wood shed above the house. Looking down we could see the shake roof which curved over the porch. Excitedly we ran down a short flight of stone steps cut into the rock garden and waited in the porch who's eaves were level with the driveway. At last we were permitted to enter. Reaching up dad pulled the string that turned on the light. There was the kitchen with it's wood stove nestled against the interior wall while a small window shed what little light from the porch onto a counter. There were two sets of windows in the kitchen, one facing the rockery and porch which did little to light the place for the eaves were low and the hill to the east was high. The South side window allowed the most sunlight but even that was dulled by the large, low eaves and two large birch trees that grew close to the house. Here in the brightest part of the room we took our meals on a kitchen table dad built. We could gaze out and watch the birds or see the squirrels chase each other up the birch tree.

To the right of the door was a narrow pantry with a sink set under a small window overlooking the north yard; a flattish piece of land now overgrown with thimble berry which faded into the forest. Beside the pantry was the bathroom which was entered by stepping over a beam! Under the stairwell dwelt an old enamel tub and behind it was a real flush toilet. The window opened out while a small sink occupied the corner on the east wall. Beside the bathroom a door fashioned from one by six lead upstairs. An archway led into the living room with it's rock fireplace. Across the south- west corner of the room were two leaded glass windows. Another door on the West side led directly to the veranda with it's view of Saddleback and the lake. The master bedroom occupied the north-west section of the house and it too had leaded glass windows placed across the corner.

We were to occupy the upstairs were two rooms nestled among the eaves. As there was no door between the rooms the three of us lived in community. You could stand upright in the middle but the roof of the house swept down to a mere three feet at the walls. It was here in the south bedroom that my brother and I slept., the beds nestled close to the window while we could reach up and touch the eaves. I often was lulled to sleep by the gentle patter of rain falling on the roof two feet from my head. The only heating devices were the kitchen stove and the fireplace, so winter mornings could be a little chilly.

The house had been built by Nels Pedderson and he was obviously a short man. Nells had obviously run out of logs or energy and decided that it was time to roof it off.

The doors were only five foot eight while some of the beams supporting the ceiling hung down around five foot ten. This didn't bother dad who was five foot six or mom who was five foot four but it posed a problem for us in our teenage years. Dad used to say, "When you're too big for the house it'll be time for you move out on your own." For the time being it was perfect and much larger than the little shacks that we had occupied for the previous couple of years.

The yard outside had been neglected but here and there blossoms sprang forth in spite of the weeds that crowded around. A little creek, about six inches wide, drained the water that dripped from the rock garden or rockery as it was known. Mom spent a lot of time that first summer trying to restore a semblance of order to the neglected flowers. The lawn was contained in a small patch between the rockery, the slope and the bank. This bank was steep and dropped off where the west veranda ended, leaving a five foot drop that separated the level of the house from the next plateau just above the road.. One enormous birch tree stood towering over the yard where the sloped area met the drop off while another grew in front of the living room window and threatened to collide with the eaves.

The remainder of the property stretched a quarter of a mile to the road and was a jungle of bracken, thimble berries and small trees just waiting to be explored. Being on a hillside everything was built in terraces with large level spaces being at a premium. By climbing the stone steps from the back porch the woodshed and parking lot could be reached. It was on this level that we planted our garden, everyone had a vegetable garden of some sort in those days. We diligently turned the stony soil and fertilized it with loads of chicken manure from the Waterfield's farm. Half way up the drive there stood another colossal birch tree that towered high above the firs and cedars and on whose branches we hung the swing. Alone in the middle of the bracken stood a cedar tree whose many branches invited us to climb higher and higher until we could look down on the house from our lofty perch. The area north of the house was less accessible and we didn't often venture there until we were older. Between the upper road and our back jungle was a very boggy area where our well was located so were forbidden to explore this area. We were also forbidden to cut down trees here and as the construction of log cabins was one of our major pursuits the area soon lost any attraction it might otherwise have obtained.

At the top of the drive where Crescent Bay Road wound around our property there was a small triangle of land bounded by the roads from our place to Waterfield's and the main Crescent Bay road. This enabled people coming from the farm and approaching the main road to turn either way without making a hairpin turn. Standing in this triangle we looked east where there was a steep bank covered with bracken that summoned us to conquer or die. Like Hillary and Tensing we set out on our intrepid attempt to scale the heights. With much slipping and sliding we forced our way up the hill pushing aside the three foot ferns. At last we gained the top only to be confronted with a barbed wire fence. Fences are meant for cattle and small boys are exempt from their warnings. We slipped between the wire and gazed down on that which we had conquered. Fifty feet below us the road lay and we could now see cars rumbling in a cloud of dust on the main road, not that there were too many cars in those days. The mink farmers truck, the Waterfield's Landrover and our own Prefect were the only vehicles regularly on the road, the remaining residents making do with "shanks pony".

We could see our house only if we were on the lip of the bank so that, once inside, we were in our own private world. The clearing behind had once been a small pasture, about fifty feet wide and two hundred long, but it was now overgrown with bracken and small cedar trees. Wild strawberries peeped out from under grasses and we spent the next little while filling our tummies with nature's bounty. It took a lot of patience to gather a small handful, but when the berries hit your mouth they left an irresistible urge to gather more. In this fashion we explored the small field that would be one of our favorite hideouts. There was only a small gap in the trees where we had climbed through, the rest of the field being surrounded by trees that made it seem like our own private kingdom. No adults were inclined to brave the steep climb so we were free to build our cabins or play at being warriors of some fierce tribe of South Pacific natives or fierce Indians out for scalps in a bloody war party. When a group of us got together we would have wars hurling the spear like bracken at each other in mock battles. When we tired of these games we would sit at the gap watching the boats on the lake while chewing on the sweet ends of coot grass.

Once or twice a week that first summer we would get into the old Prefect and head for town to pick up the mail and groceries. The old road wound along the side of the hill through the forest until it opened up at the orchard. Now we could see the lake through the lines of cherry and apple that had once been the mainstay of the economy. Now the orchards were dwindling as the river traffic dried up but they were still plentiful if a bit unkempt. Past Cann's house, round the corner past more fruit trees and on to the junction of the main road three quarters of a mile from our house. The main road ran parallel to the lake, a fifty mile track of gravel and dust connecting Nakusp with the smaller communities at Arrow Park, Burton, Needles, Fauguier and Edgewood. We crossed the bridge over Nakusp creek where we often went fishing then on past the gravel pit to the bay where the dredge was anchored. The Leary's had a house on the East side and in the summer you could hear her playing the organ hooked up to speakers so that the music reached to all parts of town.. On past the tug boats that rounded up the wood for Celgar then on up the hill to the main street.

The lower half of the town was on the lake level so this was where most of the industry gathered. The largest outfit was Celgar with it's sawmill and beside it was the Bell pole yard. A train came in three times a week to pick up the finished products and I still remember the sound of it's steam whistle as it crossed the road. Further east was the government wharf where the Minto docked and two or three private boats moored. The steep bank sheltered a motel and several houses but the main settlement was on top of the plateau that ran between the lake and Kooskanacks creek. To the east of the road was the best piece of black, loamy soil in the country where Chris Spicer ran a market garden. Half way up the hill the road levelled off before climbing steeply up the bank to Brouse and Glenbank. Here we turned West along the main street of the town which was actually paved ! The only chunk of blacktop for a hundred miles in either direction.

Like most small towns all the shops and business were located on the main street. There were a couple of blocks of houses then the Pine Lodge and it's attendant cabins occupied a block. Next door was the vacant lot where a variety of old cars and trucks were left to rust. It was a great place to spend an afternoon pretending to drive and shifting gears while making the appropriate noises. Br room. Shift up. Broom. Next gear. On all the way to top before descending again. Opposite this on the south side was the Esso station with the Grill cafe nestled close beside. Doyles meat market completed the block while on the opposite side was the Bluebird cafe where a nickel would buy a cup of coffee or an ice cream cone. Our first stop was next door to the Shell station where mom and dad always bought their gas. I never remember them ever stopping at another station.

We parked the car next to Joy's grocery where they rented freezers. We often rented one of these to store half a deer or a quarter of a cow, home refrigerators in those days weren't far removed from their icebox origins, besides, the power used to go out frequently. Shopping done we'd walk past the men's store, the hardware the telephone exchange and the drug store before crossing the street to the post office. The bank building was the most impressive building in town and housed the post office as well. On the upper floor the Masons met. We were now in the center of town and the side street north of the bank boasted the bakery, the movie theater and the legion hall. On the south end overlooking the lake was the Leland hotel, the towns lone hotel and bar. Beside the hotel was Al Butt's jewelry store and the Overwaitea while on the opposite side Hoshasaki operated the dry cleaners. The police station and liquor store occupied most of the block opposite the Overwaitea. The town's sole R.C.M.P. officer operated in digs that doubled as a court room and cells, where the town drunks could sleep it off when life at the pub got out of hand. Next to the constabulary were the town's three churches, Anglican, Roman Catholic and United, gathered together in a harmony that was common in small towns. They had a duty to the spiritual well being of the townsfolk and rarely embarked on stealing sheep from each others flocks.

From this point the town spread out for four or five blocks northward until one came to the elementary school at the northwest corner tucked in close to the forest. It was there that I would spend the rest of my school years and I often wished the school were closer to home. In those days the high school, grades nine to twelve, was further south, next to Saddle Mountain Cabins. The hospital was well sheltered in the south-west corner overlooking the lake. The only other buildings near were the doctors house and one or two others. Only the park and recreation grounds were found further on along the road that led to the dump. That was the centre of our existence for the next twelve years, a total of maybe two thousand souls living in town or on scattered farms. While life was interesting for us it must have been difficult for mom and dad. He had to live without his bowel and most of his intestines which caused him to be somewhat irritable at times. Still they soldiered on and, as being idle was not one of dad's vices, he began by raising rabbits. He had taken agriculture at one of the English colleges and after his experiences of farming in the Okanagan was prepared to make do with what little we had. At least we had a roof over our heads and some property on which to begin a new endeavour.

Rabbits multiply in the most amazing fashion so it was not long before we had two dozen of the little furry things running around the woodshed. When they were six months old we began eating them. Mom managed to dig out any number of recipes for rabbit; stewed, baked,broiled or stuffed. They were a welcome change from eggs which was our other staple. I never remember having any qualms about killing and eating the various animals we brought to the table and it is only recently that people who live in cities have begun to decry the killing of animals. The further away from the farm we live the more inclined we become to personify the food we all depend on. One way or another we managed to obtain enough food, though we never had the quantity or variety of foods that my children have today.

In those days my hero was the Lone Ranger whose deeds of daring thrilled my imagination. Television was unknown so we used to listen to the weekly broadcast on the radio. Once a week when the program aired we were allowed to stay up half an hour later till eight thirty. My brother and I snuggled down in mom and dad's bed, where the radio resided, and waited for the strains of Thychoskie's melody to break forth. Reception wasn't always clear as we lived in the valley surrounded by mountains but at night the signal bounced in all the way from San Francisco. I particularly enjoyed the music and could imitate the entire piece as I roamed through the woods or roared down the trail to Cusicks.

One spring when I was eight or nine I was in high spirits as I made my way down the steep trail. There was no school and we were all going to Arrow Park for the district track meet. I began my Lone Ranger theme song, which could be heard for a mile in all directions, as I ran full tilt down the trail. Something went wrong that day and I fell. My shout of triumph changed to a wail of pain as I gashed my knee on a rock. I picked myself up and began to make my way slowly down the trail. I was met half way down by Teddy who had been sent to see what was wrong when my song changed. I was taken in and fussed over by Marion who cleaned the wound and taped it up. Thus patched and cleaned we all piled into the car for the trip down the lake. I still have a scar on my knee that has remained to this day as it would probably have been stitched up today.

One day in the fall I decided to try and chop kindling. The only ax available to me was dad's double bit ted one which was rather heavy for a seven year old to handle. Cedar is easy to split and I managed to chop a fair pile before the blade slipped and cut my finger. Off I went to get patched up. Band-Aids were a necessary part of our existence as cuts, scrapes and bruises abounded with two active boys. I was forbidden to use the big ax and as there was no other tool to use my chopping days came to a brief halt. That Christmas I was delighted for there, under the tree, was an ax of my own. With it I progressed from cutting kindling to chopping wood for the house. That was it's primary raison d'être but it provided much more entertainment in the woods around us. With it we chopped down trees, built cabins and stripped limbs from trees to make paths through the woods. If a road wound along the face of a cliff our motto was "up and over". That way we could shorten the distance to any destination at the cost of hauling ourselves up steep inclines. If we hurried we could often beat a car to the destination.

When we were small chopping down even small trees was a chore which was managed by sharing the axe. The outer part of the tree is fairly soft so we would chop all around it much like a beaver. If all else failed once you had cut most of the way through you could always push it over. We populated the woods around us with beaver-like stumps, and in the process, learned how to care for and better utilize this most versatile of instruments. It also doubled as a hammer as we were not permitted to use dad's tools in any of our constructions. We scrounged nails from old boards using whatever came to hand in our effort to build bigger and better cabins.

If the weather was nice we were outside playing in the trees or building the hideouts that enabled us to feel free from adult constraints. There were different activities according to the seasons but most of our spare time was spent in the fresh air devising new schemes for entertainment. When I look at the time my children spend indoors with a variety of electronic gadgets it makes me realize just how far removed this generation is from ours. We still lived in that era when pioneers abounded and you could talk to live people who were the first to do things or settle this part of the world. Now we gather in concrete pillions, one on top of the other, so that a trip to the park is an occasion not the way life is lived. I'm not sure if this is progress.

OF CUBS AND CAMP

When I turned eight I joined the cub pack which was run by Fr. Smith, the Catholic priest. He was a great cub master and understood small boys catering to our need for rambunctious entertainment. Our meetings began with sixes collecting dues of a nickel a boy then we all formed a circle for the wolf howl. "We'll dib,dib, dib." the leader intoned and we all hollered back, We'll dob, dob, dob. "We took our promise to do our best to do our duty to God and the queen in an age of religious and secular obligation. After this we gathered in groups to study for the various levels of achievement from tenderfoot to two star proficiency. Our work done we turned our attention to games. One of our favourites was British Bulldog where one of the older cubs got to be the dog. On a signal the pack attempted to gain the safety of the other side of the hall before being intercepted and hoisted off the floor. The first person caught now joined the dogs and sought out others to raise off the floor. At the end there were usually one or two larger boys who were left to face the massed pack in a frenzied attempt to escape. Often it took four of us to raise the last cub, kicking and struggling off the floor. It was a great way to release energy!

There were quieter and more subtle games like Kim's game. Here a tray of objects was presented to the group for a brief glance before being covered up. Now everyone had to list as many objects as they could remember from the assortment. It was good training in observation. Another game we liked involved a soft shoe tied to a piece of rope. Everyone stood around in a circle while the rope was twirled around and around. You had to jump over the rope as it twirled higher and higher until it snagged someone. Once tangled you were out and the rope swing began until only a couple of boys were left. Patience and endurance were taught in another way. Everyone lined up in a circle, put their hands on their knees and closed their eyes. one boy was chosen to sneak around the circle, with a slipper to smack a victims bottom. Once struck the victim chased the hitter around the circle. If caught before reaching the empty place he was bent over and smacked. If he made it home safely he became the hunter and prowled around selecting the next victim. There was a large temptation to cheat by peeking but the leaders were on guard to ensure that cheaters were punished.

During the winter these activities took place at St. Mark's Anglican hall which was opposite the Catholic church ; St. Mark's Anglican was on the south side of main street. After games we all gathered round for campfire. This was accomplished by "setting a fire" with a flashlight under the wood and coloured paper above to provide the appropriate illusion. Every "six" took turns at providing the entertainment. We also sang songs or had passages from Kipling's ' The Jungle Book ' read. Every cub knew the story of Mowgli. My parents had read this to us at an early age and I can still recall having nightmares about Sher Khan sticking his head inside the wolf den and asking for the 'man cub '. Our leaders were named Akela, for the leader of the wolf pack, Baloo for the brown bear and Baghera for the panther who paid the price for the acceptance of the boy into the pack. Thus shrouded in lore and learning we set about the task of becoming better cubs as we progressed through the stages of wolf and man.

This was all training for the real thing when we would be free in the summer to put our skills to use in the outdoors. Everyone had a knife of some sort and learned how to sharpen it and carve a variety of items. Whittling was serious business. I remember having several knives that managed to get lost at inconvenient times. When spring arrived and the snow had melted we took our first hike outdoors packing wieners to roast over an open fire. Fires were serious business when I was young and you had to learn to set one because without it you could freeze or fail to cook your food. There were no camp stoves, motor homes or other modern conveniences to assist in those days. Make a fire or get cold and eat your food raw was the order of the day. Our knives were put to good use whittling shavings and peeling birch bark with which to light our campfires. Often boxes of wooden matches perished in early attempts to start a fire. By the time we had been elevated to scouts we could all start fires in almost any circumstance. Each "six" had their own fire and gathered around to cook. There is nothing like a wiener roasted over an open fire after a long hike. I still prefer my hot-dogs cooked this way.

After our meal it was time to play games of flags or prisoners base. The pack was divided into two groups who were given different coloured pieces of rag to tuck into their belts. You were allowed to tuck the flag in, not tie it tight. It had to come loose easily though be tight enough to stay while engaged in frantic running. We then dispersed to hunt the opposing team and gather their flags. Once your flag was captured you were taken to the opposing camp where you could be freed only by being touched by a member of your own team. Since the camps were well guarded this was difficult requiring plenty of stealth. The team with the most prisoners at the end of an hour or so was declared the winner.

That first summer was marvellous. I was so excited because the cubs were going on a two day camp to the Hot Springs. This was my first experience of camping and I counted down the hours as I waited impatiently for the time of departure. At last the big day arrived and dad drove me off with my sleeping bag and clothes neatly packed in his old army duffle bag. We arrived at Preemption where there was a collection of cabins at the head of the trail. Most of the cubs put their gear on the horses but the older boys, who had been there before, opted to pack their own gear. By nine o'clock we were packed and ready to depart. I remember staying with the horses in the group that trailed along at the rear but there were other groups that set out ahead and reached the springs well before we did. The trail wound around the mountain following the creek but much higher up. Occasionally we could hear the roar of water but soon we were high above the creek and only our voices and the steady clop of the horses hooves disturbed the silence. It was a beautiful warm summers day in July as we walked the narrow trail where the sunlight filtered down through the forest. Occasionally we crossed corduroy bridges that spanned small creeks sometimes stopping to drink the crystal clear water. Soon we were walking along a narrow way with banks that dropped steeply off to our left while the mountain seemed to loom over us on the right. Half an hour later the path narrowed and a sheer cliff dropped a thousand feet to the creek below. We had reached the precipice and the quarter way point in our journey. Twenty minutes later we were back to the wider trail where streams ran their courses cloaked with devils club and fern. I gazed in awe at the spiky plant that grew six feet tall with large leaves shaped like maples but studded with huge thorns. The plant is aptly named. On we went climbing steeply up a shady path before plunging down the other side always managing to climb a little higher. Where the trail was particularly wet corduroy bridges had been constructed to keep ones feet at least slightly dry. An hour later we came upon two small log cabins and here we rested for a while. I asked if we were nearly there and was told that this was Halfway. My heart sank at the thought of the long journey yet to go. Fortunately the trail became flatter and the walking was easier. At last, after what seemed like an eternity, someone gave a shout. They could hear the falls ! Soon the noise of a waterfall sounded clearly over the clop of the hoses hooves. The trail split and we took the lower path and soon found ourselves in clear sunshine again. We had arrived !

  The Hot Springs nestled in a small clearing hard up against the east side of the mountain. As a result the sun rose late and set early. Now it was bathed in noonday sun as we filed past the cabins before stopping at the round house. Here the horses were unpacked and we grabbed our gear and headed out to find a cabin. Our 'six' found shelter in one of the cabins that lined the edge of the clearing on the south side tucked gently into the forest and above the round house. Dark green firs hung over the cabins climbing in endless tiers up the steep mountain side. From the cabin door I looked over the springs that bubbled out of the ground at a hundred and eighty degrees Fahrenheit. Beyond them the Kuskanax roared endlessly singing her symphony of nature as her waters rushed down from the mountains above. Steam hung around the buildings and a sulphurous smell hung on the air permeating the camp. The river ran quickly filling the air with a constant roar but we soon grew accustomed to it and it became just part and parcel of the whole experience. Beyond the round house three other cabins stood, the sun shining brightly on the weathered logs where they faced the pool house. From inside the sound of boys laughter echoed off the mountain. It was time to swim.

We grabbed our bathing suits and headed into the changing rooms that stood on either side of the entrance. Twenty feet square and constructed of large logs; the old building had seen it's share of ablutions. I crept out of the change room and peeked into the steaming deck now covered with bodies all waiting to crash into the tiny pool. Fifteen feet long, six wide by six feet deep at the deep end the materials had been hauled in on horseback at the turn of the century. Working my way to the stairs I slowly immersed myself in the deliciously warm water and stayed clear of the deep end where bodies were flying everywhere. One brave soul climbed to the rafter beam ten feet above the water and now plunged down into the steamy brew displacing huge quantities of water that soaked the logs and ran over the deck. By now I had worked my way to the inlet where the hot water, cooled somewhat by a chilly stream, poured in. At the other end I could see where it exited via a round hole in the concrete. The water then flowed through the round house keeping the animals warm before snaking its way to the river where the last remnant of it's warmth was extinguished. Oh how the place was alive with nearly thirty boys ! It wasn't long before one of the boys stripped off his bathing suit to swim naked in the steamy waters. Soon the cry of "Bare balls away ! "echoed off the walls. Swimsuits were optional being reserved for those rare occasions when women were around. It was a great place to let one's hair down and relax.

Immersion in hot water tends to suck the energy out of you so periodic trips to cool ones body in the cold stream were called for. Half an hour in the pool left you heated through and through with your own internal furnace that defied even the cool night air. It is no wonder that by the end of a long day in the pool we slept well even in strange surroundings. I had barely been asleep for an hour, it seemed, when I was awakened by my sixer to take a midnight dip. Groggily I crawled out of my sleeping bag and shivered my way to the pool where quite a collection of boys had already gathered. We kept our voices down but soon Baloo appeared. Instead of ordering us out he joined us. Half an hour later we went back to bed and slept late.

The next morning I wandered around the springs being careful to avoid the poison ivy that thrived in the warmth. I stepped carefully over rocks that were covered with dark green slime and peered into the lower spring as it emerged from the ground. The unmistakable odour of sulphur clung to the air as I gazed into the depths of the water trying to perceive the roots of it's being. Growing bored I followed the stream to the small pool as it was known. Once my eyes grew accustomed to the dark I could see the water flowing through a trough directly into a concrete tub six feet long and two feet wide. I tried to get in but the water was far too hot. Soon the door opened and an elderly man came in and walked slowly into the tub ! I was impressed. He had arthritis and had come to spend a month in order to free himself of the pain. Some men who came were so crippled that they could not walk but had to ride in and after a month or so of immersion in the spa could walk out. As I left I marvelled at the endurance the old man had.

Swimming, or rather splashing, wasn't the only occupation as our leaders arranged for our continuing education the craft of woodsman ship. We learned the names of the trees and how to distinguish them by their bark and their leaves. Here we learned about poison ivy. If the juice was squeezed onto your skin it caused a nasty rash as some of the boys discovered to their great discomfort. We were taught to wear shoes at all times and to avoid rolling on the ground in places where the plant grew. One afternoon we all hiked back down the trial to look at the falls. A quarter of a mile out we took a steep path, more like a vertical drop off,and clambered down to a point where the falls were directly in front of us. Looking up the creek we could see the crest where the water plunged down through a narrow canyon. The rocks rose high on either side and the roar was deafening. We stood half way up and took turns throwing sticks and pieces of wood into the boiling cauldron. A rainbow hung suspended above the mists adding to the splendour of the sight. Many of the boys had brought fishing rods and spent the time fishing the pools in the stream blow the falls. It was a favorite haunt of brook trout and one might even catch the odd rainbow trout. The successful fishermen dined on pan fried fish for supper.

Too soon it was time to leave and we packed up and tidied the area before heading back on the trail. At noon we ate our lunch after a final dip in the pool and began the long march to Preemption. Each and every cub vowed that he would return again to enjoy the unique pleasures of forest and stream. The return journey always seemed longer than the trip in. The hot water had sapped some of our energy and the excitement of a new adventure was no longer there. Still the hike back was a time to walk with friends, tell tales or stroll quietly along enjoying the forest. I returned many times and even when I was older and the hike less strenuous I have always remembered the times spent there as moments suspended in time. For a while we were free to be young and alive. Once we reached high school a trip to the Hot Springs was one of the standard events of our summer. The normal routines of school and chores abated, lending a special quality to time. There was also the complete absence of mechanical sounds where the roar of the falls, the songs of the birds and our own voices were the only accompaniment to life. There is a new commercial pool now and the old springs are gradually returning to nature. All that remains are my memories of a time now gone forever as the world caroms onward.

Another feature of summer was the ten days we spent at Camp Lourdes. It was the summer that I turned nine that we first journeyed there, another memorable first. Friends of ours from Lumby were Catholics and there were always a number of locals who went with Fr. Smith, so off we went to become good Dogans for ten days. After reaching Nelson we boarded a train for the twenty mile trip along the south side of Kootany Lake. This in itself was a rare treat as we seldom went anywhere except by car. Located between two points the camp nestled between the railway tracks and the lake a quarter of a mile away.

Like most summer camps the eight cabins were unheated huts with no glass in the windows. To us they were palaces of rest and fun. On the west side, near the tracks, was the chapel with it's rough pews and wooden kneelers ; they certainly felt hard to me as we were unaccustomed to kneeling. Next came the counsellors cabin followed by the mess hall and a smaller cabin for the cook, the cooks were always women and sometimes they brought their children. The ground levelled out and there was room for a ball diamond between the mess hall and the lodge. The west arm of Kootany lake flowed past the camp and it was in these icy waters that we were expected to swim. Numerous boats were tied up beside the wharf where we eagerly vied for turns at the oars. The largest building of all was the lodge where we met for instruction in the faith and campfires if the weather was inclement. Between the lodge and the lake was the campfire, a circle of stones set on the beach where we gathered after dark to sing songs and act our skits. The rest of the area was forest where we ran on trails, chasing each other with mad exuberance.

Shortly after we left the train we were reunited with our friends from Lumby ; Charles who was my age and Philip who was two years older. They were a raucous pair. I remember the two of them wrestling on the bunks over some silly argument. Still, they were friends we had known since early childhood and they eased us through the routines of an unfamiliar environment. Through the years we were to have many different companions though the group from Nakusp frequently bunked together. I was frequently the cabin leader and enjoyed the responsibility of looking after the younger members of the outfit. Not that we spent much time in our cabins ; most of the day was scheduled and apart from rest time from twelve thirty to one thirty we were busy with various activities from seven in the morning till nine or nine thirty at night.

As it was a Catholic camp religion played a dominant role. At seven in the morning we were awakened by the often squeaky notes of a bugle or the clang of the triangle. This gave us half an hour to dress, wash up and line up for mass at seven thirty. At first it was strange to kneel on hard wooden kneelers while the priest recited the Latin mass but we soon grew accustomed to this. I began to enjoy the sonorous cadences of the Latin and even managed to pick up the responses. I remember Charles explaining the essence of the service to me.

"God, Himself, is present in a real way and we are here to honour and adore Him."

I loved to sing and the hymns added a familiar note to what was otherwise an unintelligible service. I felt a bit like the little boy who, when he was asked what the priest did at the altar replied,

"He moves his hands around a lot. He must be playing with crabs."

Except for Sundays a low mass was said and we were through in twenty minutes, freed to roam the grounds until summoned to breakfast by the ringing of the triangle. The Camp Lourdes version of the child's instrument was an immense piece of iron hung from a hook in front of the cookhouse and struck in circles with a crowbar. Breakfast usually consisted of 'mush' which was fine or cream of wheat, which I detested, and toast with a variety of spreads. Occasionally there were pancakes which were my personal favourites. Breakfast completed we hurried back to our cabin to clean and make beds before inspection. My sleeping bag was an old one that dad had used in the army and consisted of a rough wool liner and a shapeless outer covering that refused to straighten out. I envied those boys who had new nylon or cloth covered bags for while I laboured to remove the creases they had only to twitch the ends to complete their chore. Even the boys with blankets and sheets had an easier time. When the cabin was swept, the beds made and everything stored in an orderly fashion the counsellors came to inspect. Points were awarded and everyone competed for the prize of best cabin. The counsellors were smart and placed all of the days least favourite activities first. After inspection we went to the hall for religion. I was a good student so the sessions were interesting to me though I had no background in Catholicism. My brother, on the other hand, had a difficult time. One day the instructor was discussing the ten commandments and gave Marty the easiest question.

"To whom did God give the ten commandments ? "Marty didn't have a clue so the instructor began to give him hints. "You know, "he encouraged. "They went up the mountain." No response. He tried other clues to no avail. Finally the said, "You know. The man with the long white beard."

Recognition dawned at last. "I know. Santa Claus"

The class broke out with laughter and the story has dogged him the rest of his life.

Our chores accomplished we donned our swimsuits for an hour and a half of fun

on the water. Notice I said "on the water". If you actually had to enter the water it was a different matter. The river was much colder than the Arrow Lakes where we habitually swam. Being young we managed to endure the instruction periods. As soon as lessons were over it was off the boats to dry off and warm up. A number of row boats were available but they were usually commandeered by the senior campers, you had to be able to swim, there were no life jackets. The Tub was the vehicle of choice. What she had been in a previous incarnation I do not know but now she was a large, high sided, unsinkable galley. Manned by five to eight boys with paddles who drove them vigorously into the water to propel her bulk along at a lumbering crawl. Two boys in a rowboat could out run her but no one got in her way. You had to be able to swim fifty feet to join the crew as life jackets were something to sit on if we had them at all. We raced the other boats, played at being pirates and splashed anyone who dared to come near us. Too soon we were called in and it was time to move on to another activity.

After changing we played softball or read a book or just messed around. The first one to home plate was up. "Scrub" softball had definite rules. Three boys batted while the others occupied fielding positions starting with catcher, pitcher, first baseman and so on all the way out to left field. Once a boy was put out everyone moved up a notch and the boy who was out took the last fielders position. Sometime there were ten fielders so it could take a while to get up to bat. There was a shortcut. If you hit a fly ball you hoped that the pitcher or one of the basemen caught it as you exchanged places. The area of a fly ball was the most hotly contested spot on the field. Some of the boys had gloves but most of us played with our bare hands. Stopping a line drive took courage ! This sorted out the boys from the wimps. The first baseman was usually awarded one of the gloves as we had to get the ball to him in a hurry. The pitcher had to lob the ball at the batter to give him a chance to make contact. Anyone who threw too hard was yelled at to "slow down or we wouldn't hit.' It was only a strike if you swung and missed. Four foul balls and you were out. Why? I hear you saying. This simple rule prevented the better players from dominating the plate by deliberately hitting the ball foul. It was hard enough to get them out without allowing them an infinite number of cracks at the ball.

We always managed to work up a great appetite for lunch which was the main meal of the day. Fish on Friday and everything from stew to roast beef for the balance. Thus fortified it was back to our cabins for rest and canteen. We had to remain in our cabins but I don't remember ever getting much rest. During this time we were called to the lodge one cabin at a time for canteen. Eagerly we awaited our chance to spend the dime which was our portion for the day. I bought a box of Lucky Elephant popcorn and savoured every pink cherry flavoured kernel. At the bottom there was also a prize which further added to the enjoyment. This was an amazing largess for at home we received twenty five cents a week. Campers were limited to the amount that parents could send for spending money and I often heard others complaining about their slim pickings. For us it was nirvana! It was a ten day feast and we made the most of it. The money was paid directly to the camp and was debited as we bought goods. Ten cents bought a box of popcorn, one or two chocolate bars or thirty jaw breakers. Oh yes! It was indeed a wonderful time.

I cannot now remember whether swimming or ball games came next but the routines were always the same. Games involved organized softball with teams instead of our usual scrub style. Flags, soccer and other assorted games were also played. Once or twice a session we would endure boxing matches. I wasn't a very good boxer and usually wound up being suckered into fighting someone much better. Billy was one of those boys. He was also from Nakusp but was a year older, an inch shorter and twice as fast.! Luckily I don't bleed easily. There were the usual number of nose bleeds but no one was ever seriously injured. Life was different then, boys were expected to endure pain without crying. Other indoor sports followed the cubs outline of everything from ' jump the shoe ' to British bulldog. As juniors we played low organizational games and progressed on to softball and around to rappelling. Seniors experienced the longest hikes and climbed the steepest banks. I was never very good at heights but I conquered my fear and rappelled down a twenty foot cliff. It was exhilarating and remarkable safe ! I felt secure with the rope wrapped around my body and leg.

Supper was served at six then we had another round of games until seven thirty. We gathered once more at the end of the day in the chapel for Benediction. There, in that beautiful service of adoration, I fell in love with the worship of God. Everything from the cope the priest wore to the bells and incense penetrated my being ; saying to me that God was near, and if I could but reach out my soul, I could touch Him. "Tantum Ergo, sacrementum, therefore we before Him bending, this great sacrament revere..." rang out clearly through the voices of the boys and men, echoing the mystery of God incarnate. Here I began my journey in faith. "O Salutaris hostia, qui caeli... O saving victim opening wide, the gate of heaven... "held me spellbound and continues to strengthen and sustain me to this day. From that time onward I would not be content with prayer meetings or sermons, I would search for the food that perishes not. In that rude chapel, filled with the voices of men and angels, I remain to this day. The years have fled but the memories remain, clear and bright as the day I first beheld the majesty of God incarnate. Born of the wafting incense, the melodious songs and the deep devotion of those around me, that sense of the real presence has guided me always.

After Benediction we gathered on the beach as the light faded to sing songs and perform. Each cabin was responsible for the evenings entertainment and utilized the talents of it's occupants where ever they lay. Individuals sang, recited poetry or played instruments. The centre piece was usually a skit of humorous nature although some cabins stretched the limits of humour to the repetitive and boring. After the cabin entertainment we sang songs that ranged from 'It aint gonna rain no more ' to ' Kumbya '. Any new song that caught our fancy could be heard at one time or another. Mr. Smith did a very creditable imitation of the ' One eyed, One horned, Purple People Eater "complete with horn and accent. As the shadows deepened and darkness became complete with only the stars and moon to aid the dying embers of the campfire the ghost story began. Fr. Pausma was the priest whose stories filled us with the greatest suspense. Lowering his voice as the plot thickened he would scare the bejeebers out of us with a quick flip of his wrist or sudden raising of his voice. My but we did enjoy being frightened! He told stories of hands that attacked people, even when detached from their owners, of monkey's paws that granted wishes and of werewolves howling at the full moon. It was an age when storytellers had not lost their art or succumbed to the influence of television. These men spun their tales to small audiences who sat enthralled by the power of one man's voice. Only a dim shadow of unremembered years comes down to us through the hollow wires of today's technology. Sitting there in the dark with the embers of the fire our only light we were transported to earlier times when writing did not exist and all of man's frail history was passed by word of mouth, generation to generation. Over all the participants hung the spell of fire, that most primitive of human needs.

When the story ended we stood up to sing praises to Our Lady." Immaculate Mary our hearts are on fire. "reverberated off the hills as we sang to the patron saint of the camp. As the last strains of ' Ave, Maria, ' died down we headed for bed. It took a little time for quiet to descend on the camp but the voices slowly stilled, the lights dimmed leaving the world to creatures of the night.

Not all of the time was scheduled, the half hour before meals was usually free. One of the attractions was watching the trains go by the camp. Someone must have had a track line-up as there was always a counsellor on hand to insure that no foolish behaviour endangered anyone. Those campers with pennies to spare would place them on the rails so that the train could flatten them; there being nothing so interesting as a deformed and defaced coin. As for me the extravagance of wasting a whole penny was something not to be contemplated. I settled for a flattened nail or metal slug whose outlines, though thinner, were not as spectacular as the coins. It was here that I became interested in trains, a passion that would be stimulated by other rail excursions and culminate in my working for the railway for a spell. There were always plenty of interesting activities to explore in our free time and the only period that tested our patience was the half hour compulsory rest. Being cooped up in our cabins with nothing to do could lead to friction. The first year I was there I witnessed some awesome wrestling matches between Philip and Charles, something about being brothers that seemed to require resolution by conflict. One year we were subject to a tyrant of our own making, the boy who went from wimp to terror in one easy lesson. Apart from this our time was usually tranquil.

Camp lasted for ten days and the highlight of the session was the overnight trip. As juniors we usually took the launch to the beach where we roasted wieners and spent the night under tarps gazing up at the stars. Seniors, on the other hand, tackled Kokanee Glacier. Early in the morning we would gather our sleeping bags and head out across the lake where we were driven five miles up the mountain to where the road ended. A hike of two or three miles found us up in an alpine meadow with a small lake. The least adventurous of the boys camped here while we headed out on the ten mile hike to the peak. The first year we hiked until dark before camping under the trees. Early in the morning we packed a lunch, left our gear and began the ascent. The weather was lovely as it usually is in July and by ten o'clock we had cleared the tree line and could see the craggy peaks and rocky screes that lined the ascent. Mountain meadows in summer are beautiful to behold. Every plant flowers and blooms one on top of the other in a mad riot of colour. Indian paintbrush and Tiger lilies weave bold patterns of orange among the Bluebells and a myriad other flowers of every type. At noon we halted for lunch where the plants stopped growing. Gazing upwards we could see the craggy peaks above and feel the cool wind. Now the trail became steeper and we laboured to cross screes of rocks where every step higher had to be fought for. With a whoop and a holler we reached the top to find a new world of ice and snow. Kokanee glacier runs for twenty miles at ten thousand feet a vast expanse of ice on which the sun glares fiercely. We donned our sunglasses and made a short trek along the edge of the glacier but we were without ropes so any real exploration had to be forfeited. The wind blew bitterly cold and our summer gear was inadequate. As we had arrived early we took the time to build an altar of stone. Soon we began the descent making much better time on the way down. Those rock screes that had proven so troublesome on the way up became ski slopes where we half ran and half slid our way down, the rocks filling our shoes. When we reached the meadows everyone emptied their shoes and took a short rest before heading out again. The sun was setting but supper was ready when we finally arrived at base camp. We gobbled down the stew and potatoes like ravening wolves, rolled out our sleeping bags and slept like logs.

The summer I turned fifteen was my last year at camp and a few things had changed. Two more cabins had been added and our friend Mr. Smith was now a priest and presided over the camp. This did not deter him from leading the expedition to the glacier. Better organized and leaving earlier meant that we reached the mountain meadows before nightfall and camped on the slopes nine thousand feet up. We placed groundsheets on the flowery sod then headed off to explore the surrounding meadows. Three of us decided to take a climb up a small ravine where the snow still lay deep. Reaching the top of the hard packed gully we could see the others as piggies far below. On the way down we decided to ski on our boots ; the temptation was too great to resist. Slipping and sliding with little control we caromed down the steep slope steering clear of the boulders on the sides. Thomas and I had reached the bottom when we heard a loud wail. Richard had lost his balance and crashed headfirst into some

rocks. Scrambling quickly back up the slope we helped him down. By the time we reached Fr. Smith he had an egg sized swelling protruding form his head. A snow pack eased the swelling but he had a headache for the remainder of the trip.

In the morning Richard was better and we ascended to the glacier, roped ourselves together and began to trek across the frozen field. Sunglasses protected our eyes but still the glare was intense. We wore our heavy sweaters to ward off the chill winds but it was great to look out upon the endless peaks of the Cordillera. Range upon range they spread out in all directions. An hour later we returned to the lip where we built a cairn then sat down to eat our lunch admiring the magnificent view. About two we set off for the camp. Somehow the trip back always manages to be faster but less exciting. That was the last time I set foot on the glacier. I've often wanted to return.

On the last evening of camp awards were handed out. Crests with the letters of ones achievement in a variety of areas were proudly accepted. Some campers had a number of them sewn to their jackets. We all vied for the honour of best camper though I usually ended up with the leadership award. This meant that I could get the kids to follow any of half a dozen batty ideas of mine. There were awards for religion, altar serving, sports and a couple of others I can no longer recall. The final award was the Lourdes crest. This was much larger than the others and went to the best all round camper. No matter what the results we all enjoyed our time at camp and looked forward to the next year. This was my final year and I have often wanted to return. The camp is now closed and I grieve that so many good memories will never be imprinted on the souls of other campers. Though time has flown I have remained faithful to the memories and I hope that by sharing them the long intervening years will drop silently away to reveal a part of life that I cherish to this day.

SPRINGTIME

The seasons of the year dominated our activities as we lived close to nature and all her charms and tricks we knew. Like the ancient Greeks we were creatures of Earth, Air, Fire, and Water. Creatures of Earth because we spent most of our free time outside, revelling in the changing ground and walking along paths strewn with the needles of fir, pine and tamarack. We were of the Air because there was so much clean air to breathe and the sights and sounds of our habitat travelled to us along the airwaves. Of Fire because we spent a lot of time stoking the fires that cooked our food and kept us warm. There was no magic touch of the button that brought warmth when the temperature plummeted well below freezing but the honest exercise of chopping wood. Every day of my young life I cut enough blocks to feed the wood stove bringing in armloads to fill the box beside the iron range. In those days, before double panes windows. several cords of wood were consumed to keep us warm during the winter. Even in summer we needed to use the stove occasionally to cook a meal. At an early age we learned to set and start fires, both inside and out, learning the art that encourages a reluctant spark to leap into life. Not too surprisingly we grew up fascinated by the flickering flames. Lastly we were creatures of water because there was so much of it around in one state or another. Winter brought snow while spring saw it melt and flow across the land in rivulets and torrents. During the summer we spent most of our days at the lake swimming or paddling the floating logs we called boats. Autumn saw us fishing the lake or creek, catching Red fish, Suckers and Squaws.

When the weather became milder we went outside to explore the area. At first it was only the patch around our house but soon it grew to where it encompassed several square miles. In this are we were the only souls and could do what we wanted. One game that we played was called F-U-C-K, the word was spelled as it donated the secrecy of the game. In some little grove or quiet place we three would lower our pants and play with each others bottoms. We inserted our fingers into them then switched to various sticks and other implements. In this way we explored sexuality and general enjoyed the feel of our nakedness.

Of Dams and Telephones

Spring arrived slowly to the valley. First the snow changed to muzzling rain intermingled with large snowdrops before turning to pure water. Slowly the blanket of white that covered the land shrank, thawed and chinks appeared in it's armour. A few small patches of brown earth or the faded remains of bracken bravely poked through the icy pelt and soon a few hardy plants began to sprout. Occasionally Old Man Winter returned in one last assault but as April arrived he lost his grip for good and welcome greenery reappeared for the first time in six months. Nestled in the rock garden the snowdrops began to bloom, first of natures flowers to welcome Proserpine's return. As the flowers popped up my mother would attack last years dead plants removing them to free the new life now appearing. It was a season of gumboots, ice and dams.

This was the season of water, when soil and water mingled to create squishy mud pies. The earth sprang reborn but the water occasionally cascaded down the mountainsides in rolling juggernauts that tore the rocks and plants from their infant footholds. Crescent Bay road was a gravel path that wound around the mountain so vigilance had to be exercised to keep the water in the ditches. Occasionally a stream would escape it's anointed boundaries and come charging downhill tearing a great hole in the highway. This kept the highways crews busy ditching and repairing. Later when the snow had receded to the upper reaches of the mountains came the threat of flooding from the river. The lake road that wound along the shoreline serviced the communities of Arrow Park, Burton, Fauquier, Needles and Edgewood was susceptible to flooding. At that time, before the dam tamed the river, it rose a full forty vertical feet from low water so that it didn't take more than a couple of extra feet of rise to flood the road. We lived south of the town and watched with interest as the river crept closer to the lip of the road. Please rise some more, we prayed, in hopes of severing our link with school. It very rarely happened but the kids who came from further away frequently missed a few days. One thing you could count on was an abundance of water from April to June.

The ice went from the roads first where cars and trucks mash the snow and aid in it's thaw. Soon little rivers flow and puddles appear. On our early morning trek to the bus stop we would smash the ice, watching as it splintered into crystal shards or cracked like a windshield when struck by a rock. By the time we returned the ice had melted and a little more snow had disappeared showing patches of dead grass under the trees. In the forests the snow melted unevenly so that shaded areas were white and frigid while sunny spots burst forth in new growth. Ferns and snowdrops poked their hardy heads into little clearings surrounded by snow as if to say that Old Man Winter had held sway long enough and it was time to spruce the old girl up. Soon the four feet of snow on our lawn began to shrink, green patches appeared and the little rill that runs in front of the house began to flow once more. On the cottonwood and birch, buds emerged while pussy willows swelled to be picked by children as harbingers of spring. The robins tugged at reluctant worms and trilled a song that told of arriving spring and hinted of warm breezes and summers heat.

To the east of our house and at about the same level as the roof was our well. We were allowed to cut trees anywhere on the property but here, the trees protected the watershed where our well was located and prevented a large run off from the hillside above. As we grew older our dams increased in size and we moved from the ditches to the stream above the driveway. This had two advantages, the stream was bigger and we were sheltered from parents prying eyes. During the summer the stream dried up completely so it was only in the spring that we could indulge in this particular past time. In spite of the culvert, water inevitably found it's way onto the driveway and wore away the surface. For the past three summers my brother and I had spent two hours every morning hauling shale to mend potholes, trying to keep one step ahead of mother nature. Now there was a new menace. The highways department had cut some trees above our house to widen the road. Dad was furious and accused them of cutting on our property but as there were no surveyors stakes nothing could be proved one way or the other. His chief concern lay in the fact that it might adversely affect our water supply and cause spring floods. He had warned the highways boss in no uncertain terms that they would be held responsible for any damage that this incursion might bring.

Warm spring days caused the snow to melt rapidly so Marty and I played with the water. With improvised tools we built dams across the little rivulets that cut their way about our property. The climax of our efforts was the cutting of the walls so that the water rushed madly down in a torrent of power. Power ! Power to gouge the sides of the creek and sweep pebbles and small sticks away in a swirling rush of debris. The mighty strength of the spring melt filled us with joy. Of course our joy was not shared by the Highways department who had to deal with washed out roads that occurred from time to time. Still, the Canadian spirit ran deep in us as we emulated the beaver, proud symbol of industry. Like the beaver we built new dams every spring; each year the walls rising higher, the force of the release more powerful. Eventually we moved to the creek behind the house for our grand finale.

Just out of sight of the driveway we had discovered a log that had fallen across the creek. Our fertile imaginations soon put this accident of nature to good use. By cutting a number of small trees and placing than vertically against the fallen log we created a five foot dam. For days we filled the cracks with dirt, grass and other materials impervious to water. When we were finished we had created a pool four feet wide, eight feet long and five feet deep. Our crowning engineering feat was the addition of a sluice gate through which we could release the waters at will. We filled the dam half full and gradually opened the gate. A controlled stream of water rushed down the bed and shot through the culvert. Marvellous to behold ! All was going well until one Saturday. We allowed the pool to fill while we ate lunch then returned to begin the finishing touches. Mom and dad had left for town so we had the whole afternoon of glorious sunshine to work with. Holes were stopped and the channel deepened until it held an impressive quantity of water. While we were working on the upper reaches a loud crack attracted our attention. It seemed that our fortuitous log was not as solid it should have been. The dam cracked and teetered on the edge of ruin. We tried desperately to shore it up but to no avail. Of course we didn't release the sluice gate ! Suddenly the whole structure collapsed sending a wall of water directly at the culvert. Alas ! The culvert was too narrow to contain such a flow. Water poured out onto the driveway and began rushing down the steep incline gouging deep ruts. Nothing we did could stem the tide. Our summers work was all for naught. The drive lay in ruins. We did the best we could by calling Nigel and getting him to smooth out the worst effects with the tractor but it was a sorry looking road that greeted dad on his return about three in the afternoon. We sat in the living room, studiously reading and dreading his return. He burst in through the door in high dudgeon. "I told that stupid..... no good son of a bitch that this would happen when he cut those trees ! Of all the idiotic, misguided dolts in this town he's the ultimate brainless lout!"

Seizing the telephone he cranked the magneto till the line came to life. For five minutes he hollered at poor Henry before he let him get a word in edgewise. When dad was angry he wasn't very rational and now his wrath was fuelled by righteous indignation. Needless to say we didn't interrupt his tirade. The road foreman knew dad well and eventually he managed to calm him down by promising to put new gravel on the drive. Of all the crazy exploits we engaged in this was the only one that ended up being of benefit to us all, department of highways excluded. We never told dad who the real culprits were and for once he never found out or if he did he never let on.

After the snow had completely melted we began our search for a place to build a cabin. Each year the projects became bigger and more grandiose as we became more proficient with an axe. The birch, alder and cottonwood were now in leaf while the light green of the new needles of the larch added yet another shade of green to the countryside. In our garden the daffodils bloomed and tulips peeped out from under dead leaves. We had a large vegetable garden between the upper road and the drive where we laboured to turn the sod and plant a variety of good things to eat. After our stint in the garden we were ready to escape and build once more. When we were younger we settled for a lean- to on our property but we soon grew adventurous and moved further afield. One year we constructed a log cabin on top of a bank that ran steeply down to the road. We had managed to cadge some nails and by cutting small trees we built round after round until it was five feet tall. There was only one snag, there was no place for a door and manufacturing one was beyond our material means. We solved this problem by putting a door in the roof. One climbed up the side of the logs then descended by means of a log ladder that rested on the roof. Inside we built bunks and lined them with branches. By the end of May our task was completed and were ready to try it out. Four of us jammed our sleeping bags onto the bunks and here we spent the night. Notice I didn't say slept. Sleep wasn't a big item but we certainly enjoyed ourselves. We played cards and talked till well past midnight. Dawn saw us awake with only a few hours of sleep but we ate a large breakfast! The following evening we were glad to tumble into our own beds at home and and drop instantly into the deep sleep of the truly exhausted.

 Cabins were usually good for a couple of years with appropriate upgrades after a winters wear. One year when we were about fourteen we found a pile of discarded lumber that the farm had dumped near the trail that went to Duncan's. By driving posts into the ground and nailing the timbers to the outside we managed to make the largest cabin built to date. It was fifteen feet long and five feet wide but we didn't have any windows. It did have a ceiling and a roof where we laid moss and slept in the summer. In one of our rambles we had discovered a couple of old pipes and by pinching tobacco from home tried them out in the comfort of our hideaway. Being cigarette tobacco it wasn't totally satisfactory but it was illicit and that added spice to the endeavour. Here we dreamed our teenage fantasies and indulged in cursory exploration of forbidden topics : sex education not being a high priority of parents at that time.

One night we had a friend with us and were talking about sex. Both he and my brother masturbated and I marvelled at he stream of sperm the came out of their penises. I, alas, could not participate and said that I was only interested in doing things with my bum. They laughed at me and said that I would soon come to know the joys of sex.

May was usually hot. The snow had retreated to the upper reaches of the mountains and the small stream at the back of our house had ceased to flow. It had been eight months since we last swam so the first hot weekend found us testing the waters of the lake. First you dipped your big toe into the water to see if it fell off or turned bright blue. Failing these results one took a hesitating step and immersed ones foot. By slow degrees we edged into the icy waters, only the heat of our upper body kept us going. At one point or another you had to take the plunge and dive, kicking and hollering for a few feet before beating a hasty retreat. Others with more guts rushed straight in, swam around for a bit and came out declaring that the water was lovely. Once you arrived at the beach with your trunks on that first dip was required, no matter how cold the water. Sometimes the ice had only just departed from the surface but once there you were committed. Afterwards we rounded up bits of driftwood and made rafts or searched along the shoreline for a suitable chunk of wood to call a boat. One of the advantages of living in logging territory is the abundance of flotsam. Perched precariously on these vessels with our feet dangling in the water we paddled along the shore not daring to venture out too far least the boat tip and give us a second cold dunking. The end result of an afternoons paddling was usually a sunburn. We would arrive home sore to the touch and cranky. Lord help the person who slapped you on the back ! Dad was no help as he insisted on calling sunburns ' self inflicted wounds,' not the legitimate perils of summer fun. Mum could be relied upon to butter us up with Noxema or other creams to calm our screaming nerve ends. After a night spent sleeping on ones stomach the condition eased and you were well on your way to the obligatory summer tan.

Arranging all these exploits was done at school or by phone. For those of you accustomed to today's phone system where you can reach London as easily as you can your next door neighbour, and you're more likely to know someone in London, our phone system was a relic. When we arrived in Nakusp we got our first phone and I thought it a gem of modernity. I would learn later that we were in the technological backwoods and that phone systems such as ours had been extinct in cities for years. There were plenty of people who didn't have phones for one reason or another, mainly because it would disturb their tranquil lives rather than not being able to afford them. A box on the wall held a magneto which was cranked to send an electrical current down the line in exactly the same fashion and with almost the same equipment as Mr. Bell used. There were up to eight people on our line at one time and you could talk to all eight of them at once : a type of farmyard conference call! It did have it's disadvantages in that all the signals were heard in every house. If you wished to phone the farm or anyone else on the line you simply picked up the receiver and cranked a long ring a short and a long. Our code was two longs. If you were phoning from school or town you had to ring once for the operator and ask for 21R, our phone number, which designated line and ring. She would connect you and listen in on your conversation as well ! When the phone rang you didn't rush to pick it up as you do today but listened intently for the right signal. Cusicks were a long and a short, Eaton's were two longs and a short and so on to the number of people on the line.

This system worked well until we acquired a woman who spent all her time on the phone, tying up eight other people's phones. If you wanted to call out you could pick up the phone, listen to who it was then ask them to please hang up as it was your turn. This didn't always work too well as she was a sharp tongued woman with little regard for anyone else. People phoning you had no such recourse as the operator would say. "I'm sorry. The line is busy"

If it was an emergency she could break in and boot the offending party off the line. Operators worked in a small office next to the drug store filled with lines and chords. To connect a call she took the chord from the incoming line and patched it into the line of the person they wished to talk to then rang the appropriate signal. If someone else, any of the five to eight people on the line, was talking the call couldn't be made. Needless to say making phone calls could be frustrating. When my father started a new business where he needed the phone we had to obtain a private line.

As swimming and cabin building were limited to the weekends we found other activities to fill the hours after school. Climbing trees was one such past time and we had an ideal tree at the bottom of the lawn, a large cedar tree. It's many well spaced branches made climbing easy and the view was magnificent. In those days I wasn't too enamoured of heights so I would climb half way up and cling tenaciously to the limbs. Bruce never bothered to worry and he climbed higher, hanging precariously from the upper branches and declaring that "The view was great !"

From the time I was ten I had a B.B. gun, a low powered model of today's air rifles. We were given instructions on how to shoot and stern warnings to never, repeat NEVER, point the gun at anyone : loaded or unloaded. We would have been spanked if anyone had caught us doing such a thing.

Dad explained to us that "More people had been killed by unloaded guns than by any other gun related accidents."

It was a tool to be used properly with a healthy respect for the power that it possessed. We passed our time shooting at tins or bottles and even attempted to shoot those pesky blue jays that used to steal the food we set out for the junks and other small birds. At this we were unsuccessful as the range was extremely limited and the bore notoriously inaccurate. Our favourite spot was above the house where we lined up bottles on a bank and shot at them from my sister's play house. The ping of metal against glass made a wonderful sound while the breaking of a bottle was a satisfactory end to our marksmanship.

When I was fourteen I graduated to a twenty-two rifle which was a beautiful weapon. My brother and I would practice by setting up old tobacco cans, the ones with mallard ducks on them, and attempt to hit the ducks at fifty feet. Our only problem with the gun was ammunition. It was expensive costing fifty cents a package for shorts, more for longs which we used for hunting. Marty achieved good proficiency with the gun while I never gained more than a rudimentary accuracy. There were always an abundance of crows to shoot at but the wily birds always seemed to know when you had a gun. If you were unarmed they would croak raucously at you from a nearby tree but I could never get within half a mile of the black demons if I had a gun !

HOSPITAL

I was in grade three when my eyes flared up an I could not see. In those days the hospital in Nakusp was rather primitive and access to specialists was unheard of so we journeyed to Vernon where the has a larger hospital and moreover, we knew the doctor there. Dr. Campbell-Brown was a slim man who delighted in calling me "lugs" as my ears stuck out from my head. I spent two lonely days in the hallway before they diagnosed me with a non-infectious disease. Once on the children's ward I became on of about a dozen other children with various diseases. The main treatment was penicillin which was administered by a shot in the bottom twice a day. It was also prescribed to one young girl about fie or six years old who positively hated the shot. It took two nurses to hold her down while one gave her the shot. I was seconded to help in this endeavour. She would see that I would take my shot without complaining which would, they hoped, encourage her to be more placid. I'm afraid it didn't work. For three weeks I was there before being released. The only drawback was that I received very few visitors so I was glad to return home.

SUMMER FROLICS

June brought old Sol to it's zenith baking the land and causing the gardens to grow. Other shrubs and bushes also sprang up in a mad race to choke out man's feeble foothold upon the face of mother earth. Water became a necessity ; for gardens and lawns, for cooling relief from the searing heat and to replenish the moisture lost when we sweated for hours in the hot sun. A long cool drink from a creek or spring tasted better than soda pop on a long hike or after a mornings work in the garden. As children we rode our bikes to school freeing us from the tyranny of scheduled buses. Now we were caught up in counting the days to our release, we longed for the endless days of summer when books were read for fun and pens could be retired. We planned endless projects from hikes and camping to swimming and boating. Just let that old school bell ring for the last time and we are on our way to freedom !

No one slept till noon during vacation time. There were far too many things to do and so little time to do them. After breakfast we had an hour or so of chores that consisted of weeding the garden, gravelling the drive or hacking at the thimble berries that threatened to take over the lawn. Our patch of soil was very rocky and required endless amount of chicken manure to bring it to a proper state for growing food. Here we grew the summer staples of lettuce, peas, beans, radishes, potatoes and corn. Dad also grew asparagus which he diligently cultivated to satisfy his craving. It was the one vegetable that we were allowed to refuse as there was never enough to satisfy five of us. As we grew older dad invented summer projects to keep young men from straying too far from what he referred to as the ' straight and narrow.' One year we began excavating under the front of the house in a vain attempt to produce a basement. The combination of too much water from the back of the house and the fact that we struck bedrock half way through ended this project. For two years we hauled shale from the bank to the south of the house all the way to the driveway two hundred and fifty yards away. We took shifts with the rickety old wheelbarrow in a valiant attempt to make the drive smoother. This all ended with the dam saga. Summer, spring, winter or fall there were always chores to do and we were fortunate compared to some children who worked all summer on their farms.

When the afternoon sun beat down on the land the roads turned to dust bowls while heat waves shimmered off everything in sight. To escape this heat, and also to keep us away from mother's chores, we headed off to the lake. We live a scant quarter of a mile from Cusicks who lived on the lake so we would pack up our ratty towels and head down the steep trail that separated our houses. There we would spend the afternoon swimming or messing about on ' boats '. A raft was anchored about twenty feet from shore where the water was deep. It was held to the shore by a short string of boom sticks, logs tied together with chain and no one was allowed on the raft until he first swam there. Once this feat was accomplished you were allowed to tread the boom sticks and reach the raft without first having to get wet. The Arrow Lakes are a widening in the Columbia river so that there is always a current moving the water in a great, slow eddy that moves from one side of the lake to the other. In the summer the water warms up to a depth of six feet so that a dive into the lake sends you through the warm surface water then hits you with a cold chill which quickly sends you back to the surface. In the early months the cushion of warm water is only about two feet which makes swimming even trickier. Even at the height of summer there are still patches of water where it gets suddenly cold. Currents are unpredictable. There were always innumerable kids there to play with as it was a fun place to be. Marion's word was law. Break the rules and you were smacked or sent home ; the former being preferable to the treatment you would receive at home. She knew and understood children and boys in particular and as she was impeccably fair : no one ever complained. Besides she was great fun and allowed us plenty of freedom within the bounds of common sense. About three o'clock mom would drive down for her swim and we would all pack up about four thirty to return home for supper.

When we were older the Cusicks moved to town and we had to go further afield to swim. We had cut a trail across the top of the bluff to where the newly strung power line ran. Power to the town was supplied by a local station until the power plant at Watchan lake came on line. Once on the power line we could run along the rough maintenance road then along the main road to Duncans about a mile away. Dave ran the local air taxi. Mark was a year older that me and Roger was the same age as Marty so we made a formidable foursome. His daughters were younger and Pat often spent time with the girls. The swimming was the same, minus the raft, but they brewed their own root beer. A bottle of their fizzy elixir was more than compensation for the long hike.

Not everyone had cars but as dad was a mechanic we always had an old clunker that he managed to keep going. Two years after we moved to Nakusp dads oldest sister, Aunty Bett, came to live with us. She was a nurse and the addition of her income improved the family finances tremendously. In 1956 she bought us a brand new A50 Austin and with this superb machine we were free to travel. My Aunt was also a great walker and one day, for a change, she took us to the Hot Springs. Well to be truthful we lead the way but it was her idea. We packed a lunch, hiked the six and a half miles in, stayed for a couple of hours, not nearly long enough, and hiked back out ! Man were we tired ! Never before or since did we make the trip and not spend at least one night. Of course we had to show off the country so we drove to all sorts of interesting and out of the way places.

Our favourite summer hike, hot springs excluded, was to Mt. Idaho. We'd pack a lunch, usually egg sandwiches or hard boiled eggs, load the car and head east. The lookout stood on top of a six thousand foot peak near the town of New Denver, thirty miles away. The road lead past the abandoned mining town of Sandon before heading steeply up the mountain. A narrow, single lane trail, I would hate to burden it with the aura of a road, wound along the mountain snaking upwards in a series of switchbacks. I never realized how steep and narrow this road was until I revisited it in the summer of 1996. After half an hour of crawling along the face of the mountain in second gear we reached the parking lot high in the alpine meadows. We were now in true alpine country with a few stunted trees and a glorious riot of wild flowers. Every open space was blanketed with flowers from the vivid orange of Indian paintbrush to the sombre Gray of puff balls. Whole sections of the mountain were covered with arctic bluebell interspersed with purple fire weed. As we wound our way along the narrow trail yellow alpine mavens and purple heather grew side by side. Forget-me-not with their cream centres nestled under mountain saxifrage. Nowhere else have I ever seen such a profusion of flowers as if nature were making up for lost time. Indeed there were still patches of snow in sheltered ravines where little sun ever penetrated. Nature was truly in a hurry for she had but two short months to bring her creations to seed before the snow reclaimed the mountain meadows.

A mile or so along the trail we reached the summit where we sat and gazed out at the splendour of the countryside. We had arrived at that exceeding high mountain and there below us lay all the kingdoms of the earth, spread below our feet like toys. Far below lay the town of New Denver nestled beside the shimmering Slocan Lake. At the head of the lake lay Roseberry with it's mill sending a small plume of smoke that dissipated a few hundred feet up. Further along the lake Silverton and Slocan appeared in miniature map relief. At our elevation of six thousand feet we could see across the lake to the glacier that graced the slopes of the peak before ending in a rock wall a thousand feet high. Looking further afield peak after snow capped peak surrounded us stretching for as far as the eye could see. From this vantage it is man who is the lone intruder on the solitude of the vast ranges of the Rockies. Small settlements were mere dots in the incomprehensible vastness of this rocky fortress. From this lofty vantage point we could feel the awe that those early explorers felt when first they crossed this untamed wilderness. Too soon it was time to tread the rocky trail and return to life in the valleys below.

Summer was not complete without a trip to the Okanagan. We maintained close ties with friends we made in Lumby and Vernon so it was there that we stayed on our frequent trips. A journey over the Monashee pass was always an adventure though it was usually tamer in the summer. Early in the morning we would pack and pile into the Austin to beat the heat, air conditioned cars being unknown. In August the lake had receded leaving the road rough and dusty. The road was only infrequently graded, usually after a rain storm when the hard packed gravel was softened. Pot holes and washboard abounded. If you drove slowly you felt every bump while at fifty or sixty miles an hour, eighty to a hundred klicks to you youngsters, the car sailed over the top of the ridges and the only danger was hitting a large pothole at these speeds. As the car sped along it spat out a huge plume of dust that trailed behind for half a mile and crept into every crack of the vehicle. When a car came from the opposite direction both drivers pulled over from the middle of the road and went by like blown dust devils. Overtaking was tricky as there were limited straight stretches and the Austin wasn't exactly a high powered machine. After about an hour of this we arrived at the ferry where one waited unless you were lucky enough to find it on your side. The cable ferry connected Fauquier on the south side with Needles on the north where the highway continued. Onto the ferry we drove for the only smooth part of the journey then off we sped trying to keep ahead of the traffic so as not to eat their dust. On one trip we were hotly pursued by a large American car and while we out cornered it we could not match it's speed on the straights. We barrelled down the last straight stretch at seventy miles an hour, braked. then accelerated through the corner. The "large piece of Detroit scrap iron "as father sarcastically put it, failed to negotiate the curve while we sailed on free from the dust.

 By the time we reached the summit some two and half hours after leaving it was time to take a break. We often stopped on the Kettle river and ate lunch or merely stretched our legs and answered the call of nature, rest stops being unheard of in that time and place. Back into the car we piled and continued our bone jolting trip. Now it was all down hill. We sped up considerably as there were more straight sections but there was also more traffic. Our only method of cooling was to open the windows so that when a car approached from the opposite direction there was a frantic scramble to close the windows in order to mitigate the effects of the dust. Eventually we climbed the Sushwap hill and onto a paved road. The sensation was remarkable ! For three and a half hours we had endured a jolting, dusty ride. Now we were sailing along with all the windows open and nothing but the rush of the wind and the purr of the engine to interrupt the silence.

Dad often talked about the possibility of the Monashee being paved but he didn't live long enough to see it come to pass. After having worked on the first crew to keep the highway open during the winter of forty eight he missed it's coronation by a year. The Okanagan was Bennet territory and they took care of their own. While we poor second class cousins who elected N.D.P. members had trouble getting the government to straighten a hairpin curve the driveways of the Okanagan were paved ! As children we were ignorant of the political situation and only remembered the smooth roads.

We spent our time in Vernon shopping for the items we couldn't obtain in Nakusp or that were considerably cheaper in larger stores. One of those items was boots for me. When I was eight my knee swelled up and when the final diagnosis was in it appeared to be the fault of my legs, one a foot shorter or something like that. Anyway I had to endure wearing boots with inserts to correct the problem and very inconvenient it could be too. When everyone else shucked their canvas runners to plunge into the lake I was left untying miles of laces. After we had spent the morning shopping we often went out for lunch which was a great treat. A hamburger and fries ran about fifty cents and pop was ten cents. This was invariably our choice as dad ate traditional English food and shunned the North American appetite for hamburger.

Lunch completed we would head to Kalamalka lake for a swim. The beach was long and sandy while the water was warmer than the lake at home. A long dock ran from the shore out to deep water where a diving tower stood. Just jumping from the top was a thrill. Older kids swan dived and performed somersaults off the board while we watched in awe. The diving tower no longer exists, a victim of the notion that, no matter how foolhardy your actions you can always sue for damages. I used to enjoy diving and had worked my way up to ten or fifteen feet but it is difficult to find a diving tower today, even in a pool. In those days every lake had a diving board and many were blessed with towers. Pretty soon we'll be legislated or litigated into our homes. ' Please don't leave home as it is risky.' In those days you could risk your neck to limit of your abilities, sometimes even beyond.

    Usually we stayed at a friends house, double bunking or making do with a tent or the couch. Once I stayed with Charles, I don't remember why I was the only one, but we were the same age so I suppose it was logical. I was fifteen and in the evening I was invited out to a drive-in movie, a novelty for me. One of Charles' older friends had a car and we all piled in and headed for Vernon. There were five or six of us plus a couple of cases of beer. The first thing Charles did was open a beer and offer me one. I turned him down, not because I didn't like to drink but because I didn't like the taste of beer. Off we sped towards Vernon at speed of up to one hundred and twenty miles an hour, that's two hundred klicks. I know because I was sat beside the driver and gazed in fascination as the dial shot up. Throughout the movie they drank continuously and took off before the movie ended, much to my annoyance. The trip back was even scarier with the tires squealing and the car swaying as it rounded corners at maximum speed. At one point I must have looked a little scared because Charles put his arm around my shoulder and assured me that Ron was a great driver, even better when he'd had a drink or two ! Fortunately for us there was much less traffic on the roads and drunk driving was not recognized as so great a hazard. In those days it was illegal to drink until you were twenty-one so a car was the natural boozing place for many teenagers. The last thing I remember before going to bed about midnight was Charles puking his guts out over the toilet bowl !

    Upon our return home we would fall into our summer routines with renewed enthusiasm. There's nothing like a few days away from home to help you appreciate your own bed. When we were teenagers mom ran a cub pack and we were permitted to go with her on hikes to help out. Near the end of August she took her pack on a two night trip to Halcyon Hot springs. There was no road up the lake so we bundled our gear onto the M.V. Lardeau for the hour and a half ferry trip up the lake. The Minto had been retired in 1956 much to the annoyance of my parents who felt that we had lost our best link to the outside world. The town council, in it's wisdom, felt that if the Minto was allowed to die the government would be forced to build a road north. The road never appeared until the High Arrow dam was built in 1968 ! The new boat lacked the romantic aura of the old stern wheeler being but a flat bottomed barge driven by propellers and a diesel engine. Most of the boys on that trip had never ridden on the Minto so for them it was a great excursion. For me it was a disappointment.

There was very little remaining of the once proud hotel that formed the centre piece of the old resort which had burned in 1953. No one had claimed the site as the Kettle valley railroad made the route obsolete. Someone had collected the hot spring water into a small pool which was all that was left from the glory days when tourists arrived on the paddle wheeler to sample the healthy waters of the spa. As soon as we arrived we rounded up bits of wood and set about erecting shelters and building fires so that supper could be cooked. Our time was spent alternating between various activities and dips in the pool. There were treasure hunts where specific bits of bark, trees or shrubs were collected. A favourite game was prisoner's base where the pack was divided into two sides and set out to capture as many of their opponents scalps, scarves tucked into belts, as possible. The real coup was to capture the enemy flag that was planted in the heart of the base. Once captured you were hauled off to the base as a prisoner. The team who captured the flag or took the most prisoners won. Here the boys had an opportunity to practice tying knots and making fires, all of the practical skills that had been shown to us in the safety of the hall during the long winter months. At the end of two days it was a tired group of boys that boarded the boat for the journey home.

My birthday occurs in August so the beach was a favourite place to celebrate. The Kinsmen club of Nakusp had built a park on Summit lake and it was here that I remember most of the parties taking place. My birthday coincided with one of the Jupp girls from Silverton so we often met at Summit lake for a combined birthday party. The lake was a fine place to be on a hot summers day for there was a raft with a diving tower. The adults sheltered from the heat under the many trees while we enjoyed the clear waters of the lake. Later on wieners were cooked and everyone gathered around to eat. There is nothing finer than a hot dog, or three or four, when you have been hard at play and ravenously hungry as a result. It was a joyful celebration and my mind still hearkens back to those parties when my birthday rolls around as it seems to do with great regularity these days.

The woods around Summit lake teemed with huckleberries and it was here that summer officially ended. Late in August we headed out with an assortment of buckets and pails to beat the bears to the berries. For two or three hours we climbed the steep mountainside searching for bigger and better bushes. All around us the air had a cool tang that warned of approaching autumn. Leaves turned yellow and crimson, falling gently to earth in the breeze. All good things must end and the change of season foretold the end of our limitless freedom. Still there were large purple huckleberries to pick and we worked with a will to gather as many as possible. Many of the berries found their way into our stomachs but there were plenty left for pies when we collected our buckets and combined their contents. On the way home we contemplated the pie that would be produced imagining the thickness of the crust and the mouthwatering flavor of the contents. The remaining berries were canned so that, even in the middle of winter, we could pluck their contents from the shelves and remember summer.

When we became teenagers our responsibilities grew and summer ceased to be the carefree domain of childhood. Work began to dominate the scene. The farm was my first source of revenue as I mowed lawns, helped with the hay and performed odd jobs to make that vital extra money. I had a regular Saturday job at granny Waterfields where I chopped wood, mowed the lawn and did other chores as she directed. For a couple of hours I sweated for the princely sum of fifty cents an hour. She was a marvellous lady now in her late eighties but spry as could be. When I had completed the chores she fed me lunch in that fine tradition of never allowing your hired help to go hungry. Well teenagers are always hungry and a change of cooking was always appreciated. Later in the day we often saw her striding out as she headed into town three miles away.

The Waterfield's are a fading remnant of what used to be a common Canadian family. Three generations lived on the same farm handing the land from generation to generation. Granny Waterfield lived on the top of the hill while her son built a little lower and her grandson a little lower still. At one time there were four generations of the family living on the farm and when I returned in 1996 I found four generations again. Too often today the farms are split and the children separated as they head off to the cities where they become one more cog in a vast hive that swallows families and churns out human wreckage. It's nice to know that some families retain their traditional cohesiveness.

One summer when I was fifteen I worked for dad in the lumber yard for a few days. My job was to mark the lengths of the different sizes of boards as they were loaded into the box car. There were columns for tuba 4's, 2 x 6's and 2x 8's all divided again into lengths from 14 to 22 feet. I would put a mark in the correct column and when I had four the next stroke went neatly across to tie up a bundle of five. This record enabled dad to bill the company for the correct number of board feet in each box car. For this I was paid the princely sum of one dollar an hour, the same wage he paid to the man who was performed the job on a regular basis. At the end of two days I was rolling in money and stashed it in my bank account. Twenty dollars was a lot of money when the price of admission to the theatre was fifty cents.

The summer I turned sixteen I went to work on a youth crew helping to make the park campgrounds. I was sent to Quesnel where I laboured on Ten Mile lake campground. Originally I was seconded to be the bull cook, helping the cook around the kitchen and doing odd chores. In my foolishness I turned the job down as I was pressured by the other boys some a couple of years older the me. From the on in it was "rake, shovel and mattock "every day until I grew heartily sick of the routine. We did have some good times when we took a break to see Barkerville. I found the trip fascinating and the passing around of a gold brick in Wells was the pinnacle. At last the summer ended and I went down to Vancouver.

Harry Sadd

At this time I had been a server at the church and travelled all around with the parish priest. There were four churches in this parish separated by fifty miles of dirt track which we serviced regularly. One week we had an eight o'clock service in Nakusp then drove to Edgewood some fifty miles away and took another. On our way back we stopped at either Burton or Arrow Park before returning to Nakusp for Evensong. The next week it was eleven at Edgewood, two ant Burton or Arrow Park and bock for seven at Nakusp. In Vancouver we stayed at the Anglican Theological College and I had a marvellous week with other boys of a similar bent. On Sunday we went to St. James and it was here that I first experienced a high mass. It was wonderful. Shorty afterwards our priest left for greener pastures and my path changed irrevocably.

FADE TO AUTUMN

Too soon the holidays were over and it was time to return to school. To be truthful, it was always an exciting time, well, at least for the first week. Many of the kids we had not seen since June and it took at least a couple of weeks to catch up on all that had occurred during the summer. By the time were truly settled into the routine the snow covered the tops of the mountains, the leaves were turning yellow and the birds were heading south. Autumn was upon us. If we were lucky enough to have an Indian summer the days would be warm but the nights and early mornings would contain a sharp nip that turned one's breath to steam. On these days I liked to walk about the woods shuffling in the leaves and exploring my favourite haunts one more time before Old Man Winter drove me away into more sheltered climes. This was the season for reflection, when I sat alone on the top of a hill, looking out at the vivid autumn colours. Patches of larch showed orange against the dark green of their cousins the fir whose needles stayed for ever green. Soon they would fall carpeting the forest floor with a rusty blanket that would slowly fade to feed the forest. The bracken that covered the open fields became brown and the grasses withered. In the dying of life seeds dropped or popped about hoping to find shelter for the winter. In spring I knew that I would rejoice once more to see the new life spring from those hardened shells. Now they would lie dormant through the winter's chill as the dead leaves clustered around like a comforter to nurture and protect. It was our sign that, though the world was fading, new life would bloom again.

Fall in rural abode was focused on the harvest. Though we were not farmers we prepared fruits and vegetables to be stored for the impending winter. Our foray into the huckleberry woods was just one of the events that saw us store food for the winter. My mother picked strawberries and raspberries making jars of jam which were stored on shelves that lined the stairs leading to our bedroom. I don't remember ever eating store bought jam when I was growing up. We bought or picked pears, peaches and apricots by the boxes to be canned. The era of the home freezer had not arrived but we rented space in the local town deep freeze to store meat from a variety of sources. Our little garden provided food during the summer but there were others who grew food on larger acreages and allowed us to pick fruit and vegetables in sufficient quantities to preserve. Pork and beef were bought by the quarter and stored with the odd deer that we might obtain. By the end of October the shelves were filled and the freezer full.

Home canning is an art that has largely disappeared in today's urban environment where everything you need can be bought at the supermarket throughout the year. When we were young we would spend a lot of time peeling pears, peaches and cots while mom prepared the syrup and jars into which this fruit would be stuffed. Once our chores were done we would leave mom to fill the jars. The quart jars were placed in a wire frame basket that held six to eight jars then hoisted into a large pot of boiling water. After thirty minutes they were hauled out and cooled so that the lids would seat properly. You could hear the pop as the lids sucked down around the rim, assuring a vacuum. Soon another load was being boiled and metal rings were placed around the cooled jars to aid in keeping the containers sealed. In this manner all kinds of produce were preserved. My mother even canned bear meat in this fashion. The result of our labors was enough preserves to last the winter with a taste that far surpasses today's store bought goods.

Tastes that linger in your mouth and remain indelibly printed in your mind are one of my best memories of summer and fall. The indescribable freshness of new picked peas, shelled from their pods by small hands to be consumed at once or placed in the pot for dinner. Throughout the summer we would pick vegetables in season ; peas, beans, asparagus, squash, beets, spinach and potatoes. An hour before supper they were picked so that they were the ultimate in freshness. While vegetables were good fruit was even better. Every evening in late June and early July we would pick strawberries as they ripened to be consumed for desert with lashings of real cream. Our milk came whole and unadulterated from the farm, unpasteurized, un separated, UN-anything milk direct from the cow to the bottle. Once home the milk separated so that the top quarter of the bottle was cream which we skimmed off into a separate jug for use on our deserts. Chips, candy and other junk food we had only infrequently but we did have taste !

In the early fall we were recruited to go on a coon hunt. Nigel and Barbara took us on our first outing when we were seven or eight. The tools for this outing were not shotguns or twenty-twos but sacks. After dark we set out on our way to the neighboring orchards where we pilfered the fruit. While at our nefarious task we kept a sharp lookout for the farmer who could be counted on to chase one off if discovered, sometimes with a backside full of saltpetre. Stealth and cunning were what was required. The danger added spice to the stolen fruit and we often fled upon hearing footsteps, tearing up the paths, adrenaline surging, to hide in the shadows until all was quiet and our beating hearts slowed to a more sedate pace. There were rules that separated legitimate coon hunting from illegal activities.

1. You must take only what you can eat.
2. You must not damage the orchard.
3. Your must face up to any consequences if caught.

In this way we trod the narrow line that separates the purloined of apples and other fruit from the common thief. These raids took place any time the fruit was ripe in the orchards but I doubt if we ever made even a small dent in the crop. The farmer lost more fruit to windfall and insects. Cherries were the first on line and we often stretched the bounds of ripeness, not waiting for the fruit to mature. They still canned very well and we spent many evenings counting cherry stones in the time honoured fashion : tinker, tailor, soldier, sailor, doctor, lawyer, Indian chief. I'm not sure how the last occupation came to occupy the highest spot in the hierarchy but I suspect that it had to do with our fondness for the old wild west.

In October we often spent a weekend at Keefer lake on the top of the Monashee pass. The lake is the headwaters of the Kettle river and stands at an elevation of four thousand feet amid a pristine setting of balsam and pine. We drove the family car to a spot several miles from the lake, parked and were ferried the remaining miles in a four wheel drive. It was not really a road that led to the lake, rather more like a trail that alternated between hard bumpy turf and soft squishy bog. After bumping along for half an hour we entered a small clearing where a lodge and several cabins had been erected. All our gear was taken from the land rover and bundled into the cramped quarters. On one wall stood a serviceable wood stove while beside it was a table and four chairs. Two bunks stood on the opposite wall, mere metal frame and springs of the type we were used to at Camp Lourdes. Sleeping bags and food unpacked we headed to the lake with our fishing tackle. I am not nor ever have been a great fisherman but here I was content to fish. Marty and I took turns alternately fishing then rowing. We had a rule that one of us would row until the other caught a fish or we had completed one half circle of the lake. The fishing was great ! Frequently we exchanged places before completing the circle. As it took a little under half an hour to row the course we caught plenty of fish. While we fished the lake near the cabins mom and dad rowed farther up the lake. It was completely peaceful here in a way that only distance from civilization can provide. Only the call of the loon or the splash of a fish jumping disturbed the silence. By six o'clock the shadows of the trees on the still waters lengthened and it was time to head for the dock to unload our catch, clean and gut the fish before heading back to the cabin to cook them up for supper.

One year we must have made the trip in the spring for the daylight lingered till nearly ten. In the evening we would wander about the shore of the lake to watch the loons dive or see the squirrels and chipmunks scurry about in their endless search for food. We often put food out for the little critters and they were so unafraid that they would often take the food from our fingers. Once we managed to catch a couple of chipmunks and were very excited about taking them home as pets. That evening we made great plans to house and feed our newest acquisitions which were temporarily housed in a cardboard box. In the morning we opened the box to find both of them dead ! We were heartbroken! The chipmunks will to be free was so great that they had died while trying to gnaw their way out of our box. Never again did we attempt to cage one of nature's wild animals. They need to be free to live their lives where they belong ; among the trees.

On our last trip to Keefer lake we planned to spend a day hunting deer on the hills surrounding the lake. Early in the morning, before first light, we arose, ate breakfast by the light of a kerosene lantern then headed out. At first light we motored up the lake to

the north shore where a trail lead to the high country. Just as the sun peeked her head over the trees and began heating the world we reached the shore. Smokey plumes of steam rose from the water as the sun touched the lake while the forest around steamed. Fog began to hide the sun as we set off up the mountain with our rifles slung over our shoulders while the horse plodded along behind. My weapon was a twenty-two with a six shot clip which was not what I had been accustomed to using. This was to cause me some difficulty and grief later on in the day. Grouse were to be my targets as the gun was totally inadequate to bring down a deer. Dad had his thirty-thirty Winchester while Merve packed an old army issue three-ought-six, both powerful enough to handle the larger animals. We were not trophy hunters out to mount the head of an animal and leave the rest to rot but hunters of game, killing so that we might eat of the animal and so ease our dependence on store bought goods. Half a deer meant not having to buy meat for a month which was important.

By ten-thirty we had reached the open country but were hampered by snags and dead falls. In places the old dead trunks of trees rose ten feet high causing us to skirt around them, going twenty feet sideways for every ten forward. Eventually we tethered the horse and set off at a better pace. Half an hour later we split up, Merve going one way and dad and I another. The sun was near to noon and it was time to shed our jackets, tucking them into our knapsacks, while the October sun shewn clearly on the mountain meadow. For an hour or more we worked our way silently up the gentle hill, ever vigilant for the signs of deer. We were just working our way over an old fallen tree when we heard three shots. The sharp barks of the rifle reverberated around the hills. There was now no need for silence as any game would be running for the higher hills. Hastily we headed towards the area from whence the shots came to find Merve standing over the carcass of a young buck. I was disappointed that I had not been there when the animal was shot but I was soon too busy to worry about that.

We gutted the animal, tucking the liver and heart back inside to eat for supper, then trussed the animal to a pole and began hauling it back to where we left the horse. We slogged up hills and over windfalls while the sweat dripped from our faces and matted our hair. Half an hour later it was obvious that we had better bring the horse to the deer or we would be totally exhausted. I was delegated to stay with the carcass so that no other animal made off with our prize.

Dad and Merve set off across the unmarked hills to locate the horse as I sat watching them force their way through a thicket then disappear completely. I was now utterly alone in a way that I had never been before. Tucking my rifle under my arm I explored the little dell, circling the tiny pasture bordered by tall balsam fir. Soon hunger overtook me so I leaned my gun against a fallen log and began to eat my lunch. The sky was a deep blue. Across the valley rose three majestic peaks called The Pinnacles, their craggy, snow tipped peaks sharply silhouetted in the thin mountain air. For an hour I was at peace but then time seemed to stand still. Every time I gazed at my watch but a few minutes had ticked by. The wind rustled softly through the tops of a small stand of balsam but no other sound reached my ears. I strained to hear the sounds I longed to hear, the voices of my returning father and friend, but no unnatural sound broke the stillness. In retrospect it must have been difficult to maneuver the horse through the untrod wilderness but at the time I was only aware of how alone I was. I was not frightened by the outdoors and had no fear of wild animals for I had often been alone in the woods, just not quite as far removed from civilization as this. It was like waiting for a ride that never shows up while I dreamed of being stuck here for eternity. Two hours passed and it was getting late before they returned to my utter relief.

Heaving the deer onto the back of the horse we began the long trip down the mountain. I remember the feeling of relief when we finally reached the head of the trail. From here on in it would be easy, it was all down hill. Well it would have been if I hadn't taken a wrong turn and found myself alone again. I tried to fire a shot from the gun to tell dad where I was but I was unfamiliar with the weapon and couldn't figure out how to release the safety ! I felt like a fool ! It was getting dark and there was no use sitting on the trail in the faint hope that someone would come back and find me. I knew that all I had to do was to continue down hill to eventually reach the shore of the lake. When I arrived at the lake there was no sign of the boat or the landing and the last rays of the sun were sinking behind the trees. Soon it would be dark. I tried to remember which way the landing was but bogged down trying to skirt the shore. I had been calling for someone for nearly half and hour while night crept ever closer. I was beginning to despair of a reply when I heard the sound of a boat motor. Hollering and waving my hands I jumped up and down on the beach as the boat swung round a small point. I was so relieved that not even Dad's scorbutic comments could dampen my relief. It was well past seven when we finally reached camp and brought our prize ashore. Ten minutes after I had eaten dinner I was fast asleep. It was the longest day of my life.

Though we looked forward to these trips as an exciting adventure it was always nice to return home where we could snuggle into our own beds. With fall came the recommencement of church activities which were largely ignored in the summer. We were attending Anglican Sunday School which meant that by the time we had roused ourselves and mom had started breakfast we were usually in a hurry. One morning in the middle of all this hustle the Jehovah's Witness called. Dad was enjoying his customary cup of tea in bed while mother tried unsuccessfully to get rid of the unwelcome company. She was getting more and more frustrated as they never take no for an answer. There was a loud thump as dad pelted out of bed and came out rapidly tying his dressing gown as he stormed towards the door.

"This is not the time or place for you to discuss religion ! We are busy getting the disks off to Sunday school. If you want to talk religion come back some evening and we'll have a discussion. "

They left and I was sure that they would never return. I was wrong. One weeknight they returned about seven thirty. I had finished my homework so I sat quietly listening to my father discuss religion, a topic he rarely held forth on. They began by picking verses, as is their wont, and dad deftly turned than aside with other verses. I was amazed at his knowledge of the bible. The debate was still raging when I was sent to bed. I could eavesdrop on conversations as my bedroom was above the living room. Our guests were getting frustrated. They would quote a verse and would question the validity of the statement or come up with a contradictory one. Eventually they arose in high dudgeon and left, their final condemnation ringing in my ears.

"The trouble with you and Waterfield is that you don't believe in God!"

They had apparently tried a similar conversion attempt with Don but he too was a well educated man and the results were similar. They had been bested at their own game. The happiest result was that they never came again. I have concluded that this is the only way to stop these people from coming. In later years I employed the same tactics only with me they found themselves being converted to Catholicism. There is only one way to fight an idea, and that's with another idea.

Autumn is harvest time and we made the most of it. With money in short supply the busy period when farms brought in their crops and mink ranch harvested the pelts was a Godsend. Mom went to work for Chris Bird during the week that the mink were skinned and earned enough to buy the little extras that mean the difference between barely getting by and having some extras. Coming as it did in November it ensured an ample Christmas. As soon as the mink were fully grown they were skinned for their pelts as soon as their winter coats matured. They were humanely killed by carbon monoxide gas and their valuable skins carefully removed. The fat had to be carefully scraped from the skin with sharp knives, taking care not to rip the pelt. When we were younger we often went up to the farm to watch and when we were older we made money watering the animals. The mink were kept in wire cages with a wooden box inside that was their home. The inside was piled with straw while the wire mesh allowed the droppings to fall to the ground where they could easily be disposed of. Watering the little critters involved hauling a hose along the rows of pens, about nine hundred of them, and squirting water into their dishes. Food was placed on top by the handful and the mink consumed what they wanted by pulling it through the wire. When we arrived the mink would often be in their box but as soon as the hose touched the gage they would make a lightning exit to attack the end of the nozzle. They have needle sharp teeth and are one of the fastest creatures alive. Poking one's fingers in the cage would have risked being bitten and the little speedsters don't let go ! We were warned in advance and it did not take much experience to realize the truth of the warnings. Occasionally we would take a stick and poke it into the cage if we wanted to see an animal that was hiding in it's box. Frequently the mink caught the stick before we could withdraw it from the cage. It was hard work but it meant fifty cents a day for an hours work during the two months or so before skinning time. There were other sources of income to be made in the fall, mostly at Waterfield's farm. We dug potatoes and picked fruit from the orchard all for the same fifty cents an hour.

After the end of the fire season when the woods were not so dry it was time to cut the winter's supply of wood. Dad preferred larch for burning in the cook stove so we would borrow a one ton truck and head off into an area that had been logged in search of snags ; no one cuts down live trees for firewood if they can help it. Green wood burns poorly and causes the chimneys to plug with creosote. We searched for dead trees that were still standing as they were completely dry. This doesn't mean that the wood is bone dry of water but it can't be living, it takes too long to cure. Watching trees being felled has always been a favourite pastime of mine. First dad would notch the tree on the side he wished it to fall then he moved around to the other side and commence cutting until the tree began to fall. Removing the chainsaw he would step back and sideways to watch it fall. We got to stand around and admire the spectacle. Soon dad was bucking them into sections about fourteen inches long. Now it was our turn to work rolling the sections onto the back of the truck. Around noon we would sit on a log and eat lunch, hard boiled eggs, bread and Mayo sandwiches and cookies, while the blue jays and camp robbers vied for the crusts. Once the truck was fully loaded we would pile into the cab grateful for the cessation of the back breaking labor. Once home the blocks were rolled off the truck and stacked against the house under the eaves. We burned a couple of cords of wood during the winter, that's a pile eight feet by four feet by four feet. I would spend and hour or so a day during the winter to cut those blocks into the correct size for the kitchen stove.

Cutting firewood is an art that is dying quickly as fewer people use wood for fuel and the wood that is used is consumed in larger chunks in fireplaces. The knottiest block served as a chopping block and onto this platform we placed the rounds. Cutting a two foot diameter round takes skill and effort. The object is to swing the axe with maximum force and hit the centre of the block. As the knots, former branches, run to the centre one avoids trying to cut through them by hitting the bulls eye. Often two or three smacks were necessary to cause the wood to split, more if you didn't strike in a line. There is nothing so satisfying as to swing the axe and watch the block split neatly in half. Once this is accomplished the rest is easy as there is less wood to cleave and one good swing would quarter the block. If the wood was knotty, for those of us who had to cut it really was naughty, great effort had to be expended to obtain the correct dimensions for the wood stove in the kitchen. On the weekends I had to spend a couple of hours replenishing the stock of wood that was kept on the porch in case the wood box was emptied. Lord help you if there was not enough wood ! Still, it was good exercise and certainly kept us fit. It was all part of contributing to the well being of the family, even if we did grumble about it at times. In the living room there was a space heater of the type mentioned before with a propensity for roaring away at odd times. Any wood that was really too knotty to be cut ended up here where it burned to ease the winters chill.

Fire was also one of our sources of entertainment. At the top of the driveway, next to the garden, we erected a fire pit surrounded by large stones. On the opposite side of the road, about fifty feet from our fire pit was a pile of old shingles which we hauled over in drubs and drabs to help start our blazes. The secret of a good fire is to have plenty of solid burnables on hand before you start which you pile into a tepee shaped mound. The best fire starting material was birch bark with beard moss coming a distant second. As there were plenty of birch trees around we had little difficulty obtaining fuel. Once the necessary ingredients were ready one match was all that was need to start a good blaze. Once the bonfire was crackling nicely large wood was added until the flames danced two or three feet high. At this stage in the proceedings you can add materials that don't burn so well but last for a long time. Flames are fun but to create a really good pyrotechnic display you need smoke. Our favourite ingredient was cedar boughs which were readily available and could be stacked on until great clouds of smoke issued from the pit. One day we had a truly tremendous blaze going and had amassed a huge quantity of cedar boughs. More and more were piled onto the blaze while we waited eagerly for the results to show. Soon huge columns of smoke rose fifty feet into the air. In the middle of this joyous occasion the fire siren sounded. We looked at each other and wondered if we had gone too far this time. Well there wasn't anything to do but let the fire die down and hope that we could play innocent. Fortunately for us they never came. We spent many happy hours experimenting with combustibles and often burned ourselves in the process. One did learn that fire burned and that the consequences, a red welt or two, had to be endured. Certainly our parents were not going to fret over such minor pains.

Many aspects of our life revolved around fires ; they cooked our food, warmed our homes and entertained us. Today my children share the same fascination on those increasingly rare occasions when we are permitted to burn. For many city children today fire is only a menace and they cannot relate to the joys we felt as children. For them heat comes from a hole in the wall and the glow of a hotplate cooks their food. For us the naked flame in it's rawest expression of power crackled, smoked and sizzled under our control. A large part of our lives was dedicated to keeping the hearth fires burning. It is not too surprising that the ancient Greeks considered fire to be one of the four major constituents of the world, we certainly did.

WHITE WINTERS

When the last leaves rustled down from their reluctant limbs and the rain had turned the once dry ground to a soggy pulp we began to yearn for winter. The days between Halloween and Armistice day were a nether world where the joys of fall ceased before the thrill of first snowfall began. I remember Armistice day vividly because dad was born on the eleventh day of the eleventh month nineteen eleven. He often told us about his seventh birthday in England where my grandparents house had a gazebo on top from whence dad could survey the Essex countryside and the town of Maldon below. He had gone up to watch the fireworks and upon his return commented to granddad that "It was jolly decent of them to have fireworks for his birthday. "When the holiday fell on a day that created a long weekend we often visited the Okanagan or took some other trip so that this happy coincidence left it's indelible mark on us. One year we had journeyed to the Okanagan when the temperature dropped over the weekend. On our return the mercury plummeted below zero, that's minus eighteen for those of you on Celsius. As there was no protective blanket of snow on the ground our shallow water line had frozen completely. If we had been home we would have left the taps trickling to prevent this. For two days we dug up the line replacing burst sections and thing others while we made do with water from the garden pond which we hauled up through the ice. Needless to say the new line was installed much deeper and insulated to prevent a re occurrence.

All the organizations in town paraded to the cenotaph after the service in the Legion hall and as cubs and scouts we donned our uniforms and attended. Dad never participated and when I asked him about this he remarked that the had attended a lifetime of church parades in the army and wasn't about to go to another. One of the clergy from the three major denominations took the service then we all lined up for the short march to the cenotaph. In those days it was located in the middle of the side street that ran between the drug store and the Overwaitea, now the bank. Legion members dressed in their blue uniforms with their medals proudly thumping their chests, now marched to the cenotaph and stood in respectful silence. It was frequently cold and we shivered as we stood quietly waiting for the trumpet to sound reveille. No greater tribute could we bear to the fallen than our presence at the memorial year by year, in rain, sleet or snow.

Snow ! We longed for snow on those barren November mornings. The first fluttering of downy crystals sent us into rapturous delight, noses pressed against the window praying for a heavy fall. Sometimes the first snow came like a thief in the night stealing away the barren landscape so that when we awoke to look out our bedroom window the world was changed. Whether it was just a skiff or a foot or more it was always welcome, well at least to us. Of all forms of precipitation only snow has the power to magically change a bleak brown hillside into a fantasy world of sparkling diamonds and fantastic shapes. A really large snowfall erases all trace of the barren land and covers even man's intrusions, softening houses and woodsheds, hiding roads and pathways, leaving cars to appear as mere bumps like any other hill. As children we would gaze out through frosted panes and dream of unending sleigh rides or lofty snow forts. The trees, now shrouded in their woolly mantles, brought forth imaginary frosty giants striding forth to conquer the land. Each branch of lilac and birch wore a snowy jacket that swelled their limbs and caused them to bend towards the ground in wintry homage. Now lay the world still and quiescent. The snow, like a giant muffler, made normal sounds distant and far away. For a moment, an hour, tranquility descended and peace of spirit calmed the fevered pace of life. God and nature had reclaimed the world.

Eagerly we'd dress and hasten downstairs to see if school was cancelled but knowing that all this bounty would remain for us to explore on our walk to the bus stop. If we had to go to school it would still be fun to wade through foot high snow, leaving trails that marked us as the first to cross this enchanted land. If we were lucky the fall would occur on a weekend or during the holidays and we could bundle up in boots, scarves, mittens, hats and jackets to spend the day making our dreams reality. The first snows were often damp and soggy but made excellent snowballs and forts. We would start with a snowball sized chunk and keep rolling until we couldn't push it any further. Two more large balls created a base and several smaller ones were added on top. If we had friends over we would make two such forts, stock them with snowballs then ; Let Battle Commence ! The only snag with the wet stuff was that after an hour or two you were soaked through and utterly chilled. Time to call a truce and come in for hot chocolate.

After a base of a foot or two of packed snow had fallen the next good dry snowfall was truly fun to play in. A slope ran from the woodshed onto the lawn which made a good toboggan run, only we didn't have a toboggan. This minor omission didn't prevent us from hurtling down on cardboard boxes or any other piece of wood that might possible work as a sled. When I was eleven or twelve we found the perfect sled, two old fenders from one of the cars that dad used for parts. At about this time, the late fifties, a small, round plastic sled called a flying saucer was all the rage. We didn't have the funds for one of these so the fenders were our solution. The paint on the fenders was good so we inserted a wire into one of the bolt holes in front ; rope would have been cut in a moment, twisted the top into a loop and Voila ; a perfect tow rope. Our driveway was steep and about three hundred yards long so it was here that we chose to test our invention. They worked even better that the store bought saucers with the added advantage of carrying two people. We nicknamed them ' flying sampans '. We tore down the drive wriggling from side to side, sometime careening off the snowbanks and back onto the road. Over and over we climbed the hill then flew down until was too dark to see. For a couple of years these worked well and we invited friends over to participate in ' Flying Sampan parties.' At a recent school reunion I was surprised to find a friend who still fondly remembered the old rigs.

In the mornings it would be chilly in our house, there having been no fire on since we went to bed. My brother an I would climb into one bed and snuggle down to get the maximum heat. Were would spin yarns and talk of things that we would do when we older. Inevitably we explored each others body and cradled each other in our nakedness. Often we would explore each others bums, fingering and cuddling.

    A year or two later we entered into another phase of winter sports, skiing. I remember going to Sicamous to collect two pairs of skis. In those days skiing wasn't as popular as it is today and skis hadn't progressed very far. Ours were two planks with a groove in the centre and turned up points with leather harnesses. Mine were labelled Kandahar and Marty's Junior Jet. We applied plenty of Dubbin to our leather boots, strapped on the skis and away we went. First we had to pack the snow down on the slope leading to our lawn then we swished down trying hard to maintain balance. Stopping was accomplished by running out of steam or falling, whichever came first. Unlike today's skis which are totally useless for anything except downhill with a ski lift ours could be used to glide over fresh snow and we often used them for transport to bring milk from the farm. Sometimes this led to unfortunate accidents but on the whole the bottles of milk survived the journey intact. The skis had a tendency to stick so we waxed them with paraffin wax much like cross country skiers do today. We had endless hours of fun with them but eventually retired them when newer skis with firmer bindings and metal edges appeared. At the top of our property was a Y in the road with a trail heading up the side of the hill. Here we built a ski run where we could travel at will without worrying about cars. By now we had learned to stop and turn so that the curves on the run became a challenge which we relished. One night the moon was full and, being bored, we took our skis out and tried the hill. As we glided up the drive the full moon shone brightly, reflecting her pale light from every crystal of snow and thereby magnifying her power. As we reached the bottom of the run we turned our skis sideways to negotiate the steep hill. Now halfway up we stood under the shadow of the forest, surveying the tracks. It was a little tricky under the trees where the run began as the light was poor but once we cleared the forest it was bright as day. Over and over we came down, always trying to go just a little bit faster as the moon rose higher casting shadows upon the snow. We returned from our skiing, cheeks rosy and breath steaming, to warm ourselves by the fire. Oh it was a grand time to be young!

When I was sixteen downhill skiing began to become a popular sport so a ski hill was made at Summit lake complete with a rope tow. This was a great improvement over climbing the small hills around home and enabled us to ski better. The hill was the effort of three or four residents who had emigrated to Nakusp from Austria. With their knowledge and the assistance of a variety of logging equipment the hill opened in the early sixties. The only snag, from our point of view, was that we had to talk someone into driving us there as it was twelve miles east of town. There we were given our first skiing instruction and shown how to make snowplow turns and stops. This greatly improved our control which, up to this point, had been non existent. It was the beginning of the end of a simpler era. Now we needed newer, more specialized equipment and skiing became an event rather than a mode of transportation. The last two years I was in high school we even went to Silver Star in Vernon which was a tremendous experience. T-bars, poma lifts and even a chair lift dotted the runs making the access easier and the runs longer. The other element that changed was the cost. Getting up the hill quickly is expensive and it continues to increase so that skiing from urban areas is restricted to the wealthy. All our activities have become regulated and therefore expensive. Even the equipment is so specialized that you can no longer glide upon the deep snow even with cross country skis. Gone are the days when we strapped our skis on to explore the new fallen snow, to be the first humans to make tracks upon the pristine blanket ; gliding along in a silent wilderness where none have been before.

The air dominated our lives in winter and we spent a lot of time gazing at the thermometer, hoping that it would stay cold enough for the snow to stay. When we were thrust into the midst of a cold snap we would watch the mercury in the thermometer inch lower. Our faces pressed against the icy pane we would strain to read the tiny markings that notched another degree below zero. We didn't often get very cold spells where the temperatures plunged below zero so when we did it was exhilarating. Now coats and hats became a necessity and the adults warned of frostbite. Tales were told of even colder winters in days past while we listened with a mixture of awe and revulsion of stories of people who froze their limbs or touched their tongues to metal. One immediate result was that we consumed much more fuel so that more wood had to be chopped. Outside the frigid air blasted exposed skin as I struggled to handle the frozen chunks of wood onto the chopping block. If the wood was even slightly wet the ax had a tendency to bounce off the icy surface. There was no danger of feeling cold for the exercise created plenty of heat providing you kept working. We were fortunate to live in an area where there was little wind so that we were spared the really cold and windy temperatures of the prairies.

The temperatures may have been more moderate but we did get plenty of snow. Every time the snow began falling we would watch the stump of an old birch tree to see how fast it was accumulating. Dad had cut the large birch tree down as it was growing into the eaves and blocked what little light there was from entering the windows. Every hour or so we would venture out, ruler in hand, to measure the accumulations ; the more the merrier. One year it began to snow heavily in the evening and there was a foot and a half by morning with no sign of it letting up. We were ecstatic ! We measured every hour and took our skis out although it was pretty heavy going. The next morning the snow had ceased but there was now three and a half feet of it, that's over a meter for you kids. It was truly a grand fall ! No one went anywhere until the roads were plowed which took a day or two. When we ventured outside the snow reached our chests and Pat, who was only four at the time, completely disappeared ! A fast way to run some energy off your kids is to send them out to play in three feet of snow. We were bushed after an hour or so of making trails or trying to ski.

One of the major advantages of snow was that it improved the surface of our abominable roads. After the first snowfall the roads were plowed and became packed and smooth. My mother referred to it as ' White Pavement '. She whizzed around at fifty or sixty miles an hour if the roads were hard and dry, the colder it was the better the traction. The smoothness of the road and the high snowbanks created a sensation of travelling on a bullet down the bore of a vast white cannon. Snow did have it's nastier side which usually revealed itself when we attempted to gain access to our driveway. If it had snowed a fair bit or was particularly slippery we were bundled into the back of the car to supplement the two fifty pound, 22 kilo, bags of sand that were placed in the trunk of the car with the advent of winter. The classic formula for good traction is $T = \sqrt{WODW}$ or to translate, the amount of traction is equal to the square root of the weight over the driving wheels. By this formula it is easy to see that you need all the weight you can muster in the rear. With this in mind, and us in the back, we headed up the road that wound for half a mile along the face of the mountain. Mom drove as fast as she could while still managing to negotiate the curves. There was a slightly flatter section just before our driveway opened up on the left and it was here that maximum speed was desirable. Keeping a careful eye peeled for competing traffic, fortunately the number of cars that used the road was sparse, the car shot off into the unplowed driveway. Holding our breaths while the car fishtailed then straightened out we prayed that our weight would suffice to bring us to the top. Invariably it wasn't. This meant backing down the drive and onto the road to take another crack at it. Off we went again, mentally urging the car onward while the car lost speed. Just before the car stalled mom would shout.

"Out and push ! "

Rapidly we piled out of the still moving car, seat belts being unheard of, and began pushing the vehicle towards the safety of the parking area. If there was a lot of snow we wouldn't make it more that half way up. Back into the car we piled while mom or dad backed the car down to the flats to try again. This time we were told to sit in the trunk, for added effect, as off we went. Sometimes it took two or three shunts to attain the safety of the house but we usually made it. Very rarely the car was abandoned in the driveway while we walked to the house. This wasn't a good place to park as the snowplow would then be unable to plow the driveway. By some quirk of fate the steepest part of the drive was near the top so we usually emptied the ashes from the stove onto this spot to improve traction. It was always an interesting drive home in the winter.

One winter, when I was in grade four I think, I had a pain in the stomach which gradually got worse. I remember driving through the night to get to Vernon where I was hurried up and the doctor called. He came and began by examining my rectum before hustling me away to be operated on. It was near go as my appendix had nearly burst. As it was only a couple of days before Christmas I had to stay in hospital. It was hard not to be home for the holiday but Christmas morning made up for it. There, hanging at the foot of the bed, was an enormous stocking full of toys and other goodies. It almost made up for missing Christmas dinner.

It was during the long winters months when the sun sank early behind the high peaks of Saddleback that I developed my interest in games. One of the advantages of not having television was that we were forced to rely on our own resources for entertainment. One of my earliest recollections is of playing cards around the kitchen table. Dad had made a crib board and we played endless games with two, three or four players, each combination requiring different skills. There were also board games that varied from the very simple ' snakes and ladders ' to the intellectual Scrabble. Our English relatives frequently sent games so our supply of entertainment was varied. We cut our teeth on checkers before moving on to chess. Chinese checkers, a game played with marbles on an indented board, was fun as was Ludo, a variation on the games that required you to get your men safely home. There was always Monopoly to while away a dreary winter's afternoon and the game frequently lasted for more than one afternoon. Our parents played bridge and we were started on whist before graduating to that most subtle and complicated of games.

One of the big advantages of games is that you can play them with anyone. If someone didn't know a game we were always prepared to teach them. The more players you have the better and the less likely you are to run out of entertainment. Games require people to interact and by doing so you learn a number of useful social skills. Unlike television where everyone huddles around an electronic gadget fighting for control of the remote; games require you to treat your opponents with consideration and fair play. We learned not to cheat, besides cheating takes the edge off winning. Many of the games required cooperation between two players to defeat another team. We soon graduated from the mindless games of chance like fish or war as they soon bored us. Most of our contests required the sharpening of mental faculties and we revelled in the calculations of chance. Not that there wasn't a war or two over these games but even that taught us to settle our differences amicably. If you can't agree on the rules there is no game and if there is no game you are bored. One could always retreat into a book but after an hour or two we were looking for some other form of amusement.

Chris Bird was a frequent participant in our games and I have photo that he took of Marty and I playing crib. Our faces are set in concentration as we pegged our way along the board. I was eight and Marty was seven. As a child I managed to catch every childhood disease known to man so I spent a lot of time curled up in my parents bed trying to find games to amuse me. When I had run out of solitaire options I began to teach my sister how to play crib. As she was only four or five I had to count her cards but eventually she learned to play well enough to help ease my days of confinement. Crib has another big advantage in that the boards and cards are portable and can be brought out anywhere. Our parents were avid crib players when we were young which was very sneaky of them. Adding is an integral part of crib and as such it served as method of checking our math skills !

On Saturdays during the winter the Waterfields came down to play bridge and I remember sitting close to mom and watching the cards slide across the table as trick after trick was taken. While dad was a good card player he hated to lose. That coupled with a nasty temper made him difficult to play with as he would be enraged at what he perceived as stupid mistakes. On the whole they did manage to enjoy themselves and mom was well able to hold her own in any discussion of the card play. This aspect of games that can be played from the cradle to the grave started me playing bridge and has been a great source of pleasure throughout my life. Now I play with my eldest son as we carry on that tradition of playing together as a family.

Chris Bird was not much of a bridge player but he spent hours teaching Marty and I the intricacies of chess. In the beginning he would spot us a bishop or rook as we tried in vain to penetrate his defence. Of course we played against each other and were evenly matched. By the time we were teenagers we could give him a good game. One evening we invited Peter Bokis over to play and he was really very good. We lost game after game while he ruefully proclaimed, "You play too fast !" He tried to get us to take more time to really see the board and to counter each move our opponent made by looking six or seven moves ahead. One year Chris took me to a chess tournament in Nelson which was very exciting. I don't remember doing very well but the next year he took Marty who won the 'C' flight. We play occasionally to this day and my youngest shows some flair for the game.

The summer I turned fifteen I went to work for the youth crew of the forestry service where I picked up another game, hearts. Here the object is to avoid taking tricks as the heart suit is counted against you and the person with the lowest score wins. The big penalty card is the queen of spades which is worth minus thirteen, as much as all the hearts combined. If you are able to collect all of the hearts and the queen of spades you have 'control' and each player is docked twenty six. Of course you can get 'Chinese control' which means you take all except one heart, very bad for your score. One evening Chris, Marty, dad and I were playing hearts. Dad was in a bad way as his collection of high cards caused him to have more that his fair share of minuses. I had the queen of spades well protected and had passed up several opportunities to give it to other players. Dad's face took on that hunted look as he tried in vain to loose the lead. When I was sure he had the trick I tossed him the queen. He was furious and protested loudly ! It was his own fault for he had been ' hoisted on his own petard.' If he had not taken the game so seriously it would not have been so much fun to watch him squirm. By then I was old enough to relish the irony.

After four months of this we were ready for spring and even if the snows returned the melting of the snow from the roads meant that our days as ballast were over for another year. Earth, Air, Fire and Water, were ever present in our cycles of life. They were intricately entwined with the rhythms that made up our daily lives and dictated the activities we participated in. No running down to the indoor pool for a relaxing winter's dip. Our only water was frozen or so cold that getting wet meant risking hypothermia. If we were lucky the lake would freeze over and we could skate but I only remember it freezing two or three times in the twelve years that I lived at home. We lived close to nature and there was no doubt that She lived close by, influencing every aspect of our lives from school activities to work and play.

CHRISTMAS

Once Remembrance day was past the world looked towards Christmas, not with the barrage of advertising about a deluge of worldly goods, but rather with that keen anticipation which marks a truly universal festival. We were in a minority in that we did not, well our parents didn't, attend church so for us the festival was not a religious one but a family one. Most of the people would attend church sometime over Christmas, honouring the birth of our saviour with hymns and prayers, making an effort to be kind to everyone. The birth of Christ was acknowledged as the central theme of the season by one and all. At school the choir began rehearsing carols while the drama club prepared a special offering. The Christmas concert was one of the social highlights of the year for both the school and the community. As members of the Sunday school we also participated in the annual offering of the Christmas pageant. Every church and every group held their own celebration and if we were lucky we might attend two or three of these shows. The highlight of the evening, well it was for us as small children, was the arrival of Santa Claus. When the last act was completed and the cast disrobed everyone gathered around the Christmas tree. Soon the tinkling of bells announced the arrival of that most beloved character of the season. Dressed in a red coat and pants with a large black belt around his immense waist and huge boots he made his grand entrance to the squeals of delighted children. His rosy cheeks and snowy white hair and beard were surmounted by a red toque with a bell attached that rang out cheerfully as he ran. When he reached the tree we could feel the joy shining from his eyes as he settled down to hand out treats. The standard offering was enclosed in a brown paper bag accompanied by a Jap orange. I'm sure the dentist would have protested but for us it was a great treat, a whole bag of assorted candies which we delved into retrieving sticky delights and stuffing them into our mouths. It was with palpable regret that we saw him off an hour later knowing that we would be asleep when he returned Christmas eve.

Anticipation was the true hallmark of the season. Early in December enticing packages began to arrive but they were squirrelled away to secret hiding places until the tree was up and they could be allowed out on their own. These were parcels from aunts and uncles in England and I still associate Christmas with "brown paper packages tied up with string." Unlike some of our friends we were not allowed to open any of our presents until Christmas day. Would the day ever arrive? I looked forward to everything about Christmas; the concerts, the getting and decorating of the tree, the food and the presents. ' It is better to give than to receive,' was not yet etched on my young mind but it was in the great anticipation and the joy of our own receiving that I was taught this lesson. My sources of stimulation for Christmas gifts were limited to the Christmas catalog and the limited offerings of the local stores. I would pour through the toy sections of the catalogue, marking up the goods I wished I could have. One year I can remember coveting a matched set of toy pistols complete with gun belt that was in one of the stores but the five dollar price tag was way beyond my means. I wrote my wish to Santa and prayed fervently. On Christmas morning my wish had been granted. There was the amassing set under the tree. When I was older and the family had acquired a record player it was music that I most longed for. Oh to be a child again at Christmas when the imagination soars and fantastic hopes quiver in the proximity of arrival.

Make no mistake about this : Santa Claus is real. From my earliest memories comes the jingle of sleigh bells and the hearty ho ! ho ! ho ! of that jolly figure dressed in red. I revelled in the tales and songs that exulted the stature of this important figure. He always visited the parties and concerts when I was young to dispense bags of candy with an orange tucked neatly on top. Not just an ordinary orange but a Jap orange which peeled easily and divided into luscious little ' pigs ' to be popped into my mouth and savoured as the juice trickled down my throat. I knew all the tales about him and in my imagination he swelled to mythical proportions. I knew the names of all his reindeer and early learned to recite "The Night Before Christmas". I could sing Rudolph the Red Nosed Reindeer to perfection while my mind drew the portrait of Santa and his sleigh gliding across the moon with the stars behind him and the deep snow spread below like a down comforter. He was and is, so real that if you but close your eyes on Christmas Eve you will hear the tinkle of sleigh bells, the snort of the reindeer and the hearty Ho ! Ho ! Ho ! as Santa glides across the Christmas scene.

When we were small dad would arrive one evening with a tree but as we became older that task fell to Marty and I. We searched all fall to find a perfect tree then forgot where they had been as snow covered the land. A Christmas tree had to be perfect, well it had to be perfect on at least three sides. As soon as school was out we grabbed our skis and headed out to the back forty to bring back a tree. Now it is in the nature of trees that grow in a forest to be spindly and poorly branched as the taller trees block out the light. We usually solved this dilemma by cutting down a larger tree and carry off the crown. Once the tree hits the canopy foliage blossoms in profusion while the trunk below is frequently bare and devoid of branches. It takes a keen eye to tell the truth about the crown of a tree that towers forty feet above you. This little problem often resulted in the felling of more than one tree to obtain the "perfect Christmas tree." Oh the waste ! I hear you cry. We felled trees with abandon for twelve years using the trunks for fuel and cabins while making no visible dent in the forest. Today one large machine destroys whole sections now stripped of any covering at all.

Once the tree was safely home we tied and propped it into its usual corner, that's where we hid the patchy side, in preparation for it's coronation. Everyone participated in hanging the assorted decorations from its limbs being careful not to drop the glass balls that glittered so brightly in the light of the tiny coloured bulbs. When the garland had been installed and icicles draped from every limb the star was mounted on top. The lights were turned off in the living room while a hush filled the room as the tree was lit. There it was. The perfect Christmas tree. Now the hot chocolate and coffee was poured, the cake cut and everyone retired to sit and gaze in wonder at this marvellous creation.

Soon the brown paper parcels migrated to their place of honour under it 's spreading limbs while we shook each package in a vain attempt to guess it's contents. The anticipation heightened.

Finally it was Christmas Eve when we settled into our beds and pulled the eiderdown comforters tightly around us before drifting off to sleep. Our stockings were hung from the foot of the bed as we boasted no fireplace, dad having removed it to convert it into a place for the kitchen stove. In those days watches were expensive so we had no way of telling how early it was and as the sun is rather tardy in arising on the twenty-fifth of December you can understand that there were some rather early rising. If we were too early we were shooed back to bed where we whiled the time away with the contents of our stockings. Stockings in our family had a traditional arrangement. Tucked neatly into the toe was a Jap orange while a candy cane or other foodie provided necessary sustenance. Small toys or a pair of socks or other small items filled the cavity to the brim so there was plenty to keep us amused for an hour or two until we could legitimately come downstairs and invade our parents bed. Watching dad explore his stocking was a treat. He would reach in and feel around a bit before coming up with an item, say a package of cigars, then his face would light up as he exclaimed, "Oh ! White Owls. My favourite." When half an hour or so had been spent sharing the contents that Santa had provided we all set about helping to make scrambled eggs for breakfast. No one was allowed to open any presents until breakfast was completed.

By now our anticipation was finely tuned as we gathered around the tree to hand out presents. It was no mad dash to unwrap but a stately procession of wonder as only one person at a time opened their gifts so that hugs and thanks could be shared. Family gifts were opened first before we were allowed to open those intriguing brown paper parcels. Inside were a host of different items from games to books all guaranteed to provide many happy hours exploring their intricacies. They were English so they opened up a different world from that in which we inhabited which made them even more special. There were Boys annuals with tales of snowmen and Father Christmas, Noddy and the Skittles or Rupert Bear. There were Games of Ludo, Snakes and

Ladders or Chinese Checkers and one year my godmother sent me a miniature travelling chess set. When all the gifts were open mom tidied up the wrapping paper saving the best to wrap next years offerings before heading to the kitchen to stuff the bird.

Several Christmases revealed particularly wonderful gifts. The first one we spent in our new house I received an axe which was probably the most useful and well used present I have ever received. Another time my brother and I both received matching gun sets which was just what we had our hearts set on. The twin holsters held cap guns with pearl handles while the belt was studded with fake bullets. Caps were inserted by the roll and a satisfactory bang was produced along with the acrid smell of burning gunpowder. For a young fan of the Lone Ranger they were perfect. After a short period where we blazed away at each other we were gently persuaded to take our shoot outs 'outside'. When I was older I remember the gift of music. Small towns didn't have access to many cultural venues and I loved the music of Gilbert and Sullivan. I had spent a lot of time at a friends house listening to their collection and now I had some of their better known songs for myself. It didn't take me long to memorize them all, including the intricate patter songs. Christmas was that time of year when the yearnings of man were fulfilled, when the spirit soared above the commonplace to reach a deeper meaning. One year we went to Nelson to see a production of H.M.S. Pinafore. It was marvellous ! I can still remember my father bending softly towards me and whispering, "Buttercup is usually about four axe handles across the backside. "Down through the years that have followed I have kept the music close to my heart.

Of course the centrepiece of our festival was the turkey dinner. Stuffing of two kinds was prepared ; sage, breadcrumbs and onions in one end and a sausage stuffing at the other. For an hour the preparations went on while we played with our new toys occasionally being called in to help with some facet of the upcoming feast. I brought wood in to stoke the stove for the temperature had to be just right for the bird. The previous day I had cut ample wood to ensure that I didn't have to do any splitting on Christmas day. Once the bird was safely in the oven we often went visiting friends for a short time or simply stayed home and played with all of the new things that had arrived. There was no official lunch as we snacked on cheese and crackers with homemade onion pickles and a slice of Christmas cake.

Mom's Christmas cake was a marvel of culinary creation. There were currents and raisins, glace cherries and dates, almonds,walnuts,flour and eggs all combined in a large bowl. We were allowed to lick the spoons after the batter had been tamped into the biggest of mom's circular pans. For hours the heavenly smell issued from the kitchen as this culinary delight came slowly to perfection. Once cooked and cooled a thick layer of almond paste was applied to the top and then the whole was covered with white icing that dried to a hard finish. I looked forward to this cake all year round and it was a sad day when the last piece disappeared from the tin.

After snacks we were bundled up and sent outside to play so that mom and dad could work the final miracle of Christmas dinner. When we re-entered the house the bird lay on it's platter resplendent in it's coat of brown with stuffing oozing from every pore. Into the bathroom we hurried to wash our tingling hands and faces before taking our places at the table. The silver had been polished earlier and now it gleamed on the table. Crossing our hands we held the Christmas crackers in an unbroken chain. With a loud snap the crackers popped and we scrambled to obtain the wonders contained within. There were tiny silver bells, whistles or gleaming amulets ready to hang on a necklace and of course the paper hats. Unfolding these we crowned ourselves as masters of the fete. There were sage proverbs contained as well and all had to be shared. "Don't count your chickens before they hatch.", A fool and his money are soon parted ", and other equally wise admonitions. Thus crowned and amused dad began to slice the ham and turkey and the feast began. The silver serving dishes were loaded with carrots, potatoes and brussel sprouts, the last being a favourite of my fathers but unfortunately not one of ours. The ' individual cabbages ' as he called them were a bit sharp for my palette. No one complained and as we had only to take a couple, to encourage our taste buds to mature, they proved a minor obstacle. I managed to disguise the flavor with cranberry sauce and gravy. We ate until the stuffing seeped from our ears then came back for desert. Steamed puddings were a favourite desert at home and this was the best of the steamed puddings. Mom stirred them up in large batches and canned them so that they were aged to perfection when it came time to consume them. Wrapped tightly in a cheese cloth it was steamed while we ate our first course. When the lid was lifted the heavenly aroma wafted through the room. The pudding was a deep brown almost black so filled with fruit that it begged to be eaten. A small portion of brandy was poured over the shine y black ball then ignited to be brought in flaming triumph before the assembled guests. We managed to eat this along with the rum hard sauce ; sugar, butter and rum, before being filled to the brim.

Having consumed so great a meal we were in no shape for vigorous activity. Once the table was cleared and the dishes washed we retired to living room to play "The Priest of the Parish"Everyone had to pick out a colour and they became Mr. Black or Purple or Red. Dad always had to be difficult and be Mr. Heliotrope. In addition to playing the part of a parish councillor you could be elevated to the status of Beadle or be the Priest. Having sorted out these players the 'priest' began. "The priest of the parish had lost his wishing cap. Some say this and some say that, but I say that Mr. Red has it." If you were Mr. Red you had to immediately reply," What me Sir ! "The rest of the conversation went this way.

Priest "Yes your sir."
You "Not I sir."
Priest "Who then sir ?"

At this point everyone began counting as fast as they could while you had to name someone else who might have pilfered the magic cap. If you didn't make it before the count reached ten or named a wrong person, for example Mr. Red who was presently the Beadle not Mr. Red, you became the Beadle, he became the Priest and had to carry on until someone else made a mistake. The game usually only lasted half an hour or so by which time our parents were quietly sleeping so we would return to our presents. By eight o'clock the excitement of the day and the early start would have us nodding and off to bed we'd wend to savour the memories and anticipate the morrow.

The year I turned fifteen we found a new, well new to us anyway, set of skis under the Christmas tree. They had cable bindings and metal edges which were vastly superior to the old in controlling turns. Along with the skis were special boots which were much more comfortable and allowed the skis to be fastened tighter. Skiing as a sport had just arrived at Nakusp and the Austrians were giving ski lessons so that we were at last able to control our descent and ascent of the slopes. We learned how to dig our edges in and climb up really steep slopes and how to herringbone up the lesser ones. The bases were vastly superior and enabled us to attain really tremendous speeds more or less under control. Of course the faster you go the harder you fall when you do crash and our spectacular spills were the talk of the dinner table. These were the last all purpose skis I would own as they still allowed enough flexibility to pull a toboggan across unpacked snow on scout hikes or afternoon forays in the fields and trails around home. Most of the boys used snowshoes but skis had one enormous advantage in that you didn't have to slog down the hills.

Once the ski hill at Summit lake was open we spent as much time there as we could during the holidays. The town had built a rope tow up the side of the mountain and for fifty cents you could spend the day whizzing down hill and being hauled back up. It was a bit of a trick to hang onto the rope and definitely hard on the gloves which tended to wear out in an inordinately short time. We would pack a lunch of turkey sandwiches, loaded with stuffing and cranberry sauce, a Jap orange and a thermos full of cocoa and spend the day improving our abilities. First one to the hill lit the fire in the stove to warm the chalet so that when we were tired we could peel our sodden mitts off and warm our frozen hands while the mitts warmed a bit even if they didn't dry completely. No one had fancy ski pants so long underwear and wool pants were the rule. After a particularly interesting spill one tended to emerge looking like the abominable snowman ! At three o'clock mom would arrive to pick us up and we'd pile the skis and poles into the trunk of the Austin, faces rosy red and clothes utterly soaked. Once home a bath warmed our bodies and soothed our aching muscles. At night we slept like dormice hoping that tomorrow's snow would propel us on to faster runs.

One year dad took us to Vernon to ski on a really big ski hill. Silver star was just beginning to develop and had a poma lift and a couple of T- bars. The former was a round plastic button on the end of metal rod. You tucked the plastic disc between your legs and skied up to the top of the mountain. The T-bar was a similar device only two skiers tucked the bar behind their bottoms while the cable tightened pulling you up the slope. You still had to ski up the slope but it was vastly superior to a rope tow. All day long from nine in the morning till three in the afternoon we whizzed down the slopes savouring the variety of runs and staying clear of the advanced slopes which were beyond our ability to negotiate. At noon we ate our packed lunches while we warmed up. At six thousand feet the top of Silver star could be mighty cold ! Our outdated equipment looked odd on these slopes but we were oblivious to the differences. For us it was a marvellous experience. Around three thirty dad would come an pick us up, he had a heart condition and couldn't stay comfortably at elevations, and we would relax on the way down to spend the night with friends. Two or three days of this made a wonderful holiday and started us on our way to a love of skiing. Even today we all ski when we can. Nothing is so beautiful as the top of a mountain in winter. The wind whips the snow around the trees creating fantastic shapes that bend and sway in the crystal clear air. From the top of the mountain you can see across the valleys where cities appear as mere pinpricks in an ocean of craggy peaks and the only sound is the sighing of the wind and the swish of your skis.

Our Christmases were secular affairs but when I was thirteen Fr. White arrived to take over the Anglican parish. Old Cannon Mitchell had died shortly after I joined the choir but Mrs. White took over from Mrs. Mitchell and we began to learn new music. We learned to sing the Te Deum and Vinite plus the evening canticles, the Nunc Demittus and Magnificat. They were simple settings for untrained voices but I revelled in the sound of the old squeeze organ with it's pedal bellows.

"My soul doth magnify the Lord" we sang as music brought joy into my soul.

Thirteen is the age of questing. At this age a boy becomes a young man in more than physical change. Over the years I have marvelled at the resilience of youth and their exuberance. It is not for naught that teenagers have acquired the awesome stature that they have. We see the abundance of energy coupled with mood changes yet fail to see ourselves. As we live increasingly automated lives teenagers have fewer responsibilities and we have not encouraged them to take on anything new. This coupled with a young man's view that he is immortal and that nothing can harm him has adults gawking. While I had responsibilities I was not impervious to the rhythm of nature that puberty sets in motion. I now wanted to be my own man and to achieve in a sphere of life outside that of familiar family endeavours. Dad and I shared an equally hot temper and as he did nothing to check it I had only his example to emulate. It was inevitable that a clash of wills would occur at this stage in life. We had friends over Christmas day and we engaged in some rather physical play and being larger than the other child it was she who bore the brunt of it. Dad lost his temper and ordered me out of the house. I was completely unprepared for this on Christmas day of all days. I wandered alone and hurt in the snow and managed to miss dinner. It was a terrible day. Mom called me in an hour later and fed me alone at the table, my face streaked with tears. Although this experience of Christmas was not a good one some ray of sunshine crept in. The next day I was to go to Burton and sing Good King Wenclas in the church. It is a duet and I sang it with the priest's daughter. She took the kings part and I with my treble voice sang the page's part. After we retired to someones home and had a very good feast. To this day I remember that day, St. Stephen's day, as being holy and without blemish.

The only saving grace was that the next day I left early to sing in the church at Burton. In a parish that has four churches scattered over fifty miles of dirt track the logistics of arranging Christmas services becomes more difficult. The two main churches at Nakusp and Edgewood had Christmas day services while St. John's and St. Stephen's were on

Boxing day. It was a great relief to leave the house and accompany Fr. White and his daughter, who was about my age, to Burton where we sang, 'Good King Wencelas' as a duet. As I had the higher voice I sang the page parts. Afterwards we had tea and I enjoyed boxing day far more than Christmas. Ever since I have honoured St. Stephen's day, the first martyr, in my heart and soul. It was the beginning of my life in the church which has sustained me throughout the years and has made Christmas a festival where God and His son are the centre and heart of the festivities.

Apart from teenage wars Christmas was a happy time. The younger we were the more magical the time. I remember hanging on to Santa Clause and his reindeer long after others had become jaded. Hope springs eternal in the human breast and for me, a child of imagination, this was one myth I did not want shattered. It was not until much later that I would research the whole history of Santa in all his guises to realize that all myth springs from basic truths and that Santa Clause or St. Nicholas is as real as the generosity that pours forth from the human spirit. He is the personification of selfless giving that raises men above the level of the beasts and brings his soul into contact with God.

A TEN O'CLOCK SCHOLAR

Having arrived with a thump back into the world of classroom schooling, as the episode with the suspenders shows, I was caught between two worlds. Not advanced far enough to be in grade 2 but definitely bored with grade 1. My mother kept all of my report cards so I am able to gain a glimpse at those years I spent in school. Grade two was a write off. I succeeded in hiding any ability I had and to garner straight average marks for the only time in my long years of education. Whether mom and dad were too preoccupied with the matter of survival or whether I just shut out the teacher I don't know but the effects of this move have haunted me throughout the years. I was definitely not socially up to the next grade in a day and age that propelled bright students one or two grades ahead so perhaps it was just as well that I wasn't pushed ahead. There still remains a nagging question in the further recesses of my mind that had I been allowed to chase the others I could have changed the course of my life. Of such events are the turning points of our lives fashioned. The record is perfectly clear : for a whole year I was not interested in school. If any further proof is needed Grade two is the only year I could not remember the name of my teacher without looking it up and I recall nothing of import from that year.

It was, however, not an uneventful year. A whole new life had begun and a whole new neighbourhood had to be explored. Our house sat on five acres of forested land which was a vast tract of land for two small boys to explore. The driveway ended at the woodshed where there was space to store a couple of small cars. The first vehicle I remember dimly was a Ford Prefect. We must have acquired it shortly after we moved in as I do not recall ever being without a car. As we were two and a half miles from town mom would have needed the vehicle to get groceries. It was not new but it got us around when we needed to and as dad was a mechanic repairs were done at home. Between the driveway and the road was a level field and the first item of business was putting in a garden. It could have been plowed the following spring but it was certainly there throughout my years at home. To the west of this field, standing on the edge of the bank, was an enormous birch tree surrounded by bracken and thimble berries. Except for the south end of the driveway trees sheltered us from the road. It was on this open piece of land where we had our ring of stones for burning all and sundry, our private pyrotechnic area. West of the driveway was the big cedar tree which we loved to climb. From it's lofty perch we could survey the house with it's tiny of patch of lawn or spy on the cars when they came up the road. We carved dens out of dense thickets where we played our imaginary games. We were even allowed to climb the Big Hill with its mass of bracken then roll down crushing the plants in our topsy turvy journey to the bottom. Our only restrictions were that we had to remain within earshot so that mom or dad could call us. Bruce often joined us and the three of us spent hours together happily finding new and exciting ways to pass the time.

Mom had set herself the task of cleaning out the rockery or rock garden that lined the bank behind the house. It was sadly overgrown but many of the perennials still inhabited the corners blooming in profusion throughout the summer. I can still see her now, back burnt black by the sun, pulling weeds and grass from between the rocks. In the spring her careful toil would be rewarded when the snowdrops first peeped up to be followed by daffodils and narcissus. The rock garden held back the soil and water, for it was a very damp area, and was surmounted by a hedge of purple lilac. The fragrance of these blooms still brings back memories of a time when the simple pleasures of life were easy to obtain. Later there were tulips and lily of the valley with their fragile white bells and glorious scent. In the middle of this garden there were stone steps that lead from the back door to the woodshed and upper terrace. Being on the side of a mountain everything sloped towards the lake. From the veranda we could look out over the lake and watch the Minto steam up the lake sounding her whistle as she neared the town. There was always some activity going on upon the lake as log booms were towed to the sawmills that dotted the shoreline. Pleasure craft took to the lake from May to October and there were even power boats from the States that came up to visit, usually over the July long weekend. From this vantage point, some two hundred feet above the lake, we looked out upon Saddleback with it's fire lookout perched precariously on the highest peak. Here we watched the sun set, sinking over the tree clad slopes in a blaze of color. It was a wonderful place to observe nature in all her splendour.

For the first two or three years we took our lunch buckets down the trail to Cusicks where the bus pick up the neighboring children. No bus ever came up Crescent Bay road so we were obliged to walk half a mile every day which certainly kept us in shape. Climbing that vertical trail was a real challenge ! Riding the bus was a bit daunting at first as the bigger kids sat behind me and flicked their fingers at my ears which stuck out prominently from my head. It was a target they seldom refused to indulge in. We were on the first bus which meant that we had to be at the stop by eight o'clock and arrived by eight fifteen. The bus then headed out to Brouse and Glenbank to pick up the kids from on top of the hill. This area was farming land reached by a winding road that doubled back in almost a switchback to reach the flat lands between town and Box lake five miles away. After school the order was reversed and we boarded the bus immediately after school and arrived home by three thirty. This was difficult as it meant that any after school activity meant walking the two and a half miles home. Another result was that we didn't get detentions or, if we did, had to serve them at noon. For the first three years we were definitely not involved in any of the schools activities so it was up to us to amuse ourselves at home.

In grade three we had Mrs. L whose twins were also in the same grade. She began the process of restarting my brain and attempting to correct all those bad habits I had picked up. I read voraciously and by this means I managed to escape into fantasy whenever I wanted. While this was good from a standpoint of discipline and reading it did mean that I tended to neglect other subjects that I was not as interested in, like Math. We had the standard readers with their collection of short stories and poems in which the years work was stored. When the class was told to open their books and read the first story I read the first two or three. It took the teacher a while to catch onto this by which time I had read the entire years work. This tended to drive teachers to distraction. They could hardly complain about an unwillingness to work but now their entire schedule was out of kilter. We were required to have library books but the scope of literature afforded by a small school in those days was very limited. We had a better selection of books at home ! With thirty or thirty five students in the class it was difficult to spend the time necessary to channel such prodigious tastes in different directions. My parents had a far greater influence on what I read than any teacher ever did.

While I loved to read I hated workbooks. The questions weren't hard but the tedious writing of answer's, in my opinion anyway, interfered with the pursuit of the real goal ; more interesting stories. I did excel in oral reading, a staple of reading programs of the day and now sadly absent. Both mom and dad read to us and they were exceptionally fine readers, elevating the books from mere prose to artful storytelling. I suppose I was a bit of a show off as well and I revelled in doing something I liked and did very well. No show without Punch ! I would wave my hand enthusiastically to garner enough attention to be allowed to read to the whole class. All of this didn't make workbooks any more attractive. I would hurry through the written assignments then open my book and escape.

It was at this time that I remember looking forward to recess and lunch hour. Once the bell had rung and we were all sitting straight in our desks, books put away and quiet as church mice ; we were released. The primary grades spent most of their time in the woods behind the school where we chased each other along the paths or climbed the trees. There was a thin strip of trees before you came to the clearing that marked the boundary. Beyond this narrow strip the woods were off limits. This, of course, didn't stop us from exploring the forbidden acres. One had to be careful because teachers did prowl the grounds and if you were on the wrong side of the strip when the bell rang it took a mad dash to reach the school before classes started. The primary students could also play soccer in one end of the playground. There was no gym at this time as grades seven and eight were jammed into the auditorium. It would be another year before they moved to the high school to temporary facilities. This meant that during inclement weather we were stuck in the classroom playing an assortment of games or drawing weird things on the chalkboards.

Fighting was another way we passed the time. Of course there were rules to our combat which certainly doesn't seem to be the case today. Most of our scraps were wrestling matches. We wrestled on the lawn at home or on the playgrounds. Bruce was tough to beat and avoiding his scissors grip was a necessity. If he once wrapped his legs around your torso he could squeeze the breath out of you. Of course as soon as you yelled "Uncle !" he would let you go. That was part of the rules. Throwing punches was discouraged unless boxing gloves were provided. As I mentioned before boxing was a regular feature of entertainment at Camp Lourdes. We never learned how to box which was strange considering that dad was on the boxing team at his school. One year there was a new boy in our class who was smaller than I was so I cheerfully challenged him to a fight. We stood in the middle of a ring of spectators while the two of us wrestled away. I weighed more than he did but he was quicker and more agile and I soon found myself loosing until I managed to use my weight to advantage. This was one fight I didn't win and my respect for this boy went up a whole bunch. In this way we settled the pecking order in our lives, who had the right to call the shots. Teachers only broke up serious fights where the combatants were unevenly matched or where physical injury occurred. Of course no one objected to the odd bloody nose and a few scrapes and bruises, it was all part of being a man.

Grade three was coming to an end when I contracted a strange eye disease. My Right eye swelled up and appeared immune to my mother's nursing skills. I assume that it also baffled our local G.P. as I was bundled off to Vernon to see what they could do. The old Monashee highway was enough to make anyone sick even if you were in perfect health so you can imagine the effect on someone who was feeling poorly. I lay in the back of a friends car with sunglasses covering my eyes, a blanket wrapped around me as we bumped and rattled over

120 miles of dirt track. For the next six weeks I lay in a bed in the children's ward which was definitely an eye opener. Penicillin was the new wonder drug and I was treated twice a day in order to tame the stubborn infection. Fortunately I have never been afraid of needles as I was turned over twice a day so that my bottom could be turned into a dart board. One of the patients, a young girl, was not so lucky. She fought and cried every time the nurses came to give her a shot and frequently it took two of them to hold her while a third administered the shot. This tightened her muscles making the needle more painful. The poor nurses tried everything to get her to relax even going so far as to use me as a model patient for the reception of their loaded syringes.

There were other patients who were not so lucky. One boy had rheumatic fever and had spent months in hospital while others had broken legs or painful illness of one sort or another. One of the things that made my stay difficult was not having my parents to visit. The other children's parents and friends visited daily while I had to be content to see friends of the family who lived in Lumby once or twice a week. This added to the fact that I couldn't read due to my condition made me look anxiously forward to the day when I could return home. For three weeks I endured this before I was finally released about the middle of June. Now I had to return to school and try to catch up on all those hated workbook assignments ! I must have managed as my marks were good enough to propel me into grade four with outstanding marks in reading. I was back in the loop and began enjoying school again.

It was at this stage that our trio was broken up much to our sorrow. Cusicks moved to town and became proprietors of the Pine Lodge, a boarding house on the main street. This meant that we could only get together on weekends but we did our best to lure Bruce back to spend the weekend with us or angled artfully to spend the weekend with him at the lodge. There we could, if we had sufficient funds, spend the evening at the movies without that long walk home. Frequently we spent the day searching for pop and beer bottles to raise the twenty five cents for admission. The down side did not occur until summer when we lost our beach access and had to find another friend with a home on the lake. This lead us to the Duncans who had boys one year older than me and one a year younger. They also had girls about my sister's age so that we became friends in many of our adventures from then on. It was a much longer walk to Duncan's, about a mile, even with the trail we cut from our house to the power line ; the road route would have been over two miles. Of such changes are our lives made and the paths we are to take wander from place to place and friend to friend.

This was particularly true next year when a new family moved in with boys about our age. With Cusick's departure the bus stop was moved to Mackintosh's half a mile closer to town. This increased the distance we had to walk to get to the bus stop to half a mile. We made friends with Rick and Ray but it was tough going. They were not hardy explorers or makers of cabins. Rick was in my grade and distinguished himself as the only boy to cry while being give a shot. His stock fell immeasurably and in spite of the fact that they were the two boys closest to us in our age group we began to drift apart. Of course it might have been different if our parents hadn't had the same path to deteriorating relationships and, as is the case with all parental mistakes, we paid for it. It happened this way.

Frequently we went down to their place to play but somehow they never came to us. This always strains friendship as it creates the impression that 1. You don't really care for our company or 2. Your mother won't let you out on your own which is even worse. For a while we were content to play it their way but we visited less often now and after the sissy performance with the needle we reduced our friendship level a couple of notches. Over a period of a year the friendship turned to enmity and it is partly our parent's fault. Mrs. B. Was a sharp woman who seldom took no for an answer and hovered over her kids like a brood hen. We had a car and they didn't ; more specifically mom drove and she didn't. We began by giving her rides to town when we were going but then she began to asks for rides at other times and very soon mom put here foot down and the rides ceased. Another habit of hers frustrated everyone in the neighbourhood. She would talk incessantly to all and sundry thus tying up seven other phones. It was she who forced us to get that private line when dad went into business. We all listen to what our parents say and do and we model ourselves on that behaviour with frightening accuracy. The comments about Mrs. B went from mild reproach to acidic reproof. This coupled with our deteriorating relationship with the boys swung the scales from neutrality to enmity.

As children what we do may not be legal but the boundaries of what is right and wrong reside with the parents not with society. Lying was wrong and punishable with a spanking as was theft and a number of other commandments. Trespassing didn't occur on the slate as everyone went across other people's property if it was the shortest way home or if they just wanted to stroll by and chat. Having put the boys on the hit list, which made them fair game to be beaten up if caught, we spent a lot of time engineering revenge scenarios. Since they lived a stone's throw from the bus stop they either came just as the bus arrived or found another way to school. When you have an enemy it is always best to spy out their territory. We would send foray parties onto their property to see who could get the closest to the house without being seen. This activity was wonderfully close to the war games with which we amused ourselves with the added advantage of real danger which increased the heart pounding excitement.

One day after school we had chased Rick home and were lurking around the house hoping he'd have the nerve to come out and be captured. We were not afraid of Mrs. B but her husband was large man who, unknown to us was home at the time. He should have been at work. Every husband should have been at work not snooping at home to upset the plans of warring clans. I had hidden in the upper part of the porch when Mr. B chased my brother off and I waited quietly when he returned and they discussed who was left. Mrs. B. was left to patrol the area where I was by now desperate to leave. I inched my way to the exit in silence playing that no one would hear me. Just as I reached the exit Mrs. B yelled.

"He's here ! I see him in the porch. "

My heart came into my throat ! I wriggled out of the attic and ran hell bent for election, not stopping to look back until I collapsed in a heap half a mile up the road. After this the forays were much more cautious and soon after we were warned to stay away and leave well enough alone. Of course we couldn't do that. I think Bruce must have been with us as we were definitely in a belligerent mood when we set out one weekend to see if we couldn't corner us one of those rats. There wasn't really much of a chance for they stayed close to home and strictly away from our home turf. Well one thing lead to another and soon we found ourselves on the lip of their property bouncing apples off their roof. When they came out to investigate we peppered them with fruit. We arrived home feeling that we had triumphed though taking on adults wasn't really within the rules.

It really wasn't fair. The old man had phoned home. Would you believe he actually talked to dad and complained. After all, hadn't we just extrapolated the 'just cause ' and carried the family feud to it's logical conclusion ? We had, it appeared, gone too far and as a measure of how far we had overstepped the rules of conduct we were bent over and paddled then sent to bed in disgrace. It was one spanking that I felt was not justified and to some extent I feel that way today. Ti's a dangerous road to tell your children that you too are part of their feud then wonder why they carry the conflict to it's logical conclusion. The spanking definitely ended the friction as all contact between us was severed and we avoided them and their place for years. It was not until we were well on in high school that relations thawed and we met on anything other than neutral ground at school.

My memories of grade four are coloured by the peculiar addition of one boy who was mentally retarded. He had started school with us in grade one but had failed in his attempt to escape the confines of that grade as he couldn't grasp the basics. A fourth year in that grade was obviously not going to do him any good so for some insane reason known only to the principal, Mrs. W, he was placed back with his peers in grade four. He was placed in the lowest group where he was hopelessly adrift with no possibility of parole. Poor Mrs. T had to divert a great deal of her energy in keeping this one student out of mischief and at times her exasperation boiled over as she smacked him with a ruler to try and keep some semblance of order in her classroom. It didn't help the rest of us and periodically we would rebel and have to be disciplined. I remember her ruler reddening my hands for some overt behaviour.

It was still a year in which she worked to overcome my reluctance to try work that did not interest me. Math was not my favourite subject as it involved learning addition and times tables. Oh I could do the work but I didn't see past the drudgery to the usefulness that such an accomplishment brings to every facet of life. As I couldn't stay after school flash cards and worksheets were sent home and, for the first time, I had homework. In a year of drill I managed to memorize the tables and that coupled with our constant honing of our addition skills at crib gave me a good grounding in Math. By the end of the year I had made marked improvement in Math and science to go with my good marks in English. I appear to have impressed the teacher with my ability and it is a great pity that my memory only records the terrible conflict that throwing students of far lesser ability into classrooms generates. Today we have apparently learned nothing from the past and insist on perpetuating the same errors today. Throughout school we were grouped according to our abilities so that we could be challenged to achieve the most that we were capable of achieving. When all of your resources go to accommodating the lower and handicapped students the brighter ones suffer the most for they are deprived of teaching that could turn them on to learning for a lifetime.

For grades five and six I had Mr. K. and I progressed well enough to maintain a 'B' average in all the academic subjects. I never mastered handwriting as I wrote too small as if to conserve every last scrap of paper. It wasn't until I went to work for the railroad that I modified my writing so that it became legible most of the time. Spelling was and still is a chore. Thank God for computers with spell checks !

Occasional discipline was meted out by classroom teachers with a swat across the backside or hands but serious offences were punished by being hauled to the office to be strapped. This method was consistent with the ' Spare the rod and spoil the child "philosophy of the day and was no different than what we received at home. The strap could be heard throughout the school and everyone listened intently when we heard the sounds that ushered in it's use. You could hear a pin drop, even in noisy classes, as the sharp smack meant that the leather had struck someone's hand. Occasionally you could hear someone cry but we were a tough lot and rarely did anyone make a real fuss. If you erred it was up to you to take your punishment like a man. Girls were rarely strapped and the boys who were the most frequent recipients were tough. Never the less, strapping had a quieting effect on the wilder children and kept unruly behaviour to a minimum.

I was perfectly capable of kicking up a ruckus but I usually had the good sense to know when to quit. One day that good sense failed me. We were marking our homework and I was anxious to get the answers right and fudging on the results. Mr. K caught me in the lie and marched me to the office. Getting the strap from Mr. K would have been fine but to add insult to injury Miss W was there looking down her nose disapprovingly at me. I managed to take the blows without a sound and marched back to the classroom with nary a tear in my eye though my hands stung for the rest of the day. My reputation within the class went up as a result. I was also careful not to push the boundaries of prudence too far in the future.

As I mentioned before, I managed to catch all of the childhood diseases from mumps to chicken pox while I was in elementary school. One day after school had recessed for the holidays I had a terrible pain in my side. Aunty Bett, who was staying with us, diagnosed appendicitis. I don't know whether our local doctor was away for the holidays or whether mom and dad just felt more comfortable with the staff in Vernon but off we set late at night. It was another of those terrible rides with me in the back seat, bundled up against the weather, and not feeling at all comfortable as we roared across the winter landscape. It was late when we arrived at the hospital and the doctor checked me over then sent me immediately into surgery. My appendix was swollen to the point of bursting but fortunately it hadn't ruptured. Of course mom and dad couldn't stay so after ensuring that I had made it through the operation they returned home. Once more I was on the children's ward without visitors. When I checked my scar as the nurse checked my bandage I noticed that it had been clipped together with little metal clamps rather than the conventional stitching. I wouldn't be released until after the stitches had been removed and would be in for Christmas. I will say that the staff were wonderful. They provided a Christmas dinner with all the trimmings but best of all was the enormous stocking each child received. Once again Santa was real and though some of the older kids scoffed at the idea I knew that he had found my address even though I was not at home. That was proof enough for me. It certainly took the edge off not being with my family. Ten days after I arrived I was at home recuperating and we had Christmas dinner at New Years so I made up for the loss y having two Christmasses.

In the spring of 1955 my fathers eldest sister, Aunty Bett, arrived to help take care of dad as he recuperated from his cancer operation.

When dad heard the news that she was coming he huffed a bit then said. "If the old girl is coming out I guess I'd better get a job."

True to his word he invented a job that he could perform with his limited physical strength. There were plenty of lumber mills in the area and all of this wood had to be loaded onto box cars at the railway siding. He bought an old truck and had an hydraulic fork lift built over the rear wheels. Looking over his shoulder he proudly drove down the street to the lumber yard. He was an excellent mechanic and driver so the job of sitting in the cab and unloading the trucks that arrived was no problem. He had two men who loaded the lumber tallying it as they went. Once the car was full it was sealed with a metal tag that was inserted through the door handle to ensure that no one disturbed the contents before it reached it's destination. It was a good business and for the fist time in our lives we were settled and reasonably well off,

Aunty Bett arrived and took up residence in my sisters room which adjoined ours in the attic, being separated by a curtain there was not a lot of privacy. As a nurse aunty had spent many years in England as the matron of a boys school so being cooped up with us didn't phase her a bit. She went to work in the hospital and with two incomes we were able to buy a brand new car in the spring. It was with great excitement that we welcomed home the Austin A 50 with it's flying A symbol on the hood. Up to this point in time we had made do with an older ' mechanics special ', a 1946 A 40 Austin. It was certainly lively having Aunty in the house. As the eldest of the eight boys and girls in dad's family she was a dominating force. How my mother managed I 'm not sure as she was not the type to be bossed around by anyone. For us it was great to have an actual, real live blood relation with us to fill us in on some of the family history. She also helped to blunt the edge of dad's temper. Not that she couldn't be fierce when we got out of line but she knew and understood boys and was very active walking at a great clip. Many of the hikes that dad was not able to do she shepherded us into, like the nice little twelve mile day hike to the Hot Springs !

Winter was game time and it was here that we first glimpsed dad's relationship to his oldest sister. She was ten years younger than him and granddad had died when he was nine so a lot of the raising of what she referred to as ' the three little boys ' must have been left to her. Aunty Bett and Uncle Nor were born a year apart and I know that they were very close but dad and my uncles Alfred and Tadgel were the last three siblings born a year apart. Dad was the middle boy and there is a wonderful picture of them in the Maldon museum wearing sailor suits. Her relationship with them was more that of a mother than a sister hence my fathers apprehension when she announced that she was coming. From her we learned of Uncle Alfred's death at the hands of the Japanese in the Gilbert Islands where he was a missionary. Game time is family time and Aunty Bett joined in all our games and filled in when we couldn't find anyone else. One evening we were playing some game or other when dad dug his heels in. He was riding his high horse insisting that he was right and we were wrong when Aunty Bett's patience ran out.

"Charles" she said. "You always were a stubborn little boy ! "

Marty and I looked at each other in stunned amazement for the concept of dad having ever been a boy never mind a stubborn one had not occurred to us.

Spring break up is a quiet time in the forest industry as the roads are rendered impassable. We had planned a family trip for late April to the coast. Apart from one trip to Vancouver when I was very small we had never been further from home than a hundred miles. Easter must have been early as I remember having to do our school work during Easter break so that we could take time off later. As with most events excitement rises as the day draws nearer and nearer. Pat was too young for such a trip and stayed with Marion. Marty and I and the three adults piled into the Austin for this memorable trip. Both mom and dad drove fast and well so after the bone crunching Monashee was behind us we whizzed along the paved roads of the Okanagan spending the first night in a motel near Penticton. I don't remember much of the drive over the Hope-Princeton but smatterings of events remain. I remember going to a fancy seafood restaurant where dad and Aunty Bett indulged in raw oysters and other strange food. Stanley Park with it's zoo was another fascinating journey where we saw many strange creatures that had only existed in picture books or in our imagination. Here we first encountered large timber. There was the tree trunk that a car could drive through and all around us was the sea. I had never seen the ocean and the waves and scope of that much water was wondrous to behold.

One night we boarded a boat in the harbor and slept while the ferry took us to Nananaimo where we disembarked early next morning. We must have spent the day there as I remember the trip to Cathedral Grove. Even for a boy raised in timber country where there were still plenty of big trees these giants were awe inspiring. Never had I seen so many gigantic trees in one stand, their tops rising three hundred feet into the sky while our whole family could not join hands and encircle the trunks. The plants that grew beneath these firs were also larger and lusher. It was a wonderful experience then and it still is today as I often stop to wander among the ancient trees today though the rest of the surrounding forest has been shorn like a sheep. The next day it was off to Victoria. Upon checking the town, one always does a town check in any new city, we saw that a theatre was showing The Lone Ranger, my hero. Well sightseeing wasn't high enough on the list to compete with that ! We piled out of the car while mom went to buy tickets. Only one snag, we were too young to be left on our own according to the movie theatre. Aunty Bett volunteered to go with us but dad was adamant, we could watch a movie any day and we were not liable to make another journey like this. Finito ! End of conversation. We were placated by staying in a motel with T.V. We had never seen this box before and in it's earliest incarnation in black and white it wasn't nearly as good as the movie theater. Still it was a novelty and we stayed up late while the adults toured the city by night. Some spark of memory must live on and influence us in later years for I found myself drawn to return and have made this island my home.

Those are the memories of this trip that remain and we never made another like it until the year I graduated from high school. Roads were being built but most of them were winding trails that wound along the sides of the mountains. Many of the passes were closed in winter so that if you had to go to the coast you had to go through Washington. In the sixties new roads were being built and the old ones upgraded as Bennett and Flying Phill made roads, well at least the main roads, a government priority. We remained a backwater until the High Arrow dam flooded the old road and new one was built in 1968. There were still plenty of places to go and we spent the summer showing Aunty all the local sights. I t was with deep regret that we headed back to school in September.

Grade six followed the same as grade five with the same teacher. This was a bit of a rum affair as we nearly always got a break from year to year and to have the strictest teacher in the school twice in a row, well, it just wasn't fair. The one good thing about grade 6 was the arrival of a music teacher. Mr. H. new his stuff and learned about the value of notes and began the study of the intricacies of song. Before this music meant singing some well known songs or learning some simple tunes. For the first time we began to learn about singing in a meaningful way. Now we learned about note values, scales and harmony. I did well in Mr. H 's class and enjoyed it immensely. I had always liked singing and could memorize any tune, words and melody, in three or four repetitions. It's a pity I can no longer do that ! For one brief year I gained a small foot hold on the world of melody and was forever hooked. It is a great pity that Mr. H didn't stay in town long but such was the fate of rural schools. Good teachers seldom stayed long, particularly in the arts. Nakusp was a cultural backwater. The next year I graduated to the high school where the level of music instruction was even more dismal. His efforts were not in vain as the following year I joined the Anglican choir.

THE PLAY'S THE THING

Funny how dramatists and artists run in families. Oh, I know, it's all in the genes but there has to be some other component that makes one son a dramatist and the other shy. This was the way in our family. Marty tried to avoid the spotlight while I reveled in it. When I see the programs available in today's schools for the arts I weep with envy. Where were all these drama courses and choral ensembles when I was young ? Not only were they not available after school the level of instruction was dismal with a few short lived exceptions. My son gets credits for all of the work that I did after school for nothing other than the pleasure of performing. I tell you life is just not fair ! Mind you, if you expect it to be fair you're a fool so I suppose I had better stop moaning and get on with the story.

Dad had received a classical English education at a first class English public school, read private school in this hemisphere. How he came to be involved in the drama I'm not sure but sufficient to say he had the knowledge and ability and so ended up directing the the efforts of the local drama club. One of the major differences between small town drama and city plays is the fact that everyone knows the actors and half the fun is seeing them in roles that they don't normally play. Oh yes. We all play our parts in the drama we call life and some of us play many roles at many different times. With my father as director play practices were bound to be lively affairs. Dad had very specific ideas as to what was to happen on stage and when it was to take place. Being a volatile man you could hear him shouting his instructions half a block from the auditorium. His biggest curse was the actor or actress who never learned their lines until just before the performance and would invariably need prompting.

I seldom saw these efforts as, for some reason, I was never allowed a part. Whether this is a blessing or a curse I'm unsure but I think that we might have come together on stage in a manner we didn't at home. It was not until I tried directing a play in Nelson that I realized how much work and organization goes into the production. Dad helped me with this and I am grateful for having spent this time with him doing things together. Marty and dad shared an aptitude for mechanical things and I often felt left out of his world when I was a teenager, there I've gone and done it myself! Sorry, a young man. Perhaps we were too much akin to ever do more than create sparks but it would have been fun to at least share another of his passions. I did enjoy watching the performances and dreamed of acting myself.

Most of the plays were performed in the spring as there are just too many events happening around Christmas to make putting on a play feasible. There were limited performers and most of them took part in the religious offerings of the season. This worked well with the Drama festival which was held in Nelson or Trail every year sometime in April. Practices began in late January, usually once a week, and continued on for about six weeks when it was time to perform. Plays like, See How they Run or Arsenic and old Lace were favourites of the time. We usually performed three one act plays so that we could take the best one to the Festival.

Arsenic and Old Lace is the play that I remember best. The plot is guaranteed to be fascinating to young men of a slightly gory disposition. The play centres around two old maiden aunts played by Nesta Clark and Ida Johnson. These two old ladies entertain men in their parlour and, after plying them with homemade elderberry wine decide whether they are lonely. Throughout the sitting their nephew, Teddy, played by Glen Weatherhead, rushes about announcing that he is digging another lock in the Panama Canal. An elderly bishop played by Chris Bird is the first to encounter the ladies and is quickly dispatched to his eternal reward. The plot heats up with the arrival of their other nephew, Freddy, and his accomplice. These two fiends have just murdered someone who annoyed Freddy and have arrived with the body which they are desperately attempting to dispose of. The locks of the Panama canal in the basement of the old mansion appear to be the ideal hiding spot. The aunts are not pleased with arrival of Freddy and do their best to discourage him from staying.

The frantic actions of the two parties continue with hilarious results as the police are also on the scent. In between, the social worker is attempting to have Teddy committed to a mental home. In one memorable scene Freddy and the two aunts brag about how many people they have dispatched. The aunts, however, maintain that their clients were in need of being sent to their eternal reward and are shocked by Freddy's ruthlessness. In the end Freddy is caught and the two aunts are committed to the same loony bin as Teddy. They are all quite happy to go and the play ends with the bad guys getting their just deserts. It is a chilling reminder of how far we have moved, that in this day and age, the action of the two aunts is now being openly espoused as sanctioned behaviour.

The most ambitious undertaking of this small group of thespians was "Tutankhamen, Son of Ra." Egyptology was in fashion as it was not long after Carter's incredible find in the valley of the kings. The backdrop for the play was a large canvas mural depicting Egyptian life painted by a local artist. In front of this impressive scene strode the ancient king and queen as they battled with the evil high priest of Amon. Chris Bird played that role very well and for the part he carved a staff with a cobra wound artfully around culminating in a ferocious cowl-ed head. He had sequins pasted to his eyelids and they flashed balefully under the stage lights. All in all it was a tremendous production and we took it to the drama festival that year.

The opening scene occurs in darkness as the curator of the museum begins the story. My father played the part and he waited patiently, well not so patiently,for the lights to come up on him. Soto voce there was a quiet cry, "Lights"

Now my father could project his voice from one end of town to the other so you can imagine that everyone in the theater heard his plea. No lights.

A little louder now. "Lights."

Still the enigmatic flame refused to blossom. Now in high dudgeon came the cry. "Turn the bloody lights on!"

It was not an auspicious start and we did not win the festival. Still it was a great experience for us as we saw many good plays and stayed in a hotel. It was a great novelty as was eating at restaurants. I could count on the fingers of one hand the number of times in a year we ate anywhere except at home. If we travelled the Monashee we invariable packed a lunch. One play that I remember was 'The Purple Door Knob'. For some reason this unremarkable piece of drama was favourite of the entrants and was performed every year by someone. Still the exposure to all this drama has influenced my life and I love to see a well acted performance, whether it be a local high school production or a professional play.

Fire

Toasters and other electrical gadgets were just becoming popular when I was a child and some of these were remarkably unreliable and short lived. We had gone through a number of automatic pop-up toasters until dad despaired of ever having a machine that worked. He bought a simple fold up model where the bread was inserted on either side then manually lifted into place. When one side was done you turned it over and cooked the other. Dad rose early to go to work and we would hear him bustling around in the kitchen and snuggle down in our beds to delay the inevitable. We could hear him putting the water on to boil the eggs, his favourite breakfast was a soft boiled egg and toast. Suddenly we would be rouse by a desperate cry. FIRE! Running downstairs in our pyjamas we would see the kitchen wreathed in smoke, the back door open and dad standing over the sink scraping the charcoal from the offending piece of toast. Waste not. Want not. He would look up at us and glare, defying us to make a comment. We were not so foolish and quietly slipped back upstairs to change into our school clothes.

Transport

After the Minto was retired freight service in and out of the valley was handled by the Arrow Lakes Freight line. They trucked goods in from the Okanagan and returned with the diminishing quantity of agricultural goods being produced in the valley. If you needed to get to the Okanagan for any reason they were the only vehicles going and they would often take a passenger. There was no bus service and if you didn't own a car, and may of the residents didn't, it was the only way out. I remember going to spend a week with the Fishers in Lumby and taking the truck. I was fourteen or fifteen at the time and I clambered up the side of the truck and took my seat in the cab. From this lofty perch I could see things you could never see from the back seat of our Austin. We rumbled off down the road with the driver shifting gears frequently as we climbed the bluff and headed on to Arrow Park along the winding road. There we stopped to unload a box for the general store before heading out to Burton to do the same. One last stop at Farquier then onto the ferry. Here my journey took a strange twist. As we were approaching the other side Jim came and asked me if I would take passage with another gentleman. He was to pick up a passenger at Edgewood if I could. I certainly didn't know the man but I was soon seated in the front seat of his car and off we flew. It was necessary to get a jump on the other traffic is you were to avoid eating dust all the way. We chatted amiably and made a game of the posted corner signs. How much faster than the posted limit could we take the corner? It was an exciting ride over the pass but we arrived safely. It was more trusting era.

    I spent a happy week at Fishers as Charles was my age we went together all the time. One night he had a date with some of the fellows in the area. We took the older fellows car and proceeded to drink beer, at least they dank beer, I did not like the taste of beer. Charles went on and on about these new stubby bottles. We went to a drive in movie in Vernon and it was only half over when they decided to leave. Drinking beer and throwing the bottles out the car window we drove home at a hundred miles an hour. Charles leaned over to me and said. "Its all right. Gord drives better when he's had a few.' That night Charles threw up all over the bathroom and I vowed never to get so drunk.

A Love Affair

How many of us remember the first time we ejaculated. For me it came late and with a terrible fear. I had wet my pants! I didn't take long for me to recognize that the sperm that encompassed my pajamas was not urine. From there it became obvious that I had become a man. The sticky stuff that ran down my legs was an indication that manhood had been sprung on me. Our parents were totally incapable of giving us lessons in sex so they provided a book. It had useful information on dating and acne and an host of other topics but had nothing to say about homosexuality.

At this time we changed from Sunday school to singing in the choir. The priest's name was Mr. Mitchell and his wife played the organ, one of those affairs with peddles to make the air flow. I remember just a little of his instruction before he died and was replaced by Fr. White. Now we began to learn to sing the services beginning with morning prayer. After about a year I was enrolled in confirmation class and began happily to undertake the lessons it taught. When we nearly through my father called me up and told me I could not be confirmed. I was devastated ! I ran from the house crying. To give him credit he came out to talk to me explaining that he didn't want me making a decision until I was older but I could be confirmed if I would read one gospel. I picked John and began making my way through the passages. "I any man sin, we have and Advocate with the Father, Jesus Christ the righteous; and he is the propitiation for our sins." Here I found all the comfort that I needed or would need as I trod the way. I was confirmed in that little church in Arrow Park that has since been moved to Nakusp. That night I experienced a feeling of wonder such as I have never felt before, it was as if God himself had sanctified this act.

Work Camp

The summer I turned sixteen I went to work at a youth camp. These were set up around the province to do the various jobs required in setting up the campsite. When I arrived I had no inkling that I looked so much younger that my age. I got the job as the bull cook, which involved helping the cook get the meals ready. I'm not sure how long I worked there but I was persuaded to go for the normal job where each of the boys went out on separate duties. It was the worst choice I ever made. For two long months I sweated it out under sun or rain doing the manual labour required of me. Most days it would be, rake, shovel and a mattock, which meant that we would spent the day arranging the piles of gravel into some semblance of a campsite. There were better times too when we took a trip to Barckerville and wells to see the gold poured. I even got my picture take holding a sixty-five pound gold brick! At last the summer was over and I headed off to Vancouver where there was a servers conference. We went to St. James, the catholic church in the area, where I first let eyes on the seven sanctuary lamps and the incense swirling around. It was wonderful! A genuine catholic parish in the Anglican rite.

All too soon Fr. White left us and new priest came to take his place. Fr. Bruce came and though I did not know it at the time would become my closest friend. I became active in the church now serving at the altar. My voice which had been clear until that time had now broken. For a while I went up and down the parish with my parish priest as it gave him someone to talk to. It was on one of these trips that sex reappeared. We were preparing for the Paschal feast and that required us to do two services, one in the evening and the next the following morning. I was billeted with the other server and spent the night. There was only one bed and we shared it. During the night we lay together and I began to feel his bottom. He was not averse to my ministrations and soon he had an erection. We had anal intercourse and repeated it the following morning. It was great! About two years later I was coming over the Monashee and stopped by at his house. The invitation was still there and we had sex as we lay in that bed together. Our arms entwined and my hand feeling up his bottom. I never saw him again.

How does one come to pine over someone else. He was three or four grades lower than me and I tussled with him and did my best to be around him. In my dreams he came to me, like a sparkling gem, come to brighten my life. I fantasized over him in the dreams of my sleeping hours, often "coming" when I did. Over the years I got close enough to help him with his paper route and just riding double with him was treat. I would walk from my house to his, some four miles, just to be with him. Alas! I would find no solace there. We would play strip poker with the boys around. The first one striped would get his bottom spanked every time he lost. It was a way of passing time.

It was Christmas time and the world revelled in this season of joy. We had a party and invited a couple of friends over. As there was only one double bed and that belonged to my sister who was out babysitting we preempted it. We were about the same age and when the lights went out it was time to touch. I put my hands in his pyjamas, feeling his bottom and penis. He responded and then it was sex from there on in. He fondled me and I him before moving on to anal intercourse. Then it was his turn. In the morning we repeated the affair. I learned later that the sexologists recommended putt a finger up a mans anus to enhance sex. The prostate gland lies close to the surface and gives an incredible feeling. When my sister came home she was mad at me. I didn't care.

Soon it was graduation and time for me to make my way in the world. I had completed my application for Royal Roads and went to London Ont. for a ten day course and final analysis. All of us were to go to England for the two hundredth anniversary of the family company. This complicated matters as I had to fly to London, Ontario first. I passed the course and went on my way to England a happy and proud young man. Upon our return there was letter there that informed me that I had not been selected. With hurried steps my mother enrolled me in LVR in Nelson. After two miserable months living out of town I moved into town and things began to look up.

I began to play badminton at the local club and as they played three nights a week it was a good time. I wasn't the worst player in the club but I soon became more proficient. School was just up the road and was short walk rather than a long bus ride. I was trying to take two physics as well as the ordinary course load. After six months I gave up on the physics to concentrate on the remainder. The counsellor suggested that I apply for teacher college in Victoria and as my marks were good enough I was accepted.

No one was anyone in the 1960s unless the owned a car and I was no exception. For the grand sum of one hundred dollars I became the proud owner of a 1952 Austin A40. It's shocks were shot and I get to get my father to help me replace them. Once the shocks were done she was ready to go and I drove her like an E-type Jag! Once when going back to Nelson I was humming along on a wet road and tried to take the steep corner at the Roseberry bridge. The car slipped and slid, managed to just barely make the bridge, then toppled over on it's side. The next car the came along stopped to help. With three strong men we pushed the car upright, gave her a quart of oil and I was headed on my way once more!

During the week I worked on the sorting jack a Galena bay and only came down for weekends. For some time the car had needed some care and attention to the starter motor; so I took it out, gave it to the mechanic and headed with my brother for a drive. Now in order to get the car started you had to park it on a hill so you could jump start it. We spent the first night in Nelson and hills were easy to come by then headed out towards the ferry. Once on the boat there was no hill so we took out the crank and cranked it! There were stares aplenty at that you may be assured. We drove down to Spokane then headed up to Grand Forks where Fr. White was the priest. On Sunday we returned home, had the starter put back in the car and returned to Galena bay.

Another weekend I took the boy that I had sex with on that night in December and went to Nelson. We took an hotel room were we had anal intercourse alternating each with the other. In the morning we repeated the process. It was great sex. Now we come to one of those fatal coincidences that shape our lives. We had run into the very boy that I was hopelessly in love with and took him home. We drove through Kaslo to where there was little traffic and I let him drive my car. I often thought afterwards what might have be if I had stayed with the first boy, but I was young and impetuous and besides we couldn't have stayed together though now that I think upon it we were meant for each other.

The sorting jack was an interesting machine. It consisted of two large logs along the side with a raised platform connecting them. The tug would be connected to a boom of logs that needed to be sorted which in turn was connected to the sorting jack. The whole apparatus was then towed to allow the logs to come into the jack where they were sorted into two piles, pulp or saw logs. For eight and a half hours a day we worked the jack with an hour off for lunch. It was definitely boring. Not the type of job I wanted to do for the rest of my life.

There was one compensation. That was the Beaton pub were you buy a beer and no questions were asked about your age. As we were only eighteen at the time and drinking age was twenty-one this was a great advantage. As I didn't really like beer I settled for one. The others would drink copious amounts and returned home with a hangover. I marveled at the chap who could take a full glass of beer and polish it off in one swig.

University

At the end of the summer I had accumulated enough funds to go to university. I had a friend in Victoria with whom I had written letters over the course of two years. I went to the church were they went and the priest found me a place to stay. It was in a home with two other boys who were in high school. There I stayed for the next term. As it was close to the church and not far from university it was convenient for me. Into that church life I participated whole hardheartedly. The bells and incense sang a tune that reminded me of camp. The head server was a man who treated the service with reverence it commanded, with simplicity of action coupled with prayer for us sinners who journey this life together. There was also a lot of fun activities. We went hiking on Saturday to various places around the area. There was on particular hike I remember when the priests son was strolling along and seeing the wood on top of the stream assumed it was safe to walk on. Down he went getting thoroughly soaked. We hauled him out dripping wet. He was the joke of the trip and we never tired of telling him.

"Only Jesus walked on water". As it was November and rather chilly we stripped him and cobbled up something to wear.

One day in November David took me on a hike alone to Sombrio beach. We walked down the steep track, through the large fir trees and the stands of fern. It was mossy under the canopy with old rotten wood and decaying limbs now covered in salal. When we reached the beach there was no one there but us and we revelled in the breakers as they hit the shore with a crash. We ate our lunch and I cannot remember how it started. But at his first tentative kiss I was aroused. The sound of the breakers echoed to the tune of our passion. When it was over I had, for the first time, someone to whom I could talk to about sexual matters. He spent the first half hour telling me that he spotted me immediately and had only bided his time to approach me. In those days homosexuality was illegal so he had to be sure. I was the same age as he was but he was not as brash as I was, with all the brash impulsiveness of youth. We talked of hidden things to cool the hot fire of our love. He was attracted to teenagers while I was attracted to the younger teenage set. He was a gentle soul and feared discovery in a way that I never had until lately.

Throughout that year our friendship grew an we began to see more of each other. He took me to Vancouver where we took a motel with all of the security measures he felt were necessary. We walked in Stanley park and went to the zoo. We ate out and that was a great delight to me who had very seldom eaten at a restaurant. Often we spent our time talking till late at night till we had sex and went to sleep.

The next night we went to a steam bath. This place was reputed to be a haunt of homosexuals so we were not surprised when we were greeted amiably. I don't recall the steam room being particularly hot, having grown up with hot spring water it was decidedly tepid. They did have an interesting display of teenage boys on hand. After about half an hour I selected one then went to a private room were I attempted to have sex. No go. I could not even get it up to have sex with a very attractive boy. To say that I was embarrassed would be the understatement. We left but I am sure that it was fated to be. It was not love and that makes all the difference. By the end of the year David and I were fast friends and wrote to each other frequently.

I even persuaded him to come back to Nakusp for the summer and work. As he wasn't the type for labouring he got a job as a manager at the local hardware store. He stayed with a friend of mine who ran a lodge in the town proper while I lived a mile and a half out from it.

THE LAKE

It was always like that in the summer. In the morning there would be a cool breeze flowing up the valley where the roses bloomed around the house. For a while there would be the peaceful balm of breeze blowing which lasted until noon. Now the breeze died and the full heat of summer began. John turned from his reading and went inside where the coolness of the house enveloped him. Laying the book aside he began boiling eggs to make potato salad while the now cooled spuds lay waiting to be cut up. Working with a deftness he began making a pile of spuds, ready to have the eggs added then the onions and finally the mayonnaise so that the whole would be delicious. The cold chicken was taken from the fridge along with the pickles and green salad where it was laid in the basket. A bottle of wine was added, two plastic mugs chucked in and the potato salad laid on top to make the basket complete. Picking up the basket he walked out out the car, put the basket in the back seat and started the machine.

The motor started with a satisfying growl as the big six turned over and John revved the engine to ensure that all was running well. His eye went to the instrument panel and he watched the gauges come to life. Oil pressure fine, electric up to par, fuel satisfactory and temperature rising well so giving one last glance at the gauges John depressed the clutch and was off in a shower of rocks. He drove down the long driveway then headed up the highway to David's place a mile on. Pulling into the driveway he honked his horn and David came out waving cheerfully. Opening the passengers door he sat in with a grin.

"All present and accounted for. "he said.

John smiled back and cuffed David playfully on the side of the head. "So we really are ready to kick up your heals this afternoon? He asked.

"Well let me see." David began whimsically. "I suppose you could call it kicking up your heels. On the other hand there are more than heels to be kicked up." H e continued wickedly.

"Well I guess we'll just have to see about that won't we." John replied.

They turned out of the driveway and headed up the highway the engine loafing around fifteen hundred RPM. Once clear of the town John shifted down and gunned the engine. The Jag now began to feel it's oats and sprung like a true thoroughbred to three thousand and on up until John stepped on the clutch and shifted up then he continued to wind the engine through more revs until the speedometer read one hundred. With the top down it was exhilarating. Now he eased off and they cruised along at one hundred and ten miles per hour until the next corner caused him to brake before taking the corner twenty miles per hour faster than the posted speed. The Jag never flinched but took the corner as if it were a strait away. With hair flung into the breeze the two boys grinned as the miles slipped by.

John slowed down as the turn off lay just ahead. Now it was off up a narrow winding road where the surface was gravel and the car spun it's wheels a little as it gained height. A mile further on they left the car on the side of the road and hiked in to the small lake which was their destination. There was a narrow strip of shingle on the shore where others had been. The lake lay before them, still and calm in the afternoon light, the mountains reflected in their waters. Small birds sang while dragonflies spun their endless circles over the reeds that lay to their left.

David grinned and said, "Last man in is a nigger. "As he be began disrobing as quickly as possible.

It was nearly a tie by the time they hit the water with a tremendous splash. John surged out ahead in a powerful crawl and left David behind. Half a mile out from the shore they were winded and paused to get their breath. From there they could see the shoreline where the trees crept down to the water everywhere except the narrow strip of pebble beach where they'd left their lunch. Now more slowly they swam back using a breaststroke that eased their passage. Soon they were on the shore and ready for the lunch that John had provided.

Peering into the basket David's eyes lit with delight. "Chicken and potato salad. And I do believe that's a bottle of wine on top. Let's open it and taste test to be sure it's up to my standards"

Smiling John uncorked the bottle and poured two glasses. Then they were into the basket and for a while there was little talking, only the munching of meat and potato salad could be heard.

It was too hot. They had to have another swim to cool off but they swam more slowly, coming back to the shore where they finally reached bottom. John slipped awkwardly and David reached out to grab him. Now their hands met and joined into a symphony of touching. They were erect now. Hands grasping each others bottoms and feeling the cool roundness of the flesh. Kissing each other as they stood in the water now cool around their heated flesh. Hand in hand they climbed the shore and took the blanket into the shade where they lay beside one another. The touching began anew with hands feeling their penises, now shot high and ready with sweet pre cum upon them. Then David reached around John and turned him towards him, his bottom opening up to receive the offering. Deep into the bowels he sprang and David moaned in pleasure as John's penis touched his prostate gland heightening the sensation. The two bodies intertwined, caressing, caring for each other. Now the moment of ejaculation came. John panted with the effort of final completion, his penis deep inside David while David shivered with delight. Too soon it was over and John pulled out now satisfied. David turned John around and began to insert his penis into him. Now David could feel the incredible sensation of penis upon prostate. It was not long in coming. In a paroxysm of desire they were one. Each held in the moment of time, yet out of time, an inexorable orgasm of desire. One with each other, immutable.

For a while they lay there together, holding each other in the warmth of companionship. David tickled John and John responded with the same. Now they were wrestling on the blanket until both rolled off and stopped. Grinning at each other their laughing eyes holding them together.

John smiled saying, "I think after that we had better go for another swim. "

Now they splashed in the shallows not going too far into the lake. The crystal green waters enveloped them, their nude bodies sensual. For a while they cavorted in the shallows until David said.

"Let's go back to the blanket. I'm feeling sexy. Now that we've done it quickly let's see if we can do it again slowly. "

Hand in hand they climbed the bank before stopping at the blanket. They embraced and felt once again the smooth flesh on flesh that excited them. Hugging each other they began to kiss and both began to rise. The proximity of penis on penis set shock waves of pleasure through their bodies. Then David began to kiss John's breasts moving downwards until his mouth engulfed his penis. John writhed with ecstacy as the sucking went on and on. Just when he could stand it no longer David stopped and began roaming up his body until he reached the lips.

"Now it's your turn." David replied.

John began as David had with the breasts but when he reached his penis he turned him round and began nibbling on his buttocks. His tongue tasted every nook and cranny while his hands supplemented the job, feeling up his bottom and caressing his anus. His finger slipped in and David squirmed with pleasure as John's finger caressed his prostate. He lingered there until he removed his finger and began licking his anus. His tongue tasted him, licked him then dove into his anus to feel the prostate. His hands were working David's penis, now feeling his balls then running his fingers through his pubic hairs. At last he stopped and began running his tongue up David's back until he reached his head where he kissed him. They stood there, face to face, while their lingering kiss went on.

"That was great! I almost had an orgasm but you quit just in time. Lets lie down and I'll lift my legs so that you can penetrate me from above. "David said.

"All right. Let's get you in position. Up with your legs and open wide, you will love what follows." John replied.

Holding his legs John began penetrating, slowly and methodically so that their passion came together. Reaching in to hold his head John began to work slowly. David's penis was erect and touching John's body while the pace quickened. In a gasp of emotion John went off. Holding David's head John shivered savouring the moment until his penis slipped out and he collapsed on his friend. For a long time they lay there holding each other. Rolling over they continued to intertwine.

At last David said. "My turn now."

John's legs went high and David penetrated. He had cooled off and the sensations went on for a long time. At last he came and poured his love into John before collapsing down upon him. Sated at last they began to relax as the sun slid over the mountain crawling towards sunset.

"One more swim and we'd better be off." John said.

The last rays of the sun were shining on the lake when they finished. Reluctantly they got into their clothes and headed back up the trail in the twilight. Reaching the Jag they put the basket in the back seat and headed down the mountain. They drove at a more sedate pace, the ardour of their love having been quenched. When they arrived at David's place he reached over and kissed John.

"Thanks for a wonderful day." He smiled then headed into his house.

2

It was seven in the morning and John looked over the morning paper before heading off to work. Nothing new, no shipwrecks, nobody drowned so he closed the paper and set it on the counter ready for his mother to pick up. Bringing out his lunch John placed it in the paper bag and headed to the car. The Jag started and off he went driving the two miles to work. The re-bundler was an old piece of equipment that required lots of TLC. His job was to operated the boom boat that brought the logs towards the lift that the carried them up to be bundled again. Starting the eighteen horse outboard he allowed it to warm up for a minute then started off towards the logs in the holding boom. The motor was situated in the middle of the boat and by this means the boat could be turned in any direction. Pulling the boat into the assortment of logs he began pushing them towards the lift. One by one the logs came and soon the holding tank was filled.

John sat there and relaxed seeing the green waters of the lake in the early morning sun. To the West lay Saddleback, the long shape of the hill surmounted by two peaks that resembled a horses saddle that gave the mountain it's name. All around rose the peaks of other mountains, not so high, that enclosed the valley and lake within it. To the North lay the impressive peaks of Thor and Odin named for the Norse gods. It rose to a height of nine thousand feet and it's snow clad peaks looked down on the town. If you looked hard you could see Thor with his hammer swinging hard upon Odin's head with a crack of thunder. Often lightning hammered the twin peaks making the scenario even more lifelike. You could almost see the gods fighting upon the mountain at times like these.

Work continued until noon at which time they took a half hour lunch break. In the cool of the shed they ate in companionable silence. After lunch John continued working bringing logs down when a particularly large log would not fit in the tank. Getting off the boat he grabbed a chainsaw and, straddling the log, began to cut it in half. Now it would fit inside the holding tank and he could continue rounding up logs. At three thirty a boy came down to the docks to fish. He had freckles on his face but smiled at John as he went about his work. One of the others said that he had cow pie all over his face. At four o'clock the shift was over and John lingered to talk to the boy getting his name, Alfred. Getting in the Jag he drove home.

A couple of weeks later John's mother had gone to a conference in Vancouver so the place was all his. Friday he invited David over for dinner. They took their beer onto the back porch which was shaded at this time. Supper was a combination of cold treats so they continued their conversation where it was cool.

"So how was your week? "John asked.

"Well you know, The store gets busy during the summer. There are more tourists that you can shake a stick at and all of them want to come at the same time. We had a large group come up from the states and they wanted to be shown what we had in the way of fishing gear. You show them a piece and they listen very nicely and then go off to the next piece. At the end of half an hour they wind up buying nothing. "David replied.

John laughed. "Oh well! We all have to make a living some how."

"Well some of us don't have a nice cushy job driving a boat around, or shoving logs every which way." he replied. "Well I suppose you have to pay for that Jag somehow."

"Funny you should mention that. I have only three months left and it's all mine." John said.

"Really! Well you save a heap of money living with your mother. "David answered wistfully.

"Changing the subject, how about eating. I'm famished! One thing about working on the water you sure work up an appetite." John said.

"Lead on McDuff. And damned be him that stops first." David quoted.

Together they went into the house and began setting the table. There was a large ham, salad, pickles and more of his potato salad. The buns arrived steaming hot from the oven and lathered with butter made excellent eating. For a while there was little conversation as they tucked in as only two teenage boys can. The meal was accompanied by a rather fine wine which left the boys fingering their glasses as the last drops were served.

"And what's for desert ? Why strawberries of course. "John mused. "Come on better tuck in and enjoy"

After dinner they took their coffee out on the back porch, the front being too hot in the evening sun. They sat around the small pool while the crickets sang in the deep grass and the humming birds buzzed around each flower dipping their beaks into them as they came. A perky Robbin perched on a branch of the lilac and sang it's song. The rockery rose about five feet above them as they sat in the shade listening to the sounds that nature provides. Only the odd car interrupted the quiet as it wended it's way up the road to the farm above. About eight thirty it had cooled and they moved to front porch to watch the sun set behind Saddleback. Clouds etched in gold as the dying rays of the sun touched them turning them first red then yellow before fading out altogether.

About ten o'clock they found their way to the bedroom where their touching lingered in the evening twilight. Soon, their passion aroused, they began to undress each other. The touch of their flesh sent shivers up John's spine and he let himself go free, free to the elements while flames of fire ignited his body. Soon they were lying naked on the bed while David penetrated him sending bursts of pleasure though him. Too soon it was over and David slowly relaxed coming slowly out of him. Holding him close together till their hearts slowed and the world resolved once more. Now John felt his pulse race and he began to caress David's body moving in sensual circles as he raised his ardor. Once again the depth of feeling as he penetrated deep into David's body, feeling him react to the gentle massage of his penis. Holding David's penis in his right had he began to stroke it till it throbbed within. He slowed his motion to allow David to come and they both went off together.

The sun peeked it's head through the window and fell on the sleeping boys. David stirred and held onto John's naked body his arms around his chest. His body snuggled into the curve of John's as they lay on their sides and his manhood slowly stood up. He was awake now and felt John's body stir as consciousness began to come. Pushing his bottom into David he nestled down and tried to go back to sleep. Slowly David rubbed his penis and John began to stir. He relaxed as David enter him, penetrating slowly he worked his way into his body while the sweet scent of John's hair hung in the morning air. His shampoo smelled like roses and further enhanced David's performance. He came at once and shudders of pleasure ran through him. Holding John's body he slipped slowly out. Fondling him his hands ran over John's penis and found it erect so he began to work his hands.

"Try your mouth. "John said

Throwing the covers from them David began to lick John's body until he reached his penis. Now it was John's turn to writhe in ecstasy. David's tongue was now caressing the top of his penis and he gasped with delight. It was over in a moment and John lay there pouring his essence into David, his body pushed upwards into his mouth while the sensation went on and on. At last he came down, slowly and gently, and kissed David.

"I'm hungry." David said. "Any chance of breakfast? "

"Well now considering that performance I imagine we could be persuaded to conjure something up." John replied. "let's get a shower first."

They went to shower and they washed each other sensually but not erotically. David took the shampoo and poured it over John's head rubbing it in until it foamed. He worked up to a lather and then rinsed it. The fragrance of Jirmack rose from the lather and David inhaled deeply. Now it was his turn and his body shuddered at John's ministrations. Now washed and clean they dressed and went into the kitchen. Soon bacon was grilling, potatoes were bubbling and the eggs were slowly coagulating in the frying pan. Two pieces of toast apiece were in the toaster while the last drops of coffee ran into the pot. Serving up the whole lot and bringing it to the table John quipped.

"Come and get it! Roast leg of insurance salesman."

For a while the was little conversation as they downed their breakfast. Fully sated they pushed their chairs back and relaxed. The sun was fully risen and had already crept over the trees to peek into the yard. On the stump was a gathering of Robins who pecked furiously at the seed that was left there. Up in the birch tree a lone blue jay squawked noisily while the chickadees uttered their name in the hollow under the rockery. It was as if nature had wanted to lay down a path upon which their courses were laid. For a while they sat there silently drinking in the morning stillness, the crispness of the light as it grew, spreading a garment over the land. All was peaceful and serene.

"Well," said John, "What shall we do today? "

"An interesting question, "David replied. "I suppose we could go to the beach and hang out with the rest of the ruffians. On the other hand we could pack a lunch and hike up Mt. Idaho. "

"Funny the you should mention that. I was just thinking the same. The snow will be mainly gone from the meadows and it will be a lot cooler there than here." John replied.

"Well if it were done it were best it were done quickly. "David said. "What will we have for lunch? "

"Let me rummage in the fridge and see what I can come up with."

In the end they settled on cold sausages, buns and the remainder of last night's potato salad. Half a bottle of wine and some strudel for desert and they were off. It was a mere twenty miles to New Denver then it was off up the Sandon road until they reached the base of the mountain. From there the road wound tortuously around the side of the mountain until it reached a spot some five thousand feet up where it ended in a small parking lot. Here they got out and strapped on their backpacks before setting off up the steep trail. They wound their way up the side of the mountain the balsam firs rising up around them. Through a clearing in the trees they could see the mountain meadows now peeking out in the sunshine. A little further on and they could see the flowers running amok in a riot of colour. Indian paintbrush in their orange glory bloomed in a patch while the foxgloves climbed their way in purple hue. Their were yellow daisy mixed with purple daisy while in the grass, huddled down, the blue bells wound their way. Every patch of ground was covered with blooms now rushing forward as if to make the most of their short season. They stood spell bound while the riot of colour mesmerized them.

"It is certainly beautiful. "John said gazing out on the meadow.

"That it is. "David agreed.

Once more they climbed through the forest to where there were no longer any trees. The wind picked up and they put on their Anaracks to ward themselves from the chill. Now they climbed the ridge where the wind howled around them like the furies trying to unseat them. One short climb and they were sheltered from the wind in a hollow near the summit. On they climbed until they could see the top of the mountain and the little shack perched upon it. Upon reaching the top they were invited in by the warden who only seldom got any visitors. From there the world lay beneath them spread out like a jig saw puzzle with mountains everywhere and only small houses where the towns were lost in the vastness. For half an hour they chatted with the keeper until the wind subsided a little

"Well. We had better be going now. It was nice to talk with you and thanks for the hospitality." John said.

Putting on their packs they began the steep descent to the valley floor below. After half an hour later they were sheltered in a grove of firs and began to make a fire. Not that they needed the warmth but just to show the primitive need to have a crackling fire burning. They warmed their hands over the flames and broke open the picnic basket. For a while they ate in harmony and peace descended on the valley with only the whisper of the breeze to disturb the air. A camp robber came sidling up to the pair while they sat mutely watching, spell bound. As they did not move it came closer until, with a quick dart, it seized a piece of the bun and flew off into the trees. David grinned as he saw the pesky bird sitting in a near by tree. They were tired and a brief snooze followed this ample lunch. When they awoke the shadows were sliding towards sunset and reluctantly they packed up the basket and headed towards the car. The last gleam of the setting sun hit the top of the pines then headed down to bed.

Half an hour later they wound their way into New Denver and headed off towards Nakusp. The Jag ate up the miles and soon they were descending summit hill, on past Box lake and into the flat farming land of Brouse. John angled the Jag up the driveway and slowly crept up the steep hill before coming out at the parking lot in front of the house. Now parked they took the picnic basket and their back packs out of the car and headed in. The house was cool as a log house should be and they headed into the living room to relax. John fell asleep but was awakened by David about an hour later.

"Time to eat something. As I wasn't driving I thought you might want a rest. Come and get it before it pools into a soggy mess. "David said grinning.

John arose and rubbed the sleepy dust from his eyes then followed David into the kitchen. They settled down to cold ham, potato salad and a green salad. Afterwards there was a cool ice cream for desert. By now it was nearly ten o'clock and they had had a long day. They took a shower together and washed each other getting aroused in the process.

"Best get into bed before we ejaculate. "John quipped.

"So it's off to bed we go." David said grinning.

The bed was cool and they quickly threw the sheets off and began to slowly make love. It was a quiet time when they came together kissing each other before going on to complete their acts. Now snuggled down next to each other they cooled down before gently going off to sleep.

In the morning the sun shone in through the window lighting the floor. John slipped out of bed and headed downstairs without waking David. Making coffee he took his cup and strolled over the lawn. The dew had nearly evaporated leaving a mist on his shoes while walking. Ten minutes of looking at the lake now calm as a millpond then he headed back to make breakfast. The bacon was sizzling in the pan when David came down sleepily tucking in his shirt.

"Help yourself to coffee and go out into the yard. I don't want to be disturbed while I'm making breakfast." John said.

Hustling to make toast and getting all of the condiments out of the cupboards and setting the table kept John busy for the next ten minutes. Now it was time for the eggs. Three eggs each were soon in the pan bubbling away. A couple of quick flips and they were done and he hastened to put them on the plate.

"Come and get it! "He hollered out to David. "Roast leg of insurance salesman."

David came in and grabbed another cup of coffee before sitting down. Silence ensued for a while as they ate companionably. The only comment was "pass the salt and pepper or "give the milk a fair wind. "Their breakfast finished they sat back and sipped the coffee in contentment.

"Ten minutes before Mass. Better get dressed or we'll be late. "John commented.

Once more they piled into the Jag and headed for town. It was a small church of the type expected in this community. The entered and took seats near the middle. John looking up saw the crucifix and contemplated all that they had done. Was it so bad to be a homosexual? What would Christ have said had they lived in his time? The only answer came form the bible. ' Love covers a multitude of sins.' Was his love for David wrong? In the end he left that question hanging as only God could judge.

Now the service began. ' In the name of the Father and the Son and the Holy Spirit.' Let us confess our sins before God. ' Christ have mercy. Lord have mercy. Christ have mercy.' The Mass went on through the Old Testament reading, a Psalm and on to the Gospel. Father's sermon on forgiveness made one think. Have I forgiven those who sin against me? John thought about this and contemplated his life. There were always people who would rail against his kind. They kept a very low profile in the church because neither of them wanted to have any conflict. Could they survive in the church with their love intact? The beautiful hymns, the incense and the vestments spoke to a place somewhere within his soul, that captivated and held him. The old Latin hymns from benediction called out to him,

> Tantum ergo sacrementum,
> veni remur chernui.
> Therefore we before him bending,
> This great sacrament revere.

He went back to the time when he was a boy in that rude chapel at Camp Lourdes. Holding a candle or swinging the incense. The intensity of the moment, of the elevation, God on high made real so that you could touch the hem of heaven. O salutaris hostia, que cheali pandi osteum. There in the presence of God we praise you Lord of all creation.

> Holy God we praise thy name.
> Lord of all we bow before you.
> All on earth thy scepter claim,
> All in heaven above adore thee.
> Infinite thy vast domain,
> Everlasting is thy name.

Lost in reverie John missed the parting remarks of the sermon and had to be nudged into reality by David who noticed his contemplation. Now the offertory was taken before beginning the cannon of the mass. The church became quiet as the moment of consecration approached. "The Body of our Lord Jesus Christ, which was give for you preserve your body unto everlasting life" "The Blood of our Lord Jesus Christ which was shed for you preserve your body and soul unto everlasting life." Only the ringing of the bells broke the silence. One by one they knelt for communion as the sacred host was placed on their tongues. In the silence of their minds they contemplated the mystery. Refreshed they were sent out into the world to be ministers of salvation.

WORK AND PLAY

During that summer I took a mixture of teenage boys up to the hot springs. They had cut a road to within half a mile of the springs and it was now quite easy to get to. Half an hours walk and a bridge crossing and you were there, a vast improvement on what had been a three hour hike. They were an earthy lot and I sang bawdy songs to the to enlighten the way up. Once there we stripped, clothing not being necessary, and bathed for a couple of hours, dressed and returned. The summer was now over and I had decided to stay on and not go to university. David and I said farewell and promised to write.

I took a job as tug man on one of the tugs that worked the lake. It was back to Galena bay, I had just finished five days on the re bundler the headed off to start my new job. The operator of the tug was an old Japanese man whom a admired immensely. During the week end we made a raft and other things. Come Monday it was back to word on the sorting jack. I was not enamored buy this turn of events but hug on for two weeks. Now the foreman came pushing us to finish and pace was gruelling. Eventually I snapped and said that I was leaving if a replacement did not arrive tomorrow. No replacement so I left.

For three days I was exhausted. I had accumulated enough money to go to England but that didn't seem likely at this time of year. In the end I decided to go to the coast and packed up my belongings into the and started off. The Jag rolled down the driveway and I spent the night with friends in Vernon before making the five o'clock ferry. I drove to the coast and showed up on Heather's doorstep. Immediately she persuaded me to turn around and drive back so she could go to a wedding! Ah! The things that you do when you are young. I had to get a few hours rest halfway up the canyon then stopped again in Vernon. This time I had a real rest!

I don't remember whether I went to the wedding or not. Now being so close to home I decided to return and replace my worn out shock absorbers with ones from another car. Off we went over the Monashee for another trip home. Once there I changed the shock absorbers for the new set and we were off again. Then began one my most frustrating times in life. Finding a job was no easy task. Up until that time it had been easy to get a job. With nothing to show for it but a dollar an hour job at the post office for Christmas rush I went home again. Dad was ill so it was not hard to come home again and spend Christmas with my family. My brother and sister were home so a pleasant time was had by all.

The Railway

In the new year I began looking for a new job. Marty was taking a course in Nelson so it was there that I went. I revisited the Pattersons where I had roomed and he said that they were looking for operators on the CPR. For the next couple of days I studied the book and practiced taking train orders. They were taken on thin paper with several copies being produced at a time. You had to press firmly, write legibly and do it without corrections. My writing at the time was thin and spindly so the instructor gave me some hints. Start your phrase off with a printed capital then progress to a larger hand written style. It worked and soon I was copying fairly legible orders.

Next I was shipped off to Yahk were I became the third trick operator. That meant working from midnight to eight A.M. The job was interesting but there was little to do between three and five. My body had not caught up with this change in hours and a convenient stretcher was laid out in the back room. By taking a nap and hanging on I managed to hold down the post. In February I was transferred to Natal. Then dad had stroke and I was called home. I visited him in hospital and that once loquacious man was reduce to smiles and nods. I never heard him speak again. Once more the railway called me and off I went this time even further away. I now held second trick Natal and there were a few compensations. One was that I could stay, free of charge, at the engineers bunkhouse at Crowsnest some ten miles away.

It was only a twenty minute drive to work and there were more things to do in Coleman that in Natal.

At this time I received a letter from David.

Dear John.

It's funny having to write you with "dear John" as I only heard that this was the address of people going off to war. Life here at university goes on much as it has for the past three years. I am finally through with Dr. Sigmund's classes. What a bore! Never the less it has been a challenge and I can see the light at the end of the tunnel. In three more months I graduate and go on to work in the library, I've just been confirmed in this position as the staff is expanding.

I had an encounter with another boy and was he hot. Just a flash in the pan as he was off somewhere to do something or other. I still see Tom and we are getting to first base but I am hesitant to go further as he's underage. Well that's al the news for now. Let me know how you are getting on.

Love you, David

Dear David,

It was great to get your letter and brightened up my day. If this is Hell I'm sure that it's not so cold as it is here. Minus twenty with a chill factor of minus thirty when the wind howls around the place. One day it snowed some three feet and I had to catch the train to get to work in Natal. Once there I had to stay overnight in some dingy hotel before the snow was cleared enough to get back to the Crow. Enough of weather!

The agent here is biggest arsehole that ever the was. He's stuck in the nineteenth century and can't see the progress coming on him. We have to type up the Jap coal blanks one at a time even though we could make them on the teletype. He's putting in extra hours which he bills as' demur-age'. All in all it sucks! This on top of no sex as it is colder than the north pole. I miss you.

Love John

The railway posted different jobs for which you could apply, and applied for them all. In late May I received a posting of third trick Spences Bridge. My prayers had been answered! One interesting event took place in the engineers bunk house. I spied the operators copy of The Lord of the Rings and being a natural reader I began to read it. I was hooked just like Denis said that I would be. I immediately went out and bought my own copy. It was only the first book but I soon accumulated all three of them. On the first of June I packed up my belongings and said good bye to Crowsnest. As I left a chilly wind was blowing and small snow flakes drifted around my car.

Reaching home I had a few days to bask in the sunshine and warmer clime of Nakusp. Off again to Spences Bridge and the heat. If it was hot in Nakusp it was broiling at the Bridge. The first night I was there with another operator and I missed the No. 1 going one way and he missed it going the other ! Not a good start. Now imagine your standing near the track with a hoop while a massive diesel engine comes roaring at you. In the morning one of the evening operators showed me how to hoop up a train. It was really very simple. Just touch the bamboo pole to the track and hold it up in the air. No one had ever told me that. The shifts were hectic and there was definitely no time for a nap! There were twelve to thirteen trains going through on my shift alone. This being the one hundredth anniversary of confederation there were two passenger trains running with all four of them coming on my shift. Spences Bridge is in a desert so it's rather warm. I went from forty-five hundred feet to nine hundred feet, from light snow to ninety degree heat. At one point in the summer my weather report at three in the morning was "clear, calm and ninety degrees!"

Dear David,
Well here I am in Spences Bridge where the temperature is ninety and the desert air warms me through and through. There are thirteen trains that run through on my shift alone! What a change from Natal where there were only a couple of trains a day. It makes my life so much easier as there is not time to get tired waiting for the next order to come in. You are going from twelve until eight flat out.

I took one of the sleeping cars that are pulled up on the track outside the station and use it as my home. It's cheap and I can save all that money for university. No air conditioning but it's livable. One day shortly after I moved in a boy came into my car and I showed him around. One thing lead to another and before you knew it we were having sex on my bed! He is a great comfort to me and I gather that he has a relationship with one of the track hands. Out of the freezer and into the warmth, both literally and figuratively. I can't wait to see you again to have a real chat. Well that's all for now I'll let you know weather I'm coming to school in the fall.

Love, John

One time I came out of the station and was met by another teenager who asked me to be the scoutmaster. We went to his parents and talked about it, so I became the unofficial scoutmaster of the troop, all four boys. We swam and even went on one camping trip. A good time was had by all. At the end of the month I was getting off shift and stopped in at the restaurant for breakfast when who should blow in but my brother. He needed a ride up to the Cariboo. So off we went. He needed a job so we wound up going to various ranches to find him one. By the time we headed back it was nine o'clock and I was dead beat having been up since four the previous day. I went to sleep in the backseat of the car as we hummed along. After an hour or so the car began to slow down, then it really slowed down. Getting up I peered at the dash and the speedometer read sixty miles an hour.

"How fast were we going" I inquired.

"Oh. About a hundred or so" he replied.

At the end of June I moved in with the family with two sons and daughter. It was cooler there as they had a swamp cooler. This device pumped water from a cistern over some batting then blew air through it. It cooled the house quite well. I worked this shift until August then I took on the the swing shift while the operator was on holiday. This meant that I worked the midnight shift, took eight hours off then worked two afternoon shifts before taking the day shift. This meant that I was off from four o'clock Sunday until midnight Wednesday.

I alternated between going home and to the coast. But alas all things must come to an end. The reason that I got the job was that it would be fazed out in the winter. CTC or centralized traffic control was being installed which was the reason for so many men working on the rails that summer. I went down to Vancouver to see this wonder. Stretched out on a console was the whole track from Kamploops to Vancouver and with the click of a button the dispatcher could send a message to change a switch anywhere on the line.

University

In the fall of 1967 I enrolled at university once more. Before I went back David and I planned a trip to San Francisco. As we had taken his car on previous excursions I offered to take my Jag. It was indeed a superior car to his old Volvo. Off we went travelling down the I5 at a furious rate. It is here that I have to discuss our differences in driving style. While my parents had instilled fast driving as a matter of course he was the model of probity. He never exceeded the speed limit and I found his driving hard to take. None the less we took turns at driving. Once we reached San Francisco my car became ill. No other way to describe it. It had to have a new transmission. Here we were in San Francisco with no transport. We made the best of it playing strip crib to while away the time. In the evenings we would go into town to see the sights. The cable cars going up and down the hills with us clambering on to hang on the sides. In the day we took the trolley car around the city and gazed at the sights. My car was finally ready! I was late and so we hurried back. I'm afraid that I drove like a maniac with David hanging on for dear life.

I stayed with Frank who was an old army friend of my fathers. One day while sitting in the Bluebird drinking coffee Frank heard my father laugh, dads laugh was loud and distinctive.

Turning to Jack he said. "That wouldn't be Charlie Sadd would it?"

Surprised, Jack said that it was. So the two of them were reunited after nearly twenty years.

I took room an board with them and bunked in with their son. At this time dad was shifted to veterans hospital in Vancouver. Frank and I visited him there and he seemed to be little changed. While he couldn't speak his eyes conveyed his emotions. It was shortly after this visit that he died. I was in the middle of a practicum so was unable to attend his funeral. The teacher I had was good about it and we went over to his place and drank while he told me his experiences teaching. At one point he said "I would rather peddle my bum than have taught then"

In the spring term I left to take an apartment of my own. It was an arrangement between David and myself. He would pay for half the rent and I would grant him access to the place upon occasion. It worked rather well and he took his boyfriend to my place when I was out. At this time I became enamoured of C. He would come and read various material of a sexual nature then we would retire to have sex. Upon several occasions there was another boy present about the same age, thirteen or fourteen and the three of us would hug each other. I don't remember much sex when he was present but we enjoyed our time together.

Teaching

In the fall I got a job teaching at Elko. About forty miles from Fernie it was situated near the Kootany river. I was originally scheduled to teach grades one through six but as there was a large influx of new children due to arrive. Another teacher was hired and a portable brought in to accommodate all of the children. I was to have a teacher-age but circumstances decreed otherwise so I was left taking room and board with the stationmaster and his wife. They were good people and I remember them fondly. The house sat on the tracks and in the early morning hours you could hear old eighty four climb up the hill, then becoming louder, it burst upon the scene and rumbled past the house, finally fading away into the distance.

It was harder than I imagined it would be. I could not seem to find any rapport with the half a dozen kids that were all there were until later. By thanksgiving I was worn to a frazzle and ready to quit. When I went home I was tired and cranky. My mother helped me and together with the aid of some pills my sister was taking I managed to hold on. The classroom lacked books and those it had were old and worn. When

I returned after Thanksgiving I brought all my children's books with me and after that life became much easier. This class contained what would be considered "special' children by the ton. One girl was barely hanging on as she had limited intelligence. Another had been failed a couple of times and a third never came out of his shell. Nevertheless we soldiered on and now the children from the work site began coming. The class swelled to nearly twenty and I was kept busy. It made no sense to have one model so I began to teach each child where he or she was. At last I was happy and the class thrived.

There plenty of things to do in the area. Fernie ski hill was just up the road and I participated in all of it's fests. There was also badminton at Fernie high school were I drove two nights a week. It was sometimes a difficult drive as the wind drove the snow. It was cold there. Minus twenty was not uncommon and sometimes there was a blizzard raging. When we were finished we all trooped into the showers to clean and relax. The gang showers of the school were great as you could watch all of the students naked. It was after some time that I realized that the teacher was also homosexual. We went to his house were we talked about it for a while. He believed that if a student wanted to have sex then it was alright providing discretion was taken.

Nightmare

I was going to my classroom of a Saturday to tidy up some loose ends. When I arrive I interrupted three of my students stealing the funds we had obtained for some cause or another. I caught them as the were attempting to flee out the back door. I was now in quandary as to what to do. Except for one boy the others belonged to homes that were not supportive. I phoned my priest and we decided to phone the police and have them arrested. On Monday morning I received a visit from the district supervisor inquiring about allegations regarding one of the children. I was accused of molesting both their son and daughter. While he agreed that that was unlikely, I was devastated. What would become of me if my sexuality were known. I resigned. We went back to the rectory where I sat on the rectors knee and cried. I could not remain there long so after a couple of days I went back to the school where they had my children's book packed. I told them that the could keep them, rounded up my personal belongings and left.

Once at home I told my mother and sister that I was a homosexual which didn't sit well with my sister. I began a restless shifting, hoping to come up with some solution, Sleep evaded me as I drove my mind into harder and harder places. Eventually I left one dark night and drove the Monashee, now wearing yellow snow goggles! How I got to Vancouver I do not know but I remember having dinner in the Georgia hotel. I came to Victoria were I startled David with my boldness. He could not take me in as he lived with his mother. From there I went to the church were I sang. For how long I was there singing I know not but eventually the priest came to talk me into going back with him. He sat me down in his office to have a chat and I told him that I had sex with your son. Anyone else would have turned me in but he knew much and the seal of the confessional bound him to his office.

I stayed overnight with him and could not sleep. I stole out at night and invaded Heather's home were she lived with her mother. I babbled on about how I was a homosexual. Returning home I received a visit from his son which convinced him that I had lost my marbles. Soon the ambulance arrived and I was sent to hospital. Unlike now Victoria did not have a psychiatric ward so I was sent by helicopter to River view mental hospital on the mainland. There I was stripped of all my clothing and possessions and dumped into a holding tank. There were four walls and a mattress on the floor. I, who had no previous encounters with imprisonment, had live all my life outside or near it, was locked into on room. I beat on the door to no avail, My soul cried within me. Please release me! But there was no answer. Only hollow echos that rang through the corridors of my mind. There was no one to comfort me and only the long silence of unbroken days withering me. How long I was in this state I do not know. Only the angels in heaven guarded me to shield from my woe.

Eventually I came down of this manic high and was granted the privileged of being out on the ward. You were gradually inserted back into the life of the hospital, first with only pyjamas then you got your clothes back and finally you were granted passes outside the building.

I worked through the various progressions then took off and went to Vancouver. Back I was brought and put back in pyjamas to start all over again. One of the methods by which you were integrated back to the fold was to have you try tobacco. You had various types of tobacco you could try from roll your own to pipe tobacco. I chose a pipe because Gandalf smoke one and with it I could blow smoke rings. I know that it sounds terrible in this day and age but it was there that I was hooked on tobacco. Eventually I was brought back but still no one even mentioned homosexuality.

After a month of this my mother came down to visit me and was I glad to see her. My ticket for release. Eagerly I inquired when we were going home. It was then that she told me that she could not get me out. I was devastated! Throwing my hat down I cried.

"I might as well kill myself! "and ran down to the bottom of the property.

Sometime later a concerned nurse came to me and by that time I had calmed down. It appeared that I had been committed involuntarily and only through the hospital would I be released. Back to square one again. It was then that I began to look at some of the goings on around the hospital. Certain patients were routinely shunted off for electro shock therapy and once I recall seeing a patient flopping around like a fish out of water after this procedure. I was horrified. But now there seemed to be no way out except through this route. For a time I resisted any notion of going through this procedure. Eventually I relented. It was the only way I could get out. How many times I was put through this I do not know, but eventually I was freed.

Once more I had no inkling as to how to deal with my homosexuality. I left the hospital with no follow up and not a clue as to what had happen to me. In these cases I was prone to another attack. One of the clues that you are going into a manic state is that you are hyper sexual. Sheila Hamilton describes this in the following passage.

"Hyper sexuality is one of the most troubling and challenging symptoms of bipolar disorder. Doctors Fredrick Goodwin and Kay

Jamison reviewed the literature and hyper sexuality and concluded the 57 percent of people with bipolar disorder report difficulty controlling the urge to have sex with someone other than their partners.

Research by Barbara Geller M.D. And colleagues in an NIMH financed study at Washington University in St. Louis found that 43 percent of children diagnosed with mania exhibited hyper sexual behaviour. The subjects of the study were ninety-three children with mania whose average age was about eleven years.

"Hyper sexuality can be a component of hypo mania an elevated condition in which the bipolar patient feels energetic and charismatic, and inhibitions drop. Hypo mania can be an enjoyable mood state that is like a recreational drug." 1

1. All the Things we never Knew, p59

Railway again

I picked up my car and went back to work for the railway. I worked quite a while in Yahk. My mother had bought me a tent and as it was summer I tented in the campsite. For a while I was shunted back to Natal and stayed in the engineers bunkhouse. I had one unusual sexual occurrence during this time. A young man picked me up and we went to his place. He couldn't have been too old as he was straying with his parents. I stayed with him sharing a bed and we had sex together. It was the only time that I ever saw him. Back to Yahk to finish the summer. A cousin of mine was working on a banana boat that periodically stopped in at Seattle. Saddling up my old Jag I started off to meet him. On the way the car started going through a lot of oil. The next day I took it up to Canada and bought a used Austin 1100. It was definitely a much slower car and it came perilously close to overheating as I went through Moses Lake. I reached home only to find a letter telling me that my license would be suspended. All this and heaven too! When I reached Victoria I went to see the deputy in charge.

He looked at me and said. "It seems you have a heavy foot."

I replied. 'Yes I had a heavy foot but that I had a new car that wouldn't go fast.'

He allowed me to keep my license, for which I was immeasurably great full, and went on my way.

I lived in one room in a rooming house. In those days you could have a sink and a one ten range where you either had half of two burners on, a whole burner on or the oven on, not the works. I suited me fine as I was at university and had little cash. It also provided a place where David and could meet to have sex or just talk bout life in general. One evening he brought his flame around and we enjoyed three way sex. There is not too much to talk about that year and at the end of April I decided that I had enough money to last me next term so I went to England for the whole summer.

I stayed with my cousin in Ireland who had a farm just outside Lisdrumbroccus. With both of us working we managed to put down more hay than he had ever done before. It was good to have a labouring job and we put up more hay than ever before. Working with the hired hands proved quite a challenge. I could not understand one word in ten. Between the accent, which was as broad as could be, and the local colloquialisms it was touch to figure out. At the end of my stay the hired hands young son gave me the ultimate compliment.

"My but your Irish has improved." he said.

Six weeks later I took a plane to England where I spent the rest of the summer visiting my numerous relations. On my was back I stopped in at the ranch in the Cariboo where my brother was working. We talked about the things that brothers do then headed into town for a drink. The man at the bar turned to Marty and said. "You'll have your unusual." Then turning to me said. "Can I have some ID please. "Marty thought this was hilarious and roared out. "That's my older bother you know." This was after the drinking age had been lowered to nineteen!

D. C.

I took my usual room in a house not far from the cathedral and worked on my degree. One of the profs that taught me gave me a job developing curriculum. It was designed for the primary grade and involved a number of pictures with different places and peoples on it. My job was to make a list of questions that would enhance the pictures.

It was quite challenging and I enjoyed the work. It gave me the idea of putting my slides of Ireland into some sort of order an making a unit out of it.

Winter was now upon us and as I had just returned from Christmas I was feeling rather low. The depressive side of my bipolar was kicking in. I was in a state where everything seemed melancholy. I didn't have enough energy to read. At this point D. came to me. He was now singing in the choir at the cathedral as a chorister which was located a block away from where I was staying. One day he dropped in unannounced in order to get a ride back home. We chatted and I began to wrestle him, putting my hands up his sweater. At this point he said.

"All right. Let's do this properly."

Before I knew was was going on he had stripped naked and was laying face down on the bed. I didn't take long to join him. He proved amply supplied with all of the tools for sex. He was primed for sex and I did not disappoint him. I had anal intercourse with him which he enjoyed. In my state of loneliness he was a balm that I could not refuse. For six months we were together and we enjoyed sex together. We went on trips to sea world and the museum. His infectious laugh and ready smile were there to put me at ease. I got to know his parents well at this time. On Friday nights we would have hot dogs and other times we just laughed and had a good time. D. was the youngest of four. He had two grown bothers and a sister some years older than himself. It did not take too much imagining to see how David had become acquainted with sex in the fashion in which he had become accustomed.

The shift in my mood was instantaneous and feelings of well being climbed back into my brain. When the affair continued and we began to feel comfortable I began to recover. My mood switched from that of depressive to one of almost mania. Whether it was good for me or not remained to be scene.

"Bipolar disorder diagnosis requires patience on the part of both the patient and doctor. At present, only about 20 per cent of patients receive full diagnosis in a year or less."(2) If that is the rate at which we diagnose patients this day I had zero chance of receiving help.

2. The Everything Health Guide to Adult Bipolar Disorder, p42

He was very straight froward In all his doings with and infectious laugh and a giggle that turned me on. Once we went to visit a friend and he embarrassed me by asking questions in that brash manner he had. As the weather warmed we went skinny dipping in the haunts around Victoria. We also spent a few weekends camping; my tent proving to be useful in ways that my mother could not have imagined. At the end of June I left to become a counsellor at a summer camp in Alberta.

School

After the sessions of camp I had become good friends with Tom Payne. We went to the same church and out of that crowd of evangelicals we were the only Catholics. In the fall I headed up to Edmonton to try and get a job. I soon became a supply teacher and things were settling down. One afternoon I took two of the campers of a football game. On the way there were were rear ended by a drunk with no insurance. The back of the car was a write off. I took the car to my mechanic who said that they could fix the car by changing the motor and transmission out of it into an new body.

Soon after that I got a call from Hinton school district for an interview. Taking Tom's Pinto I rolled out and being successful I hurried back to pack my things. The classroom teacher was having a baby and left in mid-October so I was the designated replacement. I worked there until my car was ready then drove to Edmonton to pick it up. It was slower trip back. At Christmas time I turned for home once more. It was snowing and minus eighteen, twenty five below today, as I headed out. Over to Jasper then on up to the Columbia ice fields and the top of the pass. Fifty miles out I saw the snowplow turned around and headed in the other direction. I stopped and asked him if someone was coming the other way and he said yes. I headed out. The 1100 had little clearance and I slid upon occasion fighting to push snow and maintain control. Fortunately, the other plow arrive and I was spread any further hassle.

Now I had another problem. As only one side of the road had been plowed I was forced to drive carefully on it taking to the deeper snow when oncoming traffic showed up. At the the top of the pass it had been plowed both ways and I hurried on. The 1100 was not built for cold weather. It was all the heating plant could do in those temperatures to keep the ice off the windscreen. I barrelled along with no visibility on either side. Finally I reached to No. 1 and headed down the strip that would put me there. It wasn't plowed. There I was with no visibility and coming down onto the busiest highway in the country. I clung to the side of the road and prayed. With a honking a car gave me a berth to get onto the highway. Shaking all over I pulled into a rest stop for a coffee and lunch.

I was now driving on the No. 1 and though the surface was better the trucks kept spinning up snow so that it became hard to see. For two hours I fought with the icy conditions until I made another pit stop, poured more coffee into my frozen body then headed on. It was getting dark when I final reached the north road and felt that the journey was at an end. Not so. I climbed up one particularly steep pitch only to spin out, Back down the hill I went to get a run at the hill. This time I made it and rolled on home about seven o'clock. It was a journey I never wanted to repeat.

Christmas at home was it's usual good time of friends and family. After two weeks I returned to Hinton via Edmonton as I did not fancy trying the sky way again. I spent the night in Edmonton and the next day I proposed a ski trip to Jasper to a young friend of mine. He and I set off for Hinton reaching there about supper time. I made supper and we talked for a while before going to bed. We had sex which was surprising and good. The next day we spent the day skiing and for the first time I didn't freeze as we went up the lift. Once more we had sex then I put him on the bus to go home.

From there on in the winter was cold. Temperatures of minus forty when the air froze and you had an ice fog. Even with the car plugged in it barely started. There was no escape from the cold. It permeated everything that we did. And for three solid months our only contact with the outside was skiing. And some days it was too cold to do even that. At the end of March it was thirty below! Easter was coming soon and I longed to get away. I wrote to David and he booked a motel in Victoria for me. Driving south through the Yellowhead I spent the night with the Gibson's before heading on to the coast. The motel was out of town in an out of the place spot. I immediately contacted D. parents then D. and I went back to my motel and had sex. The next day I moved in with the Sexsmiths and spent the rest of my time with them. They were fun people and I was a lonely young man. D. and I had sex that first night but I couldn't refuse the Sexsmith's invitation.

It was too short a respite. Soon I was back in the land of ice and snow. Gradually it warmed up and I began to think of camping once more. I arranged for a camping trip with one of my students and another friend. Bernie came come with me to spend the night. There was a spare room and I should have made up the bed to give him a place to sleep.

"Oh the snakes walk at night. That's what they say. When the snakes come out. It is time to play. The gun I had was held within my hand. No I didn't plan to give them any warning for the devil on my shoulder had command. "

There were two bedrooms in the house and I sat their trying to decide weather to make up the bed in the spare room. "O the snakes walk at night, that's what they say. When the sun goes down, the snakes will play. No I did not plan to give them any warning, for the devil on my shoulder had command." He slept with me and I had anal sex with him. It was over. Later I was given the choice of resigning or being fired. I resigned. I phoned my mother and said that I had done it again and she told me to come home. I said that I would but only after the term. Driving back to Edmonton were I spent a miserable month and a half. I sat around trying to write a novel but my only thoughts kept wandering back to that scene.

I was jolted back to earth. All my promises to keep from this type of behaviour went down the tube and I was standing in the ruins of my life. As Dr. Haycock remarked. "Behaviour therapy is one method for treating borderline personality disorder. One goal is to get patients to view the things they say and do- and the things that subsequently happen to them- in less extreme terms. Antidepressants and mood stabilizers are sometimes used in concert with individual and group therapy." 3

3. The Everything Health Guide to Adult Bipolar Disorder, P51

"Almighty and most merciful Father, We have erred and strayed from thy ways like lost sheep, We have followed too much the desires of our own hearts, We have offended against thy holy laws, We have left undone those things which we ought to have done, And we have done those things which we ought not to have done; And there is no health in us. But thou, O Lord, have mercy upon up miserable offenders." 4

4. Book of Common Prayer, P 4

I drove myself to write and achieved some measure of accomplishment. For six weeks I remained there with only my thoughts and a song on the radio that seemed to fit my mood.

"Sylvia's packing she catching the five o'clock train. And sir won't you call back again. And the operator said twenty cents more for the next three minutes. Please! Mrs. Avery I just want to tell her goodbye! "

After six weeks I returned home and spent the summer trying to recover. I worked for the village collecting camping fees at the towns campsite. I went around each evening taking fees then returning them to my mother. At that time she was the village clerk. I made friends and took several groups up to the hot springs to visit and marvel at the woods and the quiet tranquility of nature's bounty. Near the end of the summer I was taking two kids and had another boy who was stranded without companions. He was an odd boy who had stolen several things from my mother's home. At the end of the summer we took a camping trip were they let their hair down. I had sex with him though I know not what became of him later.

PAINTER

I returned to the coast where I took a room in a rooming house. I tried to find work but only found a job selling adds for a radio station. Then I got a call from my brother who had connected with someone who was setting up a painting business. As I had no job or prospect of getting one, it was an intriguing prospect. We were going to make our fortune spraying Kenitx on houses. As the opposite room was empty James took this and we had the whole top floor. It was a wicked winter. With temperatures dropping down to minus thirteen with a howling wind. The walls might have been made of paper for all the good they were. We just barely kept warm with the oven on full. The landlord complained but as he couldn't provide the heat we needed he was out of luck.

At this time I was apprised of a hearing in Edmonton regarding my resignation. It was too far to go so I didn't. The hearing was held and I lost my teaching certificate. I was feeling very low. Gradually I recovered and it was partly due to having new job. At the end of December a friend of mine said that he had a house to rent but that he would have no trouble renting it. I jumped at the chance and said that we would rent it. We received a two bedroom house for the same price we had paid for the two rooms. As this house had a full basement in which we could store our equipment and mix up our paint. We were painting up a storm and making money. Early in the spring we split the team and James took a client of his, Mike Peters, and went out on his own. I took another of his clients and started on my own. The work went well and I began to make good money. I bought a Rover 2000 to replace my tired 1100. It all went south when Mike tried to mix his own material. I tried it out and it slid off the walls! Oh well! Easy come easy go.

David and I continued seeing each other and after James left we had the whole house to ourselves. The passage of the act making homosexuality legal meant that we were free from the law but society was still against it. The church was against it and as we had invested a large portion of our lives in living within the church we were still cautious about declaring that we were; that would have put us in a bad relationship with the church. It was a catch 22. We continued to remain closeted.

On the anniversary of the Trudeau decision that the state had no right to be in the bedrooms of the nation we went out to a club and partied. All care went with a few drinks and we were having a great time. One thug who had seen our enthusiastic scenes objected to our company, so we we decided to leave. When we reached the door one of the men threw a puch at David. He buckled over and I had to get him out of there. We stumbled along the street until we came to a bench where we rested. In a short while David felt all right and I drove him home. That night his mother phoned to say that he had died. I was shocked! One moment he was with me and the next he was gone. I went wild in my grief. The only thing that I could do for him was to swing the thurible at his funeral. Even my pain could not be shown for then our love would be revealed.

In the fall I decided to buy the house and with a bit of negotiating that's what I did. I began painting with paint rather than textured coating. It was a hit and miss affair and I wound up doing other odd job to make ends meet. In 1974 I decided to go back to university to complete my degree. In order to afford this I took two boarders in and supplemented this by teaching badminton in the local rec centre. I had no one left to turn to. I decided to take counselling to see what I could make out of this mess.

Dr. Jones was a fully capable man and he asked me all sorts of question regarding my previous sex life. He asked me whether I wanted to remain homosexual or go straight. I had had enough of being homosexual so I opted to go straight. Little did we know about the difficulties of a man going 'straight'. For him it was the obvious solution to that problem. We little knew how it would play out.

We worked on this problem for the balance of the year and I tried valiantly to comply. I forsook all sexual contact with men and instead picked up a young lady off a badminton court. We had to have something in common. Through out that year and into the next I courted her. Finally I proposed. I said "Do you want to make the biggest mistake of your life." And she said yes. We arranged a wedding for June and in the meantime we played badminton together going to several tournaments. In May she had bad spell, she was a diabetic, and we had to cancel our plans to go to England. In June we got married in a full nuptial mass. My sister was somewhat annoyed as she thought that weddings took twenty minutes. Off we went on our honeymoon. Tom Payne hid the car as we didn't trust her three brothers. Now we were off, sailing on the Princess Margurite, the last of the steamships to ply the coastal waters. Four hours later we arrived in Seattle.

To say that I was anxious on our first night would be the mild understatement. Wonder of wonders it turned out better than I imagined and sex turned out to be wonderful. We camped down the Oregon coast stopping at Ft. Stevens then moving on down the coast. We decided to take the No. 1 along the coast as it would be cooler, our car having no air conditioning. Down we went to Ft. Bragg where we spent the night. The next day we headed out for San Francisco only a few miles down the coast. It was not a great distance but it was like a dogs hind leg, twisting and turning along the coast. I took us all day to reach our destination. Reaching our motel we inquired as to where a good restaurant was. The owner directed us to Joe of Westlake. Upon our arrival we noted with satisfaction the waiters all wearing tails. When we came to be seated it was in a booth and when we ordered prime rib it came with a choice of" french fries, spaghetti or mashed potatoes" ! No baked or roasted spuds were available. Still, it made a very memorable meal.

I showed her all the sights that David and I had explored years earlier. Then it was off up the I5 to return home. As evening fell we headed up the pass that goes to Crater lake. We camped on the way where we encounter little squirrels and chipmunks. In the morning we completed the drive up to the lake. It was at this point that Lesley began to have trouble breathing so we hastily departed. We reached main road just before Bend. Outside of Bend we got stuck behind a logging truck and as Lesley was driving we waited for an opportunity to pass. A long stretch of highway appeared and she floored it. At ninety miles an hour we roared past the truck and on our way. I always kept my pipes in the ashtray and when we reached the boarder the guard asked to look at them. He sniffed them expecting to get whiff of marijuana. No such luck. He waved us on through and off we went to Christina Lake. On the morrow we reached Nakusp and spent a pleasant couple of days with my mother before heading back to the coast.

Once there we settle into married life with all of it's foils and foibles. The next summer we bought a new house and rented the old one. We were playing badminton together and getting to know one another. At one point were ran a tournament together. There had been a break in at the hall and the kids involved were identified. It was agreed that I would spank them and no further action was required. At a break in the tournament I took them home, they pulled down their pants and I spanked them six times. It was over and I had quite forgotten about it. Now one of those boys is calling it a homosexual act!

In the winter of 1978 Lesley began loosing her sight. Spots appeared in her eyes and laser treatment seemed to do no good. As winter turned to summer her condition worsened. By June she was certified legally blind. You cannot imagine the stress something like that puts on you. One day you are going onward and the next life is turned upside down. Now only one of us could drive and we could forget playing badminton where we first met. We sold her car and I was obliged to fill in as the sole driver in the family. I went manic at this time.

Lesley took some time to be with her parents and by the end of the summer we had managed to put the worst of it behind us. We took a long holiday up to Edmonton to visit friends. As we both smoked at the time we found our way to the coffee shop to warm up and have a puff. Our visit over we took our leave and bombed back to Victoria. I had bought a Rover 2000 and it purred along at ninety miles and hour back to Jasper then on to the coast. We stopped at Kamploops where I had an aunt who was getting on in age but welcomed us.

It was at this time that R and R came into our lives. I took them hiking and camping and they came over to our place to play games. Rob was funny and full of mischief. We got along well together and soon left Rick at home on our excursions. It was on one of our camping trips that I first had sex with him. It was an unusual time. Rick and Rob had lost the replacement for their father who had skipped out on them going to Australia. Rob and I needed each other in this time of crisis. We clung to each other I holding him and he giving me all the love he had. It was a symbiotic relationship. He was oriented to oral sex and I to anal. We had sex upon occasion though out that year. We went skiing and camping together. Once we went to Manning park with Lesley and a friend of hers. We skied but man was it cold! The next day it was colder still and we decided to pack it in and head for home. It was cold there too. I had sex with Rob. I loved him. In the spring it was baseball season and one day I went to visit Rob. There he was with the coach of the team and I instantly recognized him for what he was, another homosexual. I could not compete with one who had moved in with their mother. I departed the scene gracefully. I kept track of them as they moved to a house and even tried to see them but it was a failure. I gave up.

Throughout that year I began teaching again. I got a job doing home schooling in the Saanich school district. I taught kids who had dropped through the cracks. With trepidation and not much hope I applied to get my teaching certificate. To my surprise the deputy minister had been wondering whether I would apply as I was now married and well on my way. I went on the supply list and taught in various places. For three years I taught and was it different. The NDP had removed the strap and the kids seemed to be in charge of the classroom. On we soldiered and the cases became more acute. It appeared that the principal now had the authority and no other. If he was good, the school was good. I taught in one school where the principal stood at the bottom of the stairs and scowled at the kids. The next year the school got a new principal and the teaching was fun again. One day I was subbing for the librarian and was having a particularly hard time with one of the students. Doug Shaw came in, took the boy to the office where he received the worst tongue lashing I have ever witnessed. He shamed the boy. I tutored a lot and gradually built up a client base. One particular event shook me up. As I was now in the union the meeting had a proposal to take less in salary so that more subs could be hired. It was shunted off to make some minor adjustments. When it came back it had to pass by a two thirds majority in order to get back on the list. It only received sixty-two percent. I was appalled!

I continued painting in the summer months and became more proficient as the years rolled by. In the fall of 1980 I received a phone call from Rob. John had left, and they were once more in an apartment in Esquimalt. Gladly I took him back and we had a short affair until Christmas when he decided not to continue any more. We broke off amiably and he continued to come to our place and play games. One night when he was fifteen or sixteen Lesley was out, probably spending the weekend with her parents. Rob came over and we played games until it was time for bed. We got close together and began to strip. His hand was on my penis. As we slipped into bed where he sucked me off.

In 1981 Rick came to me asking for a job. I gave him odd jobs until the summer when he began to paint for me. Ross was the chief architect and Rick worked under my tutelage while the bulk of the work was performed by Ross. At that time my wife was in hospital with our first child, diabetic pregnancy being complicated things. I was in lust and as Rick made no objection we had sex. When Lesley came home Rick held the baby and said, "I could have lots of these." He baby sat Roy and I was in love with him. In the fall we began to play badminton and go to tournaments. We would go to the hall, play badminton for a couple of hours then retire to the showers. I made sure that the door to the hall was locked. His body sent shivers of pleasure through me. I touched his body as I washed him. The scent of his shampoo was intoxicating. For a while I was carried back to my youth. Then we had sex.

At Powell River we took a room it a motel, went out for supper then came back. We began to roll around hugging each other and kissing. I took down his pants and sucked him off. When I had finished and the sperm was hot in my mouth he gave a little giggle. Then he turned over for me to have anal intercourse with him. We repeated the performance the next night. On the way down we were laughing and joking with a car load of kids. We stopped at a gas station to fill up and Rick jumped out and began filling my diesel car with gas! We halted the filling immediately and searched for a garage to empty the tank. While this was going on we had supper. It was rather later when we returned to the road.

Over course of the year we had sex but sometimes he was willing and at other times he seemed to take a negative attitude and we had no intercourse. One day we were having an argument about sex as we drove through the countryside. Upon reaching the trailer he said. "I'll have anal intercourse with you if you don't have it with me. "Now a brief lesson on anatomy. The prostate gland that regulates sex is located in a mans anus. Sexologists advocate that a woman insert her finger into her husbands anus in order to properly stimulate him. As he penetrated me I received a multitude of shocks. It was a an incredible feeling. He continued penetrating me while holding my penis and I went off in his grasp. For some five minutes he continued until he too went off. It was an incredible night.

Towards the end of the second year we were to take a camping trip to Cowichan Lake where my in laws had some property. Rick asked if he could bring a friend along. Knowing that this meant no sex I still agreed. We had our supper, I can't remember what we had. I had a bottle of something, what it was I do not remember, and after dinner I left it on the table and went to have a nap. It had been a long day. Sometime later I woke up to find the two of them gone. I searched the place finding them in a ditch with C. R. sucking a very aroused Rick. It was rather a public place for this so I took them back to the trailer. There upon C. R. took my pants down and began sucking me. He kept saying "Come in my mouth! Come in my mouth! "I did my best to comply but as he was sucking so hard I couldn't go off. Eventually we were through though I still had not gone off. I went to him and had anal intercourse with him. ' in vino veritas'

One trip that we took took out from among the rest. We went to a badminton tournament in Kelowna and it was agreed that we would only have sex one night. It was a hard tournament and I don't remember whether we won or lost. It was late in the day when we finished our final match so we roared back to the coast. We missed the last ferry so we took motel with a Jacuzzi tub to soak our sore limbs. It was very relaxing and the sex afterwards was great.

Another painting season had come and I was preparing Rick for his driving license. We practised at the university and eventually graduated to the road. When he took his license and passed he was so proud. As I had no need of the car I gave it to Rick to take home and bring back in the morning. came back devastated. Your mother had thrown a fit and would not permit you to have my fourteen thousand dollar car. She got over it but I still remember your crying at the time. Eventually she relented and you took the car upon occasion. We drove to Vancouver to watch a Lion's game and spent the night in a motel. By this time we had agreed to have sex only once on an outing and this was the night. The next day we drove over to Nanaimo were we spent the night. It was getting late in our relationship and I sensed that it was coming to an end.

From this age I can see clearly now what was going on. Rick came to me knowing that I was a homosexual and deliberately traded his body for money. That's the only way to put it. He was so sexy and I was still entangled in my wife's blindness. The lust that overcame me was real and I make no apology for it. On the other hand Rick was enamoured of all the good things that came with money. He even wanted to quit after the first summer but as he could not find another job it was back to work for me. At least he didn't stay with me and had not to place his body in jeopardy so frequently. This is what happens when greed tangles with lust and the two engage in combat. I have long ago put my lust to rest but Rick could not admit his greed. Today with a trial in the offing to decide the outcome he continues to hide.

Denumont

I was still teaching badminton but now I was looking for replacement for Rick. I seemed to have found him when it exploded in my face. The cops were called and I was hauled in to have an interview. They told me that I was looking for another partner which jived with my thought. They knew about my relationship with Rick and now everything was coming unglued. I stopped and took a deep breath. I asked them to put away their pencils and then I confessed to everything. They told me that they would be contacting Rick and Rob. I went home to my wife and confessed everything. My doctor got me counselling. Thankfully neither of the twins said anything only saying that I was a touching caring sort of person. There was hope left in life for me, a sinner. From that day to this I have had no sex with anyone outside of my wife.

We were mad, I know, but we decided to have another child. Secretly hoping for a girl my wife went into her second diabetic pregnancy. It was not to be and Martin was born in October. Martin was a hand full. For the first eighteen months he woke up every two hours. We took turns feeding him, changing him and rocking him. I was frazzled and tired as well. How we got through those first months I do not know except that we were young and healthy. Les said then, "If he had been born first he'd have been an only child" At eighteen months he began to sleep through the night. Now we had a different problem. Lesley's eyes were becoming sore and in particular one eye. It was glaucoma and later that year she had her right eye removed. An eye that did nothing but hurt was no asset.

It was then that I began to notice a trend in the papers. It began with the Noyes case and continued to get worse. I remember being over at a friends house and she was commenting on a case she had seen in court. The young man was accused of sexual assault conducted his own defence. He admitted that he had touched the girls bottoms. When the sentence was brought down he got five years. I can remember Lorna was aghast. Now I began to be worried. If they were handing out sentences for those offences what would they give to me who had sinned more than he. Soon the situation went from bad to worse. They began looking years in the past and handing down harder sentences. I began to think of moving my family to England but I could not deprive Les of the support of her family.

In the end I stayed. In 1989 a bridge playing acquaintance of mine asked me to look after his nine year old son for a weekend. What I didn't know was that they had changed the law regarding sexual contact with a minor. It now read 'touching for a sexual purpose'. Foolish me! C came and took a bath with my children but when he came out he had a towel sketchily draped around him and came and sat on my lap. He played badminton with us upon on the weekend and we showered together, my son and C. In the summer they borrowed my car to pull a trailer full of goods down from Yahk. We waited without hearing a word while I fumed at the delay to our vacation. At last they arrived and we were off. I knew that the kid was not good for me but I continued seeing him. I kept pushing him away but then there would be another request to have him sleep over. In the fall of 1990 the cops came to arrest me. The magnitude of my own folly was revealed to me in a blinding flash. In the cop car he tried to get me to confess. He left me in a cell and I prayed to God with my fingers acting as decades of the rosary.

"Hail Mary full of grace the Lord is with you! Blessed are you and blessed is the fruit of your whom Jesus. Holy mother of God pray for us now and the hour of our death. Amen. "Over and over I recited this mantra.

Sometime later Cpl Black came back to finger print me. Now he stuck the needle in most cruelly. If only I would confess my crime I could be spared the months of separation. My wife and family were being question as we spoke. In anger I finally burst out.

"Damn you all to hell ! "I was so angry that I could not even address my priest who for some reason was waiting there for me.

I was returned to my cell where I spent the rest of the night in fervent prayer. The next day I was taken to court were I was arraigned and set free to go to my wife. Her experience with the social worker was horrible. They asked her all kinds of question regarding our sex life. We finally phoned my brother and, bless his soul, he came right away even though he was in Montana at the time. I was not permitted to be with my children. Off I went to spend a couple of nights at the rectory. When James arrived we had a long talk and as he was staying with my wife I felt better about that situation. Two days afterwards I moved into my motor home to do a job for Lorna. For six weeks my wife and I communicated with each other while the children were at school. Eventually we got back to court and the ban against being with my children was lifted.

I returned home but life is not fair. For a couple of nights we raked leaves and were home together. Now social services assured us that they could take our children away if I continued to be at home. It was the last straw. After six weeks of waiting that which I had most fervently desired had been taken away. I broke! I became manic. I did all of the things that you shouldn't do. I crawled into bed with my wide at three in the morning and howled until there was no more pain. Eventually I ended up in the psychiatric ward. It was a time of searching and sorrowing. I flung all of my misguided efforts into trying to solve a unsolvable puzzle. I remained high for quite some time, even after I got out of the hospital. They took my visiting privileges away which was of no concern as SS had effectually done the deed. Christmas saw me still high but all I could think about was the knot that seemed to get harder and harder as I went along.

I was getting out my manic phase and beginning to become depressed. Come February I was in a full blown depressive state. At that time I went to to see Fr. Hanley as I was seriously considering changing churches. I remember that he said that; "If it's the one thing that Catholics know about it's sin." It was comforting to know that sinners would be able to thrive in the Catholic church. From then on we went to St. Pats. Our family received a welcome there that we were grateful. None the less It was still a stressful time. I have recently found a book of my writings from this time and here are some quotes from it.

Sunday, Feb. 4. Went to eight o'clock mass and felt refreshed.

Feb. 5 I was home but my children are with their grandmother. Went to work but could not concentrate. Had a beer with Rick. My god, guide me through another day in peace and joy. Heal my wife I beg of you.

Feb. 9 I was getting support from Sister Eileen, my sons grade one teacher and wrote to her. Went to Vancouver where I stayed with Peterjon and received quite support. Had a visit with Don and he told me of his troubles. In the afternoon I drove to the mission and signed in as a guest.

Feb. 12 I awake the the sound of bells. Mass at six fifteen and then breakfast and prayer. I can repay my debt for this place of prayer and faith with it's beautiful music. Everyone finds their way here eventually.

Feb. 14 I must leave here today so hold me Lord. I went to mass and then to breakfast before saying goodbye. I phoned Les from the ferry and praise God she missed me ! I need her now at this time of crisis.

Feb. 19 Awoke feeling depressed but I played bridge with Keith and felt better.

Feb.23 Depressed. Went to work from my motor home and tried to come to terms with this anomaly. How can I get out of this mess. We all go out to Romeos for dinner and I spend a quieten evening with the kids till eight the back to the motor home where I become depressed again'

Mar. 1 Les is in the hospital again and the kids are with their grandmother. I come home and spend time there before visiting Les. Awake at five so I take a pill and sleep till seven. I am loosing weight as my body tries to handle the situation. Another poor nights sleep.

Mar7 Les is home so I move back into my motor home. Played badminton with Rick and went home early. I keep telling myself that "with God all things are possible.' Roy wanted to win the lottery to "get dad out of jail."

Mar. 8 Went to mass at St. Pats. It was an unquiet dawn. Fear is overcoming my rational mind. Lord help me! Martin'"s card meant so much to me: "I love you dad. I love you. "I don't know if there pills are helping me or hindering me.

Mar. 14 Another depressed day until I saw John who helped me. I must replace fear with desire. Deeply troubled for my children. Why me Lord! My routines are broken as I am not at home, can't sleep to re-start.

;Mar. 21 Forest woke me up at five to go out which was not good. I'm tired and it's raining so no chance to paint the dormers. I saw Les and took a walk but nothing helps. I am in my own home but the place seems dull and lifeless; so wife and no kids. I'm loosing my children to the hatred of my mother in law.

Mar. 23 A day without structure as I have nothing to hold on to, nothing to grasp like a straw in the wind. I live only to see my wife and my children but now I must get a pass to see them. How long must this go on.

Mar. 23 We get the boys and go to St. Pats where all is strange and the gospel too long. I play bridge in the afternoon but there is no sweetness in to victory.

Apr. 15 Plea for my case for there is no return. I must go on. I MUST.

There in ends. All my frustrations peeled like an onion. From then until my pleading guilty two months later I shrank into myself, holding onto the hope of seeing my kids once again. My wife was in hospital and I did not know whether she would come out again. I sank into the depths of despair even going so far as to attempt suicide. How I made it until the end I do not know.

At some point my priest asked for some pictures that I had taken of the kids. They were of the kids bathing nude. I considered them sacred and was outraged when they showed up in the police files. Now it became a matter of how to extricate me with the least possible damage.

A court case was still a possibility but the chances of getting off were slim. Not only that but I had to consider my sons. They would be called to testify with all of the resulting damage. In the end I pleaded guilty to two counts of "touching for a sexual purpose". In June it was over and I hurried to get my children from their grandmother and began to start a new life. The house was sad and lonely as no one in the neighbourhood came to see us. Eventually we sold and bought a house on Richmond St.

KNIGHTS

It was the end of my participation in the Anglican church. In March I joined the Catholic church. My kids were already in St. Pats, still, it was no easy chore. I was leaving the beauty of Cranmer's prose for the "You Who" mass. When I visited Monsieur Hanley he said the one thing that I have never forgotten. He said "If it's one thing that Catholics know about it's sin." I joined St. Pats congregation and joined in all of the events. On Sunday we joined the bowling league and became active bowlers, including my wife. The fact that she could bowl was a marvel to most of the people. In the fall of that year I was invited to join the Knights of Columbus. As I had always considered myself a catholic the question of being a good catholic gentleman was a no brainier. I served at the altar and as I knew more about the service than most of the servers it was assumed that I had been a catholic all along. When it was discovered that I was not a catholic it was quickly remedied and I was a catholic in fact.

The Knights turned out to be my Savior. I participated in all aspects of the council and rose through the ranks to become Grand Knight. Once I had reached this summit I realized that the Knights were a most extraordinary group. Their charitable works were many and varied. Many members that never attended meetings were very involved with charitable works that I never new. Supporting widows, supporting members or just praying for someone. I was humbled by the scope of work done quietly and behind the scenes. O there were the affairs when we ran a dinner or had breakfast with Santa or ran a bar-b-Que for the school. The times when members got together for fellowship and the many degree ceremonies where new members were welcomed along in their journey to knighthood. All were fun and entertaining but the real work was done by those unsung members.

Harry Sadd

As I rose in the ranks of the Knights I began to look at the issues that confront man. It is a difficult time to be a catholic. The scandals about priests have shaken the church. We look at things very differently from those who are not of the faith. Confession and absolution mean nothing to the outside world. In a sense we are looking at the world backwards, not looking for long life but a life in which the compassion of our Lord shows through. I was privileged to write about some of the issues that confront our world. Here are some of them.

O COME LET US ADORE HIM !

It was then that Christ came to us as a lowly and vulnerable child. Herod sought his life not knowing that "My kingdom is not of this world. "In the city of David he was born to symbolize the power of Israel that was by now faded under the boot of Rome. He came not to restore the glory that was Solomon's but to restore man to God. A strange assortment of people came to worship him and they encompassed everyone from the very wealthy Magi to the lowly shepherds. In this we may take heart for it is to all of us that He came both rich and poor. His earthly father was a carpenter and he laboured as a child in that trade. Most particularly He came to the poor in spirit who find this life a vale of tears and sorrow.

The Knights of Columbus were founded to perpetuate this ministry to the poor and needy, particularly to the poor in spirit who need comfort in this secular age. Too often we sit in our insulated homes and we do not see those who are shut out of life either through poverty or loneliness. The richest man cannot buy happiness and the poorest can be filled with joy. It is this paradox that makes the message of Christmas timeless. Christ stands by the door of our hearts knocking for entrance so that he may imbue us with His spirit to the end that we may go out into the world and comfort the lonely.

We have just completed a very successful year and you will be asked to forward your ideas to the council for the spending of funds to fulfill our mission. We who have much of the world's wealth must share with others this bounty so that the Church may be strong to minister to the poor in spirit, so that we may raise up the feint heated, comfort the lonely and bring God's peace to this world.

May God bless all of you in this great work of His that we have begun and may the peace of the Christ Child dwell in all your hearts now and always.

THE TEN COMMANDMENTS

Hear the law of God which was given to Israel in old time. You shall have no other gods but Me. "This is an easy one to follow, after all we don't drop down and pray to the sun the moon and the stars or do we ? We are much more sophisticated than the people Mosses led so we tend to have more sophisticated gods. We believe in the power of science to rectify man's problems though we know that man's nature remains the same. Jesus said "The poor you have with you always "which is a funny statement in that we believe in His omniscient Word. There are many poor people in this country yet we provide basic necessity to all so how can there be poor people ? Christ was telling us to worship Him not some social system and that by so doing we would lift up the spiritual and material well-being of our fellow man. We are called to serve God first for unless the power comes from Him all our efforts are in vain.

2." Thou shalt not make unto thyself any graven images... thou shalt not bow down to them nor worship them, nor serve them... "Hey man ! I don't worship idols. All that stuff about Baal and Zeus is for the birds. But Christ says "Lay not up for yourself treasures on earth where moth and rust corrodes but lay up for yourself treasures in heaven, for where your treasure is there your heart is also." I have the most difficulty with this commandment for I know that I have many material possessions. My car and my house take time and money and it is easy to justify spending money on these idols rather than increasing my giving to the church or the poor. There are times when in my mad scramble to provide what is good for my wife and children I miss the point that all life is transitory and it is not what I have on this earth that counts in God's eyes but the uses to which I put those goods that come from God alone. What would I do if some catastrophe wiped out all my worldly goods ?

3 We don't swear do we ? Or if we do it is in mild terms so what does it mean not to take the Lords name in Vain. Often I find myself going through the service with my thoughts on anything but the Name of Jesus. At the name of Jesus every knee shall bow, the hymn says, and I am often lost in the fog bank of my own world when I should be bowing the knee to my lord and Savior. Do we pray to God for some vain thing or do we concentrate our prayer so that we mean with our hearts what we say with our mouths ? Do we love God with all our heart and mind and strength 4 Sunday is the Lord's day and in this increasingly secular world we are fighting a battle to hold onto It's sacredness. The shops are wide open and nearly everyone around us does one of two things ; goes off to work or sleeps in then spends the day in play. There are two extremes to avoid in this commandment and the first is the total disregard for the worship of God on the day He established for the redemption of mankind. In my grandfather's house no work was performed on Sunday as the day was completely devoted to prayer. We have to remember that "The Sabbath was made for man not man for the Sabbath. On the other hand I have often found myself on holiday with the real temptation of missing mass because I am having a good time or it is inconvenient to find a church in a strange place. Recently we have made an effort to find churches and it is remarkably uplifting to worship with strangers in the unity of the Eucharist, to be welcomed at their coffee hours and to know that no matter where we go we can find a spiritual home.

5 We live in an age that shuffles the old into homes so that they don't impinge on our lifestyles or interfere with our ordered existence. The state has usurped the role of caring children and too often they are shunted into homes with only the company of other elderly people. In biblical times this commandment worked both ways, the parents had to care and honour their children for the children were required to look after them in their old age. Today we have pensions and many of the elderly are well off but are we guilty of shuffling them out of our lives or do we encourage them to visit or even live with us when they need, if not our money, our love and affection ?

6 You shall do no murder. Note that this commandment does not say, "You shall not kill "else the Israelite would still be camped around Mt. Sinai rather than knocking down the walls of Jericho and subduing the holy land. It has always been a duty to protect and guard the weak from the powerful aggressor. Christ says "Greater love has no man than he lays down his life for another ". We are not called to be pacifists but to be soldiers, to carry the cross of Christ into the world and, if necessary to die defending His honour. We are called to spread the gospel of Peace but man is frail and we need to protect the widow and orphan for while might does not make right the right must be maintained by might.

7. Adultery is the sin of our age. We have stricken it from the record books and tried to rearrange our laws so that it completely disappears but to no avail. Every day we look out on our world and see the effects of adultery on the children who are plagued by broken marriages and marriages that never took place because we denied that adultery has any power of sin. In study after study marital infidelity is the leading cause of divorce yet our laws show no hint of remorse. We are caught at the extreme of the pendulum where rather than saying, "Go and sin no more "society says go ahead for there is no sin. How can we as Christians unravel the sorrows that disobeying Gods commandment has brought upon us ?

8. Most of us were brought up in an era where the little that was available had to be stretched in order that everyone could have enough. Theft was a temptation which was quickly discouraged. Today shoplifting costs each and every one of us hundreds of dollars a year as stores have to increase prices to cover the losses. There are other forms of theft that are more subtle. The urge to cheat on one's taxes, to short change our employer by not giving fully of our services or to charge more than a fair price for our services. I have been surprised by how often the waitress is stunned when you tell them that the bill is out in your favour and that they haven't charged you enough. Yes we have all been tempted to let the error stand, particularly when times are

tough. When we are honest God rewards us with His blessing and the knowledge that we have been ambassadors for Christ's kingdom.

9. There was a time when an oath meant something, that ones word was binding without resorting to pen and paper. I am distressed by many aspects of life where the media, advertisers and even the legal system tries to manipulate the truth for their own ends. We are all familiar with the results ; the product that bears no resemblance to the add, the harm a biased news report causes or the scandal when a drug dealer goes free on a technicality. How well do we keep the promises we make ? Do we consider our word to be binding upon us ?

10. What does it mean to Covet your neighbours house ? Does it mean that you really like it and that you wish you had one like it or does it mean that you like it so much you would do anything to get one ? If you look up the word you will be directed to other places such as envy and malice. To covet your neighbours possessions is to desire them so much that you hate the possessor. It is this hatred that so destroyed Communist Russia. The desire to spread the worlds goods around is a very Christian philosophy but the operative words in the Christian lexicon are love and freedom. We are not compelled to give away all that we posses and no Christian is compelled to give to the poor, rather, it is the act of love that prompts the acts of charity. If we have not charity, St. Paul tells us, ' We are as a sounding brass or a tinkling symbol.' Covetousness is the opposite of charity for it would hoard all the worlds goods unto itself. If we are covetous we are empty and hollow, ' For it is in giving that we receive and in dying that we are born to eternal life. '

These are the great commandments of God and lest we become too concerned with the details Our Lord has reminded us of their overriding purpose. "Hear O Israel you shall love the Lord your God with all your heart and with all your mind, and with all your strength,this is the first and great commandment and the second is like unto it : you shall love your neighbour as yourself. On these two commandments hang All the law and the prophets."

In November my wife required triple by pass surgery. In December we picked up the pieces and carried on. Christmas has always been a special time. A time of love and hope when you look after the kids and spread joy throughout the world. A time for healing the wounds of time and concentrating on being a new person. For me it was just such a time. I had emerged from the cauldron and was purified by it's fire, I began the difficult task of putting my life back together. I was going weekly to a session designed to asses your life as a sex offender. You were required to list all of the sins you had committed. I was coming head to head with these anomalies and didn't like the look of the current view of them. What I had considered to be a consenting affair was now considered a crime worse that murder! Still I plowed onward hoping that this would be the end. For five long years I was subjected to conditions on my freedom, not counting the brutal eight months I was forced to live apart from my family. Now I had the chance of making some restitution in my commentaries.

ST. MARY MAGDELENE

It was a difficult convention as conversation whirled around the resignation of Fr. Philip Jacobs and about the various accusations of child abuse sprouting up throughout the secular press. Most of these accusations involve cases now twenty or thirty years ago and it is certainly impossible to recreate the truth at this late date in time. More distressing are the figures being bandied around regarding the compensation of these "victims." It is a strange phenomenon that all of the complainants seem to have found their encounters to have permanently shattered their lives. Of course we all know that sex sells newspapers so it is in the financial interest of the papers to trumpet the sins of the clergy.

All have sin and fall short of the glory of God. We are frail humans who have to deal with the frailties of the flesh. Society has set aside the old barriers of sexual behaviour and condones all kinds of sexual affairs between consenting adults, permits the use of abortion as a contraceptive and is debating the killing of the terminally ill. For our society to reach back thirty years and condemn a man on an allegation strikes me as the ultimate hypocrisy. How many of these complaints are made for financial gain ? I am reminded of Christ's comment to the Pharisees. "You Hypocrite ! First take the beam from your own eye so that you may see clearly to take the speck from your brothers eye."

We need to look at this problem from Christ's perspective, not the worlds. We know that the man erred. We know that he obtained forgiveness and that his work here among us was exemplary. What then would Christ have done ? Well we know the answer to that one. They brought the woman caught in the act of adultery and asked him to judge. Here is the judgment.

"He that is without sin, among you, let him first cast a stone at her. "When they had left he said. "Woman, where are your accusers ? Has no man condemned you ? No one Lord. Then neither do I condemn you ; go ; and sin no more." John 8

St. Mary Magdalene represents the heart of our faith, the forgiveness of sin. Today Mary Magdalene is usually a man and the world stones him, denying the saving grace of Christ. May we within the church not turn our backs on the Magdalene's of the world !

MAGDALENE

In the garden of death he lies,
Seeking the church of light.
In the darkness of sin he cries,
Mourning a mission so bright.

From shadows deep in the past,
Comes the arrow that pierces at night.
The plague of his soul that will last,
Till the end of the mountains of might.

Doomed by the righteous of earth,
To wander this valley of tears.
Torn by the barbs of rebirth,
Crushed by today's new seers.

Can you feel in your heart his pain ?
Does the Savior not speak to you now?
You, without sin, you may train,
The stones that will crush his brow.

Abortion has been sanitized so that society looks on it's perpetrators as just another doctor performing his duties. Any mention of the fact that they are committing murder is swept under the carpet. It has been one of the church's most adamant stands. Abortion is murder, plain and simple. All attempts to publicize this fact is met with extreme measures. They have enacted bubble laws to prevent protesters from even going near the site. Mary Wagner has protested this state of affairs and as a result has spent considerable time in prison.

STAND AND BE COUNTED

Raise up Your power, O Lord, and come among us, and with great might strengthen us, so that we may come to the aid of Your afflicted children. Give us grace to battle all the snares of the devil, particularly we ask for your help to defend the unborn who die before their time has begun. Grant this through Jesus Christ our Lord.

Last year one hundred thousands souls perished at the hands of abortionists in this country alone. For every hundred live births in this province there were thirty one abortions. When the Supreme Court of Canada struck down the abortion law the number of abortions sky rocketed from 71 thousand in 1990 to 106 thousand in 1994. For a society that says it cares about children this is a strange way to show it. A week ago a baby was stolen from a hospital and everyone mobilized to find the child and punish the kidnapper. Had that child been killed a few months earlier in an abortion clinic no one would have known and very few people would have cared. The difficulty with this kind of off again on again morality is that it sends mixed signals to the general population. On the one hand life is sacred, but on the other hand it is dirt cheap. As Catholics we have an obligation to stand up and tell the rest of society that this wrong and make every effort to change the attitudes of others. That's what evangelizing is all about. The trick is that we have to do it with love.

On Sunday October the 5th we will once again gather on Bland St. between Tolmie and Cloverdale to protest the massacre of the unborn. I urge all of you to join us at two in the afternoon for an hour to bear witness for Christ. This is a family occasion and I urge you to come with your wife and children. Two years ago the abortionists attempted to disrupt our protest so YOU KNOW that your stand is being noticed.

Do we care for the life unborn ?
Are the morals of Christ still alive ?
Does society's apathy wear us down ?
Is our time too precious to strive ?

Our Savior still stands in the Garden,
He asks us to watch and pray.
Can we spare Him and hour now and then,
Will we stand by His side and stay ?

For the life of the unborn is short,
Soon this flame will reach the abort.
My friends we must stand and protest,
For Christ needs your voice at His behest.

God willing we will make a difference in a world where values are tuned upside down.

FAMILY

Roy wanted to join band and his grandmother found a saxophone for seventy-five dollars. With this instrument he joined the band. Under the direction of Mike he flourished and Mike even taped our first Christmas tape. It was a combination of Roy playing the piano with Martin and I singing. We had bought an old upright from the church. It weighed a ton and getting it into our new home was a challenge. It had a very good tune and Lesley and the boys learned to play on it. Roy moved on to St. Andrews where he did very well. He was a natural scholar and excelled at school. He joined the band and sang in the choir. In the morning he got up on his own and biked off to school some six miles away. We became involved in the musical aspects of the school. Choir fundraising and concerts were the staple of our lives. When Martin graduated elementary school it was obvious that he would go to a program of music. Of to Oak bay he went and Roy went with him. The money we saved was spent on music lessons.

For Martin it was a tougher road. He hit out at his classmates and was hard to handle. It was at Christmas of 1993 that he sang a verse of We Three Kings. He sang so sweetly that the whole school picked up it's ears and listened. In the spring of that year he sang in Joseph and the Amazing Technicolor Dream Coat and sang the narrators part well. Now I had to find him music lessons. As money was hard to come by I settled on sending him to Michael at the Anglican cathedral. I would pack him off to the cathedral then head off for the eleven o'clock at St. Pats. As their services lasted longer than ours we had plenty of time to pick him up. For three years he continued with Michael getting stronger and more proficient every year. The piece that young choristers sang was the first verse of Once in Royal David' s City. He sang it well. Another more difficult piece to sing was the Miserere mei,

Deus or psalm 51, where the soprano goes up to the C above high C. It is sung on Ash Wednesday, the church's solemn feast of penitence. He sang it well and I still have the recording of it. At Christmas time we made a tape where he and I sang various carols. In the fall of that year we enrolled him in Oak Bay as funding two students in St. Andrews was prohibitive. We also switched Roy into Oak Bay and gave them an opportunity to play in a large band and some smaller ensembles. We also looked for a voice teacher. I phoned a teacher who was taking students and took him for an interview. I sat at the kitchen table not knowing what was to come as I had never done this before. At the end, about ten minutes later the teacher came out and said." I must have him!" So it was that he took lessons from HP.

LET IT SNOW

Now we come to the year of the great snowfall. We were quite pleasantly surprised by the small fall of snow that fell just before Christmas as it makes the world quite different. The kids had a great time and were out making snow forts and throwing snowballs. We even took the Death mobile out for a spin. Let me explain. Upon renovating our den from what had been a bar we wound up with a surplus padded piece of board about three feet by five feet. Having plenty of excess skis around we placed two skis on the bottom and christened it the Death mobile. It took three husky boys down the hill at Beacon Hill and a tremendous rate. Thus tired out from all their exertions we retired home where it had begun to snow. We shovelled off the driveway ready for church on Sunday and retired to bed. This is what happened.

It must have been the continuous refrain of Bing Crosby's White Christmas that started the affair. We had been playing it along with the old stand by Let it Snow for days and the kids were getting quite exited. Christmas day dawned and we had our first white Christmas in decades so I took out my video camera and recorded the event. On boxing day Greg and I took our kids to Beacon Hill park in frigid minus five degrees weather with a howling gale that made it feel like forty below. We had recently repaired the Deathmobile, our home made toboggan, and were eager to try the slopes. It worked like a charm and because it had a four foot slab of padded plywood on top, even Greg and I managed to slide down in style. We had taken bets on who would go the furthest with Greg assuring me that I couldn't possible loose; not with all that mass behind me. Knights like that are soo appreciated, particularly when they are right. A good time was had by all and we headed home to warm up the frozen bodies.

We made the fatal mistake of wishing for a bit more snow to cover the grassy spots. On came the snow while Victoria brought out the Five Old Ladies With Brooms to keep the roads clear. Now it was a race to keep the drive clear while the boys made huge snow forts the like of which would be at home in Saskatchewan. Saturday we cleared the drive of snow and were all set to go to church Sunday morning. Somebody forgot to tell Huey, he looks after the weather, about Sunday mass. We awoke in the morning transported to Siberia. Honestly ! It couldn't have been sunny, mild Victoria. We did manage to clear the five foot drifts from around the doors but by that time even our intrepid snow builders were tired, tsk, tsk. We spent the day with our feet up on the mantle piece listening to Russian carols and waiting for the next tornado to transport us back home. We really needed those ruby red shoes.

Wednesday the wind blew us back and I hope that your home arrived back safely. Now I think I'll go upstairs and pour a large glass of rum and egg nog and meditate before the fire. God does have a way of slicing through our complacency and keeping us on our toes.

Throughout to year we remember certain events of our Lord's life and specified times. For Christmas we journeyed through Lent finally reaching Holy Week. Let me bring you back to that time some thirty-five years ago.

HOLY WEEK

I still remember the first time I served during Holy Week. I lived in a small country parish that covered four churches in communities separated by fifty miles of dirt track and a ferry in-between to complicate the journey. It took an hour of hard driving to reach Edgewood, providing that the ferry was not just leaving for the opposite shore. I was fourteen or fifteen at the time and the trips were my form of adolescent rebellion, I was the only member of the family that attended church. It is a lonely occupation being a priest in a small isolated community and I kept our priest company and assisted in whatever ways I could with the services ; I served, read lessons and assisted Fr. Bruce to vest.

Maunday Thursday we headed out for Edgewood as soon as school was out and had supper with one of the parishioners. Mass was at seven thirty with the church filled with light and the fragrance of incense, my particular task and joy. Throughout the service the glory of Christ shone around us as we obeyed His great command "take, eat for this is my body, do this in remembrance of me." Our celebration completed we extinguished the candles, stripped the altar then turned out all the lights leaving only the flickering candle before the sacrament to light the church. In silence we left the church and went to a friends house to spend the night in preparation for the Good Friday liturgy. At nine we were back in the now bare church to tread the road to Calvary. After the service we drove back to Nakusp where we repeated the service at three. Easter Sunday there was Mass said in Nakusp for eight and eleven before we journeyed south for a service at two in Burton and another in Edgewood at seven thirty. By the time we reached home around ten o'clock we were both tired but filled with a sense of peace, that peace which passes all understanding.

Now, thirty five years later, I am preparing once again for the journey in faith though I will not have to spend so much time in the car. Here and now is the culmination of our Lenten sojourn. Easter is only relevant when the great trideum has been properly observed so that as we have travelled with Christ from the upper room to Gethsemene and on to Calvary we may share in His glorious resurrection. May the glory that is our ultimate victory over death ring through all of us this Easter. May we truly rejoice on Easter morning. Alleluia ! Christ is risen.

MOTOR HOME

We had a motor home and made use of it on various holidays. When I bought the rig I took out a mortgage to pay for it, so on the back was, Myrtle the Mobile Mortgage. On our first trip to the U.S. we stopped at a park were they had swimming pool. As it was spring break the weather was not good. They were in the process of becoming a private park. The next morning we took the tour and realized that they had a park in Oregon as well as this one. We joined up. Our first trips were to the La Conner park where the kids went fishing and we spent time in the shops. We went swimming and it was here that Martin learned to swim. On other trips we went to the science centre and Woodland park zoo. We would spend the morning looking at the elephants and monkeys before heading back to the motor home for lunch. Thus fortified it was on to the planes where the giraffes poked their long necks about in a lumbering gait. There were lions and hippos swimming in a small tank, gazelles and wildebeests and all of the other denizens of the plains. Next we moved to the pool were penguins of various sizes swam. On to the ocelots and cheetahs before heading to the bears and wolves. A whole day of different animals.

Another favourite was down to Nehalam Bay where the other resort park lay. The night before we would clamber into our motor home and go down to the docks to be first on the six-thirty ferry. Customs came to clear us about five thirty and by six-fifteen we were on board. The sun was rising over the Empress hotel as we backed out towards the Johnson street bridge. Past the parliament buildings, the wharves and hotels that lined the harbour, on past Ogden point and finally out into the straights. An hour and forty minutes later we sailed into Port Angles were we disembarked and headed on our journey south. Through miles of reseeded timber then of to the eight mile bridge that crosses the mouth of the Columbia. On past Seaside and Cannon Beach before reaching the park. The kids liked to go crabbing off the dock and spent hours pulling up mainly immature young crabs which they returned to the sea. They rented boats and for two dollars you could spend a couple of hours fishing or crabbing or just heading up river. We attended mass in a little church just up the street then headed out for central Oregon. In the middle of nowhere there was a park affiliated with ours and for two dollars you could spend up to seven nights there. It was peculiar in that it had a small amusement park attached to it. The kids had fun while we relaxed. Now it was on up the I5 before turning east and heading for Morton. RPI Mt. Ranier was a roomy park like being in a B.C. Campground with trees surrounding the sites. We built a fire and roasted hot dogs and marshmallows over it. It was from here that we took a trip to Mt. St. Helens where we saw first hand the devastation caused by the blast. It was quite a scene! Tuttle lake was no more only a greasy slimy residue remained. The next day we took the scenic route back past Mt. Ranier. We rolled along through grassy meadows with a magnificent view of the mountain. In a small village somewhere along the way was steam train. Leaving Lesley to read a book in the motor home we clambered aboard. It was an old forestry shay and puffed its way along the rails to a small lake. There had been a sawmill there but now it was deserted and only the crumbling ruins remained. Once back at the motor home we headed back to La Conner.

One summer we decided to take a trip to Yellowstone national park. We booked RPI sites at Moses lake and just outside the park. Off we went spending a rather hot night at Moses lake before heading up towards Montana and our park. The park turned out to be full and we wound up spending the night with no hook ups at all, not even power. We were not amused and set out to find another park. We found one in Wyoming and left the next morning to explore Yellowstone. Old Faithful was as reliable as usual, going off right on time. That night we spent the night in a regular park, which was a novelty, then headed out in the morning. We visited the limestone rocks then headed on to explore the mud pots and watch the buffalo bask in their heat. Leaving the park we passed by the Grand Tetons before going through Jackson's

Hole and on to our campsite. Star Valley proved to be a great place to stay and we ate at the local dairy which had fabulous food. On going along the highway the signs were most amusing; Grantville, population 349, elevation 6245. One town had an arch made entirely of deer antlers. There were hundreds of them! They climbed up the side then rolled on over the road before cascading down into a smaller arch. Quite unique. Back at the park there were bumper boats to amuse the kids. We never regretted going there. Too soon it was time to go so we headed off through Idaho and on to the Columbia before reaching La Conner once more.

It was great having our own motor home. Lesley could read her books as we went along and the kids could hop around, go to the bathroom, sit still and read or just watch the scenery float by. Technically it was a twenty one foot motor home but at the ferry I would cheerfully say twenty feet and more often than not they would let it pass. I those days we went mainly through the states as gas was cheaper and you didn't have to climb all those mountain passes. To get to Cranbrook where my sister lived one had to go over five passes whereas if you went through the states you climbed once. Beside all of that there were multiple RPI campgrounds we could stay in which made the journey more of a holiday. One trip we made to Edmonton where Tom and Bonnie lived. Went up through Cranbrook then hit an RPI campsite halfway to Edmonton where they had a small lake and paddle boats. Having made it to our destination we relaxed and talked bout old times. Next day Martin and I were taken by Tom to the railway in Stetler. There we bought engineers caps and Martin got to ride on the locomotive while they were sorting out the train. It was an excursion train with a theme. I don't remember what the theme was but in was enacted by several people on the train. We reached a small town and disembarked for supper when we were served Alberta beef. On the train we clambered and off for Stetler. It was indeed a memorable day. A trip to the Royal Glenora club was one of the highlights. There we relaxed in the steam room then sat down to a very good lunch. Soon it was time to leave and we piled into our motor home and headed back through Jasper and the Yellowhead pass. One more stop at Helmecken falls in Wells Grey park. The the water poured down at twice the height of Niagara and swirled its way down among the rocks to finish in a plume of mist.

We travelled all around western North America and had a wonderful time. From Cranbrook we often journeyed to Nakusp along the narrow lake road that meant that we didn't have to climb the sky way. At Crawford Bay we took the ferry to Kootany Landing before heading out to Kaslo and New Denver before reaching our destination. We visited the hot springs again and I took the kids on the short hike to the old springs. The small pool was still intact but nature had claimed most of the larger pool and all of the cabins. On the way back we stopped at the falls climbing down the narrow path over hung with large firs. We gazed at the power of the falls where the noise was like a mighty monsoon roaring down upon us. We often stayed at the Bligh's parking our motor home in their driveway. Dick was a character and could always be counted upon to amuse Martin. I think that he and Martin shared a lot in common and Dick could see himself in days gone by. It was a reasonably flat drive down to the coast through Revelstke, Kamloops, Spences Bridge and through Hope. We certainly saw the country.

PAINTING

I had always painted since my brother and I had first made that venture into Kenetex. There were always the people for whom it was a pleasure to do business with. I garnered a number of clients for whom I did repeat work. One of them was the cathedral. I started out by painting the interior of the building. This required six stages of scaffolding mounted on wheels and we moved the pews slightly to enable the rig to reach the walls. At thirty-five feet the painting began and we worked our way up to about forty or fifty feet. The challenging part involved taking a support from the stylized crown of thorns to reach the bits in behind. Once we reached the sanctuary the task became harder. There was one part which we could not reach with the scaffolding so we put a twenty-eight foot ladder on top of the scaffolding and went up form there. Certainly not WCB regulations at all !As is usual I had to file my tax return and the end of the year which I faced with a certain amount of trepidation.

TAX TIME

I run a small business so naturally I filled out my application to become a tax collector. This form says that if I make over thirty thousand a year, gross, I am required to collect taxes for the government and remit them quarterly. This involves adding up all the money collected and subtracting all the money paid, taking the input and subtracting it from the output, multiplying by ten then squaring the result. This figure minus ITCs, ADJs, and assorted minuscule charges is the Net G.S.T. owed. You tear off the top, send in the bottom, along with all your profits, to Rev. Can. and hope they don't double your assessment. As you go to place the form in the envelope you receive a stern lecture not to bend, staple or mutilate this form or face a penalty of three months in Northern Saskatchewan,,, in the winter. Nasty minds these bureaucrats have. They know how to coerce. The interesting part is that if you make $29,999.99 you don't have to perform this dance. Now you know why there are so many great bargains for cash in the marketplace.

So much for the collection end now on to paying YOUR FAIR SHARE OF TAXES. My wife and I like to file a joint tax return as only I can read the instructions, they're written in Egyptian Hieroglyphics. This is strictly taboo. As far as Rev. Can. is concerned your marriage certificate has been annulled and mailed to the Vatican. You each have to make out separate forms, only one of you claims the kids and any other deductions, and if you dare to talk to them about your spouse's form they send you back to Northern Saskatchewan. I claimed more than my allotted R.R.S.P. this year and did I ever get it in the neck ! My head was on the block so fast I had to move it to N. Sask. just to get them to let me explain ! From my chilly igloo I made call after call to the tax office in order to get my sentence reduced. For three months the line sent back a busy signal,so much for the government listening.

Finally, in desperation, I wrote letters to my M.P., the Minister of Finance, the janitor of the House of Commons, anyone who might be able to return me to my loved ones. Finally someone phoned.

"Look here." I said with all the patience of Job. "My wife has three thousand dollars of extra room in her contribution so just transfer the balance to her account. "

"Who told you she had that much room ?! Have you been Reading letters we sent to your significant other ! SHAME ON YOU ! You will not be allowed to claim that deduction, you never will so send us the extra five thousand dollars and the fifty percent per month interest P.D.Q. or you know where you're headed."

A frosty rime formed on my glasses as she said these words and I shivered inwardly at the cold, callousness of the woman on the other end of the phone and went back to my desk to re-work the forms.

In order to make the forms simpler the old method of taking your income and subtracting your deductions was changed to a system where you have to convert your income into rubbles, multiply by PiR squared and place in the box. Next you do the same thing for your deductions only you have to DIVIDE them by PiR squared. There are no deductions for children anymore, only some vague promise of a tax credit, if you're eligible. Finally, after six months of exile we finally agreed on a figure and I was allowed to return. Next year we're moving to Hawaii.

Through the years we painted the windows of the hall, the rest of the interior and the inside of the hall. When the front doors of the cathedral needed painting I stained them and painted the metal hinges. In the summer of 1990 they had a one hundred and fifty foot crane in to do the roof. This was an excellent time to paint the louvres in the bell towers when a crane would be on the site. They were grey and rather worn, standing out like a sore thumb. The architect picked the colour and sent it along for me to inspect. It was a greenish colour and I couldn't see how that would fit in. As we were doing it in an elastomeric coating it would be there for a long time. Once on though it looked like the stone and fitted in so well that I was completely blown away. It still looks wonderful some twenty-six years later.

TAX TIME 99

Here we are once more in that mystical land called tax return. Once more I open the envelopes and began inserting figures into the little blanks that pop up in unusual places. On the front of the form is the warning: "As a Canadian resident, you have to report your income from all sources both inside and outside Canada. If, in 1998, you owned or held foreign property, or had certain dealings with a non-resident trust or corporation, see the guide for details. "It doesn't matter whether you paid taxes on this money you have to declare them here at home so dear old Miser of Finance can get his hands on some of this loot too. At the ominous words "certain dealings "I break down and chew my finger nails for half an hour. Let me see ; did I buy something from the mail order catalogue or perhaps I went south for a vacation and consorted in foreign shops. Mercy Me ! I'd better go have a cup of tea and calm my nerves.

Two days later I round up enough courage to return to the forms all the while trying to ignore the icy feeling that Someone is Watching me. On I go to the page where I declare my income. When this page is completed a loud klaxon horn sounds warning me that "It is fraudulent not to declare ALL your income. I duck involuntarily and quickly add another five million dollars to my income. That dread task accomplished I quickly deduct the paltry sums that I have been able to put away in an RRSP and move on to the next page.

Now here is where the bureaucrats really get creative. In the old days you listed your family income, were allowed deductions for spouses, children, tuition fees and other incidentals, and deducted same from income. This, of course, is far too easy so the deductions have been renamed, "Non-refundable tax credits." As it's name implies you are guaranteed not to get a refund. First you receive a "basic personal exemption "which hasn't been changed since 1892 inflation notwithstanding ; then you move on to spousal deductions, disability deduction (if you are completely blind, deaf, mobile or dumb) I just fill it in under the dumb section ; CPP, UI, tuition and medical expenses. I do all of this and notice that, despite Mr. Martin's assurances, my deductions haven't increased. This causes me to search the form once more to find, hidden under infirm dependent, a supplemental amount. Of course this means that I have to flip through the schedules in a vain effort to identify which one. Here, in the hallowed halls of high finance, I find the formula that is used today in place of an increase in basic personal exemption. This half page form starts out by slotting me five hundred dollars, which sounds lovely. However, I now have to take my spouses income, add it to my own, subtract it again and then add five hundred dollars to the deduction before subtracting my income from it then taking the square root of this result and dividing it in half.

I trust you understood all of that because I'm NOT going to repeat it. Now I fill out the full page version of the Federal Tax schedule then the Provincial tax form and the Provincial tax credits, all five bucks worth. I am now instructed to double my income, multiply my tax credits by.017 then subtract the two. This figure is then squared and I am required to send a cheque to the Miser of Finance for Eight Million dollars. Happy tax time!

I had other jobs that kept me busy. One of them was painting and re-painting my dentist's house. When I first came to the job it had been sand blasted to take off the Kennith. Kennith was sprayed on over everything, as I can testify to, and was a bitch to get off. While it came off in flakes in certain places it clung to others like it was holding on for dear life. Once off it was painted in several shades of purple with white and grey trim. It looked awesome! Every few years we changed the colour or added new trim bits. Another project that kept me busy was Lorna's houses. She had amassed a number of houses and together with her own house it kept me busy. On day she called me up as she wanted to wallpaper the ceiling of her dining room. As the surface was not flat we had an interesting time with the wallpaper. The surface of the ceiling had bumps on it that caused the wallpaper to stretch and this in turn caused the pattern to be slightly off, We solved that problem with little pieces of pattern stuck over the offending pieces. This gave it a uniform look. All in all in looked awesome.

Together with the run of the mill painting it kept me amused and in money. Some of the people were friendly and others not so much. Some insisted that we were fed lunch as that is how the workmen in their lives were treated. The most difficult time was had with the Chinese who's command of the language was somewhat limited. One particular lady wanted her house stained in the same colour. I asked if she had the number and she replied no so it was off the the paint store with a sample of the existing siding for them to match. We began working the morning and decided to spray the west side before the sun could hit it. We started spraying and the colour seemed a little too blue, however, we sprayed one side. Her husband came home and said it was marvellous. On we painted until a little after four when the lady came home. She threw a fit. That was not the colour at all.

"Then what was the colour." I demanded.

"Just a minute." she said and going into the garage, which I was not permitted to do, she took a can of stain off the shelf! I was fit to be tied.

I must say that working as a painter was very rewarding. You were allowed to take someones house that looked terrible and turn it into a work of art. The most satisfying aspect of this job is to go around town and see the houses that you have painted still there in all their glory. As time goes by there are fewer and fewer houses that have not been repainted. I still go by the cathedral and marvel that the paint put on some thirty years ago is still there looking as good as new.

LANDLORD

In the summer of 93 I became a landlord having bought a piece of property from a friend. It was an older house that had a suite in the basement. This meant that it broke even and we confidently expected that the increase in housing prices would give us some profit. I was not to be. In a trade like those you see on Trader Joe's we swapped this house for a larger house in another part of town. This new house had a number of bedrooms and three floors. The problem was not renting it out as much as it was screening the tenants. Within this house was an assortment of humanity that cover the poorer side of the spectrum. Most of the tenants were on welfare and come welfare Wednesday the house could be counted on the be very lively! I employed a caretaker who got a reduced rent for looking after the place as well as the best room in the house. It was a fairly comfortable situation which went along for some eight years. As I was doing the community a flavor, as I thought of it, nothing could go wrong. Every once in a while the fire inspector would come around and check the place out. With nothing major involved, a new fire extinguisher here or a broken fire door that needed mending, we went comfortably along. I collected about five hundred dollars for my part and considered it a fair wage. The homeless were housed and I made a little too.

In 2003 that changed. The city, in it's wisdom, began to take a dim view of rooming houses. I received a visit from a new fire inspector and he assured me that I needed sprinklers. This was a novel approach and as the sprinklers would cost a lot of money I ignored his request. Now the electrical engineer was called in and he declared that I wasn't up to code. This in spite of the fact that he had visited a few years earlier and declared that he knew the electrician who wired the place and that it was just fine. It became obvious in contact with a number of other landlords that the city wasn't interested in compliance rather it was shutting down all of the rooming houses. One land lord who owned several houses said. "I thought that we were doing you a service. "And he shut down all of his rooming houses. A city has it's own peculiar set of denizens, those who live just below the poverty line. They are there even though you don't see them most of the time. Now without anywhere to go these people were forced out onto the streets. This culminated in the tent city of 2016. And for what? If they asked us we would have lived with a reasonable set of rules. For a fraction of the cost that the city and province are paying to house these people today we would have gladly accepted a grant to fix up these places. As it is millions upon millions of dollars of taxpayer money is going to house these people.

THE DECLINE AND FALL OF AFORDABLE HOUSING

When I left home to attend university I rented a room in an older house. It had a fridge, hotplate and hideabed which was all I needed. No matter how humble one's home is one's castle.

Time passed and one by one the old houses were torn down to make way for towering skyscrapers or more modest apartment complexes. Slowly the affordable housing disappeared like smoke from a bottle. Business licenses were required for any house with more than four people and that meant regular fire inspections. Now these officials have vast discretionary powers to order the installation of everything from battery operated smoke alarms to sprinkler systems. If you have a mature, reasonable inspector there are usually no problems but one visit from someone who doesn't like the look on your face or who woke up in a bad mood can cost you thousands of dollars in unnecessary fire systems. Slowly the licensed facilities began to dwindle. The pedantic enforcement of the bylaws and the insistence on permits for minor alterations further eroded the supply of reasonable accommodation. As the licensed places declined the unlicensed places proliferated. That was fine with city hall, they had no responsibility, and apparently, no concern for the homes of the poorest segment of the population. Where do you get rental accommodation when your income is five hundred ten dollars a month ?

In 2001, as the NDP Government in British Columbia was leaving office, they sent a memo to Social Services to investigate the accommodation of their clients asking them to check on the safety of the accommodation. Armed with this request the fire department of Victoria began to visit rooming houses and issue orders to the landlords to increase the level of safety equipment. Many of these places had operated safely for many years and had passed fire inspections. Now new orders were issued for the installation of fire doors and fire alarms that cost thousands of dollars. The landlords were in a bind. Many gave up and sold the properties. The rental accommodation for low income people began to shrink.

The mayor and councillors wrung their hands at the ever increasing number of homeless and the number of people sleeping on the streets. Meanwhile the fire department and by-law officers were busy shutting down rooming houses. Once they decide that the house has to go they begin to send letters to the owner asking him to remove such necessary items as sinks and stoves. When the astounded landlord asks for the reason for these requests the stock answer is, "no permits." Now since the sinks have probably been there for fifty or sixty years it is not surprising that there are no permits. One landlord had a house with seventeen rooms but as there were no permits for the bathrooms he was required to remove them. When he applied for permits to regularize the bathrooms they refused to issue them. Although he had an engineer certify the building they disconnected the power. The house is now derelict and the city is threatening to have it torn down. One city inspector insisted that the Electric Plus had been installed without permits so the landlord had to check with Hydro and then back to city hall. There were the permits. Strange that this wasn't the first place the inspector looked.

One landlord had a visit from the inspectors who insisted that, if he was to keep his license, he must upgrade the fire system and have "an electrical survey, structural survey and plumbing survey." He spent several thousand dollars on structural surveys, plumbing inspections, wired smoke alarms and electrical inspections and felt that he had complied. Four months later the fire department arrived and ordered new systems. It constantly amazes me how a building that has passed fire inspection for many years with only minor hiccups can suddenly require several thousand dollars worth of new fire alarms. If you don't comply but ask for reasons why the sudden change of heart they take the owner to court. This, they know, will cost the landlord in legal fees as he tries vainly to comply with regulations that contradict each other. A room, under provincial regulation, is deemed to be occupied by two people though they know very well that the people renting these rooms are single. One landlord was hit with 24 thousand dollars in 'necessary' fire equipment.

Now suppose that a landlord complies in order to protect his investment. Next comes the Coordinated Enforcement Team. You will soon be visited by the; By-law Officer, Health Inspector, Fire Prevention Officer, Animal Control Officer, Building Inspector, Plumbing Inspector, Electrical Inspector, City Police Department and the Verification Officer from the Ministry of Social Services. At the appointed time all these officials arrive and begin disturbing the tenants. They swarm the house like locusts then disappear to confer and make their reports. Of course it is too much to expect that they will all arrive at once so one or two show up later when the landlord is not there to keep an eye on them. This leaves your caretaker in an awkward position.

Now the letters begin to fly and they often deliver them in person or wrap the letters around your door frame rather than leaving them in the mail box. One landlord had his house inspected and passed as electrically safe. When he questioned the order further requirements were imposed. When he discovered that the person who originally wired the building was an electrical inspector he suspected something was wrong. His electrician finally tested the house and the entire top floor had not been rewired yet it passed inspection not once but twice.

The health department hates dirt of any kind and insisted that all his carpets had to go even though they were cleaned just prior to inspection. A landlord's neatly bagged garbage was declared a health hazard and the bags of old clothing awaiting a trip to St. Vincent's were deemed to be a nesting place for rats. After two months of visits he finally satisfied the inspector.

Having satisfied the health department and with a certificate of electrical soundness from your electrician a landlord should feel comfortable. Wrong! One day later they issued a disconnect order. While the unfortunate landlord was scrambling to find out why the power was to be disconnected, out went all the lights. No warrant is necessary, no judicial appeal is in place, and no reasons are given for invading the homes of you tenants. One landlord's lawyer finally obtained an answer of, "No permits for the rooms." What the permits for the rooms had to do with the electrical safety has not been shown. In order to provide power this landlord rented a generator and had his electrician hook it into the house according to code. After three days the electrical inspector arrived at 4:30 in the afternoon, disconnected the power and walked off with the generator and cable. The Electrical Safety Act requires a written notice to be sent but no notice of any kind was give to the landlord. Most of the tenants left so he tried to keep the vandals from busting up his property by hiring someone to camp in the place with propane heaters. Now the fire department came and issued an order to evict everyone immediately, again without written notice. They kicked down the doors causing several thousand dollars worth of damage then boarded up house. He is now officially closed. If you think that this cannot happen to you then I urge you to read the Electrical Safety Act and discover the truth. They can and do disconnect any house and from this judgment call there is no prior warning and no protection under the law.

It was no use. The city closed us down leaving a giant hole in the rental market. Each of us did what we had to do to keep afloat. For me it meant fixing the place up so that it could become a single family residence again. We put both houses on the market and as our house on Richmond sold first we moved into the newly renovated house. Not that I have any complaints as the house was free from the mould that plagued the other house. We built a suite in the basement and carried on. So much for social responsibility.

Now, some fifteen years later, we see the result of this short sighted policy. The landlord of a large house is gone and though there are still some people renting out housing the clientele is considerably better. Today with the housing prices sky rocketing the result is obvious. Tent cities are springing up all over the place, and it doesn't look like it's going to get any better and time sooner. To accommodate these people will require massive amounts of money and even then screening the tenants will be an horrendous task. Most of these people require extensive rehabilitation before they could fit comfortably in our society. As the sky scrapers rise higher the density becomes greater and people are no longer in a village. We grow further apart and more isolated as the years go on. What will become of us I do not know.

ON HER BLINDNESS

In 1978 she began to go blind. I did not know anything about it at the time but black spots were beginning to form in her eyes. She had laser treatment in the spring of 1979 and I continued to hope that everything would be all right. In June of that year she left the house to go to a doctor's appointment and when she came back she was hysterical. She railed at me for not having got out of bed to drive her. It was only then that it hit me that her problem had become acute and that she was blind. Shortly thereafter she was declared legally blind leaving us to pick up the pieces. She was fortunate in that she worked for the federal government at the time as so was eligible for a pension. We struggled during the summer and she went to live with her parents while I took a vacation back home. In the fall we were back together and going along with this new situation.

She made application for a guide dog and was accepted for a school in California. In August of 1979 She returned with a guide dog. Bebe was a lively puppy and the cat took one look at her and headed for the basement. My brother was with us and we talked away about her experiences. Soon a little nose appeared over the lip of the basement. Inch by inch the cat crept closer to the dog. Then, making an heroic dash, she made a bee line for the dog, swiped at her tail then scooted back to the basement. Bebe did nothing. We laughed at the cat's antics and the dog was made a member of the family.

All was not well, however, as Lesley had become used to sleeping by herself and now we had the dog in our bedroom as well. She was constantly grooming the dog and seemed to have an unnatural affection for the animal that left me on the sidelines. For about a month I put up with this, growing more and more hostile, until one day it exploded and I told her what she could do with the dog. I was at my limit. It seemed to clear the air and we worked out an arrangement so the dog could sleep in the kitchen giving us much needed privacy.

We had put our names up to adopt but after two years we were told that no one would accept a blind person as an adopter. As the reason we wanted to adopt in the first place was to prevent her going blind it did not seem now to be any barrier to our having children. We began immediately and were rewarded with our first pregnancy. I was so excited that I could not hold it in. I was to be a father. In the spring of that year she had some complications, I don't remember what they were now but it involved being in the hospital on bed rest. I visited every day though the separation was hard. It was at this time that Rick came to me asking for a job. Oh it's easy to rationalize taking this young man, and he was a young man, of fourteen into my home. What ever had gone on with John left him vulnerable. I bribed him. When the summer came he stayed with me and I had sex with him. It was the beginning of a relationship that lasted two and a half years. "The love of money is the root of all evil "I raised a monster. "The evil that is done lives after them, the good is oft interred within their bones."

On the night of her delivery I was summoned to the hospital as they were concerned and were going to take the baby by C section. I wandered through the halls of the hospital until shortly after midnight the call came. I had a son. Nothing could fill me with such pride. I phoned my mother at two in the morning to tell her the news. I was a wreck most of the next day but fortunately Ross and Rick were there to carry on the trade. I remember sitting up in the hospital, gowned and holding my son. His little ears stuck out just the way mine did. Visiting Les shortly after the birth she could not share my enthusiasm. All she could say was, "I hurt !" In three weeks she came home and we began our life as a family.

Roy grew by leaps and bounds being in the 98 percentile for height and weight. As his parents and maternal grandparents were large people this was understandable. Bebe became integrated into this family as well. I soon got used to my wife's independence and she roved all over Victoria talking to school children and young adults about blindness. If we needed a baby sitter Rick was always available. We went skiing and that was a real challenge. Skiing downhill requires someone with sight to guide you as the person cannot see. It's just like skiing in a white out. The first year we went skiing I took her back to Silver Star where we had been when she could see. Bebe stayed in the ski patrols hut while we were out and one of the instructors took Les out for a lesson. At the end of or trip they presented Bebe with her own ski pass, complete with picture and card! We continued to do the things that we had done before she went blind and except for badminton we managed fairly well. The downhill skiing came to an abrupt end on day at Mt. Washington. We were skiing down the last slope to the lifts when Les began to go straight downhill. I yelled STOP at the top of my voice. No response. I quickly headed towards her but by this time she had resorted to her usual method of control. She sat on her skis. This made them go faster and even more out of control. Finally she ran into a tree. Fortunately she was not badly hurt and recovered after a short stay in the medical room. End of downhill skiing.

It was cross country skiing for her from then on. She travelled throughout western Canada going to meets, particularly ski for light. One weekend we took Rick as a baby sitter so that we could concentrate on going around the course at Mt. Washington. We stayed at the home of Fr. M in Courtenay where I made an interesting discovery. Fr. M was gay. He later moved to Victoria and we had many interesting chats.

Bebe was a constant delight. She would pick up some food that she was not supposed to have and gently slide up to you, with a look on her face that said you had better take this from me. Once you had pried the morsel for her mouth she was all right. Sometimes she would play with Roy when we let her out in the yard. He would be riding on Hell Cat and attacking her with a sword made from a stick. But Bebe was too smart for him and grabbing the hood of Roy's jacket she would wrestle him down to the ground. This infuriated Roy and he would come into the house crying that "Bebe had knocked me down" Most of the time she was very protective of Roy. One example of this was when Les and he were staying at her parents property. Dad was burning brush and not paying too much attention to his grandson. After a while he turned around and they were gone. Immediately they scoured the neighborhood which was mainly bush with nearest house being half a mile up the road. Eventually they found them with one shoe off wandering in the bush. Bebe never left his side.

In 1984 Martin was born and we became a family of five, two kids and a dog. As Bebe was allowed into all places were people were allowed it was hard to think of her as a dog. At this time Roy was off to pre- school and you could often see Les with Martin in a backpack and Roy holding onto one hand as they waited for the bus. Roy was definitely not shy. On one occasion a patron was being condescending say it was a blind dog and how everything went well. Roy piped up. "My mother's blind not the dog." We had our problems with Martin. He woke us every two hours through the night until he was eighteen months old ! My wife said the that if he had been our firstborn he would have been a single child! When we got over that hump life settled down. We had to retire Bebe and as we had not taken a holiday except for camping, we decided to go to Disneyland. As the school would be paying for Les' flight we arranged to fly to San Fransisco and rent a car for the drive down to Disneyland. As Fr. Henstock live not far from Disneyland we stayed with him. We had a wonderful trip then drove back to San Rafael were Les was to train with her new dog. We dropped her off and returned to the airport and off into the skies to Victoria. When she brought the new dog home it was obvious that it was a larger dog. As he entered the house he casually swept the top of the dishwasher.

One evening Les told me to get a banana muffin from the counter. I went but could not find any.

"Are you sure you made them ? "I hollered.

We discovered then that Forest had cleaned them off the counter. Thirteen banana muffins! When we moved to our new house it was necessary to put the dog in his cage, a fenced in area at the back, to do his morning business. Martin would go down to let him in and the dog would barge past him getting upstairs before he did and promptly snaffled his lunch or breakfast! Martin never learned and lost numerous lunches that way. Another time we had gone camping at French beach and walked Forest along the edge of the water. Now you have to remember that he was a California dog and his encounter with water had been in his water bowl. Now we lead him onto the rocks that lined the rock pools and he gingerly put his paw in the water. Taking it out he shook the water off it as if to say "It's wet! Don't make me put it in again. "It was the funniest thing to see a large Labrador retriever shake his paw the way.

When I was arrested Les stood by me. The winds of Hell were howling around me yet she remained firm in her faith in me. Once more I was having a bipolar attack. I was so manic that I got around the police and attended a banquet that opened the hall at the cathedral. After supper I was arrested and brought to the hospital. I was not a happy camper. Throughout the next month in the hospital there was never any discussion of my being bipolar. They talked about stress and never even once considered that I might be manic. The euphoria of this state lasted until early March. Now the fact that I was separated from all of my friends and support turned me into a depressive state. At one point I considered suicide. From Lesley's supplies I got a syringe and a supply of insulin, injecting a full needle into my arm. I wanted no more to do with this world and rationalized that my children would be better off without me. I slept the day away and to my disappointment I was still alive come supper time. At this time I was going home for supper and was surprised at how hungry I was.

Sometime later Lesley went back to university to pick up some courses and see whether she could still handle the load. She took psychology courses at first and the first book was a real shocker. It had been written by a man who obviously didn't know the first thing about English. As I was tasked with putting this book on tape you can be sure that I cursed at the text. For some reason or other he seemed to write in long sentences. One sentence took up half a page! It was worse that the rumblings of St. Paul. Never the less we survived and Les passed the course. It was an interesting time and though she didn't take many courses she had success in the ones that she did take.

We picked up the pieces and went on. Our home had become a desolation within the neighbourhood so we sold it and bought somewhere else. I went back to painting and getting back to work after so long a period of inactivity was hard. Martin was the most affected by this and we had trouble controlling him until he discovered music. Les continued to lawn bowl and as much as possible we carried on as before. About two years later I received a mug from Lesley that summed up all the I had gone through. "When someone you love has gone through a trying time and come through it all, we are proud of you. "We had managed to come through this time of trouble with the help of the church and the grace of God.

It was at this time in life that a man has to acknowledge that he is mortal. As cancer resided in my family, both my parents having died of it, it was decided that I should under go a Colonscopy. The preparation for this procedure is medieval at best. Let me see if I can explain it.

COLONSCOPY

The interior posterior regions of a man's anatomy should be treated with great respect so when I received the instructions for this procedure I was rather miffed. The date and time of your arrival at hospital are clear then the water turns murky. "The day prior to the procedure, be on clear liquids only." Now to me a day is twenty-four hours but not to the medical people. They want you to fast from supper two days before the operation. Now the fun part. "in the morning prepare the Golyte solution as instructed on the bottle and place in fridge. At six P.M. begin to drink (2 litters only) of the Golyte solution.... drink an 8 ounce glass every ten minutes. Rapid drinking of each glass is preferred instead of drinking small amounts continuously." Now the bottle comes in four liters so half your precious money is wasted but the real travesty is the name, 'Go lightly." There is no such thing as go lightly as consumption of this amount of fluid on an empty stomach will guarantee that the fluid will be ejected from your anus at half the speed of sound. No mention is made of the effect this has on your orifice so I talked to my friend who has had the procedure. He smiles sympathetically and tells me to be prepared for diaper rash ! "Get yourself some zinc ointment." he muses. You're going to need it ! "

    I go home to mull over his words of wisdom before putting two and two together and realizing that coating your backside with Vaseline as you would your baby's should prevent the worst of the ravages of this excursion. My wife sagely advises me to stay close to the toilet, another precaution not mentioned in the notes so I cancel my bridge game. I prepare to drink the solution which announces that it is flavoured. Unfortunately the flavor resembles castor oil and it's effects on an empty stomach are equally repulsive.

An hour later I have consumed the require two litres and my stomach begins to rumble so I head to the bathroom, take copious amounts of Vaseline and apply liberally to the aforementioned orifice and wait. The rumbling in my tummy is a combination of verbal protest at the lack of food and the abominable drink. Suddenly fluid rushes out which makes your feel like you have dysentery. One more line needs to be included in the instructions, "replace toilet paper with blotting paper." Well blotted I re-coat and wait for the next onslaught. At least they have the timing right and by midnight the explosions have subsided and I'm off to bed. At three in the morning I have another round anal water pistols.

Six o'clock comes too early and the next round of insult and injury is foisted on my poor stomach which is loudly protesting the prolonged absence of food. It's not good to make a man go without food for too long; he gets cranky. If the Golyte was bad the oral enema is worse and we settle in for three more hours of anal water pistol, praying that I don't have to go while I'm en route to the hospital. Of course the road to the hospital is torn up and I bounce nervously in my seat while my son navigates the hazards none too gently. He inherited his grandparent's lead feet. Into the hospital where the nurse calmly informs you that "Baby's are born full of poop and this is the first time in your life that you're not full of shit!" I counter by complaining about the paucity of instructions.

Once the I.V. is inserted the rest of the procedure is routine. I awake some time later and head to the nearest subway to placate my abused stomach. Now if the doctors will only publish this little tome and hand it out to all future patients life will be much easier.

By 2004 we had moved into our new home and Les began to weaken. We had by this time slept in different rooms as our mutual snoring woke each other. Now she was restricted to a wheelchair and I pushed her to Zellers to shop. We stopped at the restaurant for lunch then headed home. Now she began to be disoriented and I found it necessary to put locks on the doors so that she could not get out and ramble around. At one time she had been found by a neighbour, wandering around, not knowing where she was. I was awakened at all hours of the night to help her get up off the floor or assist her to the bathroom. For three successive nights we had to call the ambulance to get her out of a diabetic coma. The last time I couldn't get her up off the floor so the paramedics concluded that she had to go to the hospital. It was over. She went into hospital and never came out again.

For a month I visited her in hospital until she was moved into a nursing home. It was quite nice and she had her own room where we could talk away the hours. I was, by this time, retired so apart from my social responsibilities was free to spend time with her. We decided that I needed one day off a week so for six days a week for the next three years I visited her. At first we went on walks around the building looking at the flowers and gardens. Glengarry where she was placed had wonderful gardens, rhododendrons, tulips, daffodils and a myriad of other flowers through which we went my describing the beauty that was all around us. After a couple of months they moved her into a double room which caused some problems. The woman she was with could scream with the best! Les continued to decline finally having to be lifted up to go to the bathroom. A year and a half later we were moved to Mt. St. Mary's and what a difference. There she had her own room and only the residents on that floor had meals together.

I had taken the time to feed Les most of her meals which freed up one of the staff. On Sundays I would arrange for a handy dart and we would go to a restaurant where we spent the time eating and sharing our moments. During the summer I would push her wheelchair down a couple of blocks to the Spaghetti Factory. We tried to go to a different place every week but eventually settled on the Ross Bay pub in Fairfield. As her supper time was early we had an early dinner which made it easier to get into the restaurant. Sometimes the boys would join us when we went to Cora's for breakfast. When there were a lot of us we booked the dining hall on the main floor and ordered in. For two years we went along visiting on Tuesday and staying for mass at ten o'clock. Another thing I did was read to her. Although she had talking books and once a week someone brought new books from the library we read the books I loved to read. A Christmas Carol at Christmas time and other stories from time to time. We were halfway through the Honour Harrington series when she died. In the evening of June the 25th 2014 at two in the morning I lost my wife of thirty eight years. It was the eve of her anniversary and her birthday. You don't know what you've lost until you loose someone dear. A large hole had appeared in my life. No longer would I go to the nursing home and take Lesley out for dinner.

A MUFFIN FOR BREAKFAST

I had buried my wife and now had gone into a routine. I went to church in the morning and played bridge in the afternoon. By the time I had made supper it was time for a nap and then retire to watch television. This went on until Wednesday August the seventeenth, at which point I was arrested for sexual assault some thirty -five years ago. I called my lawyer and then went into the interview room with Sgt. Ross. She began by showing me a picture of Rick spouting nonsense and accusing me of assault. The memory of him that I had differed radically from what he had experienced so I said that it was complicated. I spent the night in cells and on the morrow was bailed out on my own recognizance. I immediately went to see my priest and told him what had occurred. I continued to go to church until Sgt. Ross splashed my face across the papers. I was then confined to going to church when there were no children present. This continued for two months. At which time I went before a judge to get the bail order changed. The prosecutor and Sgt. Ross objected strenuously and we were not granted the changes we sought. In a peek of fury the bail superintendent cancelled my permission to go to church. This caused a major problem as I was used to going about five times a week to daily mass. In response I went to the priory where no children were present. At Christmas I had had enough and began going to daily mass again. No children were present so I had fulfilled the requirement of the law.

I hate to calculate the money spent on my case. The time involving prosecutors and the police would be enormous. Just the jail time comes in at over seven hundred thousand dollars. Nevertheless Sgt. Ross continued to diligently work away at my case. By the time she finished she had definitely come to the conclusion that I had been a homosexual. None the less it was all some thirty five years in the past. Here she managed, and I can only imagine what hatred she had for me, to concoct the most amazing tale of sexual abuse ever seen. With lies and half truths she had me sent into prison with a record that Jack the Ripper would have had a hard time with. She had worked on Val who was staying with me so that the poor girl did not know which end was up. Then she charged her with threatening the Prime Minister! Nonetheless, she had managed to achieve her main goal which was to put me behind bars. Val had managed to look up Rick's number, I didn't even know you could do this, and ascertained that I had been going to church. This was all she needed to get a warrant for my arrest. It was good that I was in Penticton when she came to collect me as she had to wait until I returned.

It all began one June afternoon when I was on my way to bridge. I had no sooner turned onto Esquimalt Rd. than the police siren went off. They pulled me over and directed me to go into the A @ W parking lot. Two detectives then re- arrested me, cuffed me and brought me to the precinct. Once there I was released from my handcuffs, reprocessed and allowed my phone call. I waited in the cells for a couple of hours, they take your watch away, until my call came to talk to Sgt. Ross. For two hours she tried to pry a confession from me. She talked of things she knew nothing about and all I would say was "no comment. "At 4:15 she gave up and sent me back to my cell with this comment. "You shouldn't have gone to church "Well I'm sorry but to forbid me church when I needed the support most was not going to happen.

The cells are underground so no natural light is allow in. Time stood still. I passed the time singing, the cell made a neat sounding board, and sleeping. Eventually 'supper' arrived, a ham sandwich, juice box and a cookie. I ate the white bread but disdained the crusts; the cookie I saved for later. It was the usual night in the cells with the banging and shouting. The only indicator that night was over was the shift change about 6:30. Breakfast consisted of banana bread and a juice box. I waited anxiously for my trip to the court house. The charges against me were : contacting my accuser and going to church.

I waited and the court house and was immediately shown in to see my lawyer. Lunch was a very good sandwich, juice and a cookie. We went in and no bail hearing, I was devastated. The hearing was put off till Monday. Oh well! Off we went to Wilke. The processing there took forever. Super was a baloney sandwich. I was so tired all I wanted to do was sleep. It was not to be. I was put in a cell with someone coming off a heroin high. Through out the night he kept shouting, "Shut the fuck up! "What interested me was his calling out for God as he lay there half asleep. Periodically throughout the night he said "I'm going to pound you." In the morning he had at me with his fists. I fell to the floor. Two nights without sleep was just too much. Fortunately the guards came and took him away and I had the cell all to myself. The only casualty were my glasses which suffered a scratch to one lens.

Heroin Addict

To this time of quiet reflection remembering all.
A tired body dragged from one cell to another,
Till only the tiredness of my soul remains.
Hate filled, hollering, yet I am here in hell.
' Shut the fuck up "streams from the bunk below,
Only solace of a brain wracked by heroin,
Yet oddly vulnerable through the cracks of time.

A whimper of a long lost soul in purgatory,
Hailing an god he doesn't know, revealing
A chink in his Armour. "Oh! God help me."
From the catacombs of mine un rested body
There comes a blow, followed by more blows
Till I fall on the floor shattered and alone.
He's gone. Blessed relief of weary body,
Collapsed on my bunk, too tired to think

NIGHT TIME

In the darkness of the night,
When the shadows close about.
The pain of the now released.
Heroin takes control, surrounding
My mind and turning it to dust.

When I cry in my sleep
Noisily asking for help,
From a god I do not know,
From one long forgotten,
Hope from the rays of God.

I was free of him so I relaxed, watched television then slept some more. At five they changed cells and put me in a pig pen. With only a broom I tidied up my cell as best I could. That evening I was let into the common area where I could at least have a shower. The next day breakfast was served and I had a muffin and a cold cup of coffee. C'est la vie. I returned the cereal and toast that came on the tray. At supper time I was moved again and moved into a cell without T.V. Now the regulations state that a prisoner who has not been committed can not be placed in the same cell as one who has. It was the first time Mair had me and I'm sure he thought that I would be suitably punished. The cell next door was empty as I could testify when they put me there on solitary confinement.

At least the window opened and fresh air came through like a breath of life. Without TV I set about to order my day. First I read my office, the comfort of Gods word before reading and breakfast. This came about ten O'clock and was bacon and eggs. It also came with a sandwich which I returned. I alternated reading, and as there was no one else to bother me, I sang hymns. And the morning and the evening was the third day. Next morning was the same except that they served pancakes and sausages. As there was no one in my cell I sang the office. Reading and singing filled most of my days. Sometime later I was called to see my lawyer and he gave me the bitter news; no bail hearing until July the 20th. Oh well, I thought, as long as my reading material held out I was fine. This was a problem as I had already read two books and was well into the third and fourth, I would phone Roy to bring me some books from home. Monday I phoned Roy and made a list of what I needed. He would see me on Wednesday. We went into the video court where the bad news was confirmed. I spent the rest of the day reading and writing poetry. I had been reading with my varilux lenses which provide only a small section for reading. I was looking forward to Wednesday when my reading glasses would arrive. That day I read knowing that my reading glasses would come so I phoned Roy to add other things to the list. I keenly awaited the arrival of Wednesday.

On the short eastern wall was the phone. The phone system must have been rigged up by Monty Python. First you dialed one and got a disembodied voice telling you to dial the number. Once dialed you had to put in your CS number then the voice told you to give your voice activation. That's when the fun began. Upon saying your name a Machievellien voice would say, "I'm sorry. Your voice recognition failed." Once more you had to give you voice activation. You only got three shots to pass or the system shut down. Now you had to start the whole process again. Once you had achieved voice recognition the phone began to ring. Once it had the person one the line it gave out a stern warning that you have a call from an inmate in a correction facility. The person on the other end had to listen to all of this before answering then had to press buttons in the right order before being connected. For this service they charged ninety cents and gave you thirty minutes. Eventually I changed my voice recognition from Harry Sadd to simply HS.

FAITH

> In the winter, dark and dreary,
> When my heart clings to me.
> All my being longs for peace
> Cool taste of summers release.

Stand I not alone but with Thee,
Like the cool shade of an oak tree.
Shading from the heat of suns ray,
All my fears now gently calmed away.

TIMES PAST

Alone amidst my thoughts, a quiet time of meditation.
The soft whisper of the breeze through my cell calls me.
I think of times past, of journeys long forgotten,
In the dim recesses of time my mind recalls, remembers,
The faint whisper of children playing amid the forest,
Deep silence hangs around the hill where once I played.

Alone midst the towering cedars in a glade,
Nestled among the bracken and fern I lie,
Arms folded, the sun dappled glory of summer
I contemplate the stillness of the forest floor.
High above the clouds scud by, birds chirp their song,
While I peacefully dream of times when I am free.
Jul 2017

GODS GRACE

Alone yet not alone, for Thou art with me,
The solitude encompasses me, as in an oak tree.
In the silence of my mind, cool waters by,
And all my yesterdays, now fully grown to fly.

Not the brashness of youth, now grown to maturity,
But the still, calm voice of God, serenity,
Grown in the fullness of God, upholding, uplifting.
Through the silent hours of the night, revealing.
Jun. 2017

I have, so far, only dealt with the materialistic side of my imprisonment. When it first occurred back in June I expected to be out on Monday. After the trauma of the first day I began to sing God's praise. It is a funny thing that I was thrown into prison with this stinging reminder, ' You shouldn't have gone to church!' Well here I was and you would think that I would be devastated. Not so. When the lawyers said that they would not have the particulars for some time I was ready to remain. I was God's prisoner and I would remain here as long as it took to get before a judge. After the third day I had no TV. The one in the cell had been removed. So I set about getting the books I required. It took longer than expected. For some arcane reason TV was streamed in day and night but books were not allowed, except for books that you had to buy at Chapters. I scoured the common room looking for books. A bible was found and a pitiful supply of other titles. My Library at home was unreachable, and it might as well be on the moon. Nevertheless I had my bible and was able to say morning prayer and evening prayer for, after forty years, I had memorized all of the canticles. You can even look them up in your bible. I have just completed my 287th reading of this office. It has been a great comfort to me although the world outside has spun once more around the sun. Singing has always been second nature to me since I was a kid, I sang throughout that first week when no other source of entertainment was available. The second habit was more problematic, no whistling! In the jail I whistled incessantly, no human power seemed able to stop it. I was constantly in trouble for whistling, it was quite unconscious. When I was happy I whistled. On ward N with 40 people on it this problem became endemic. I would go for a while without whistling then some inadvertent action would trigger it. I tried to sing instead but that invariably lead to whistling.

Now I want to go back to he physical layout of my cell. The ward contained a dozen units each containing a bed or two stacked one on top of the other. It had a TV on one wall which was blocked in and changing channels required the use of a pencil. Stuck in the various slots it would change channels, turn off or on or adjust the volume.

You put the pencil in a different hole to do different things. In one corner sat the toilet and sink while the other contained a book shelf, two hooks and a desk which faced the window. This then was my home for the foreseeable future. The cell block was divided into two sections with the correction staff in the middle. There were two tables, one that seated six and another that seated four. Down the corridor that lead to the exercise yard there was a table that had been used as a computer table but, alas, it was long gone. On the North wall ran a steel table with sink and a coffee machine and two fridges, one for "normal" inmates and one for protective custody inmates. They were both locked and you had to get a guard to unlock them. Further along the wall was the door to the outside world were you went if you had to go to video court or for health care. At the end of the wall was a door that lead to the exercise area. It opened out on a small courtyard which was surrounded by twenty foot walls with barbed wire on the top. There in that 20 by 30 foot area I took my exercise. Over half of it was pavement but a small patch of grass grew along the building now growing six or seven inches high. There were windows on the West side that overlooked the old wardens house, the berm, fence and road that lead around the grounds. On the South wall were steps going up to the second floor, a room that had originally contained books and a washer and dryer but now contained only cleaning supplies and clothing. The remainder on the wall was taken up with the four single bed cells. Down a short corridor was the shower and the staff washroom. My cell was on the top floor and had a window that looked out onto an old house with some newer ones in the background. In the evening I could hear the children playing.

Tuesday was clear and I phoned Roy to update the list. Most of the day I spent reading with time spent singing my praise to God who never failed me. The next day I spent anticipating Roy"s visit. Apart from an hour with my lawyer I had been a week without company. The hour came and I walked down to the interview room, my heart filled with hope. We talked and exchanged news for the better part of and hour. Roy remarked that we never have conversations this long at home. The bad news was that nothing could be brought into the jail.

He did get to take all of my stuff home and so could do my banking. I couldn't even get my reading glasses in! It would be another week before they arrived. What sort of outfit feeds it's inmates TV yet does not allow books in ?

I returned to a cold plate of food but as I was not hungry I left it. We got out about 2:00 and I went down and heated it up in the microwave, hot ham, baked potato and vegetables. Then I went up to my cell to reorganize my life. I was sure that the books in the library would not last and as the TV seemed doomed to not appear I would very shortly run out of things to do. As I had no cash it was necessary for Roy to put fifty dollars in my canteen account which he did promptly. I could now order the clippers and coffee that I deemed necessary to keep me going. That day I read the paper, went for a walk, took a shower and had fish and chips for dinner. Friday I went to the psychiatrist assuring her all was well. No one impinged on me nor I on them.

A NEW CELL

At 4:00 they moved me out of the cell once more. This time it had a TV and was just in time to watch the football game. I was there until noon the next day when I was moved to an open ward. My notoriety had come before me as the very guy who had punched me out was on the ward. This was indelicate but we worked it out. I was to be on the top bunk but felt that I couldn't make it so pushed my mattress on the floor for a couple of nights. Again No air. The opening mechanism had been wired shut. July the 1st, Canada's one hundred and fiftieth birthday and here I was locked inside. For the rest of the day I read and played cards with Bear. At first I was quite content to read and quietly asses the situation. I would sit by the window with my book and watch the cars stream by on Wilkinson road. On Saturday morning the was particularly hard when I knew that my friends from church would be going along on their way to the Crooked Goose for breakfast. I read a lot of books during my time in jail with titles ranging from science fiction to history to religious tomes. The chaplain brought me books and I managed to read nearly all of them. ' A Prayer for Owen Meany', The Genesis trilogy by Madeline L'engel, Angela's Ashes and 'A Politician for God' about Wilbur Wilberforce's efforts to end slavery. In addition to these I read 'The Lord of the Rings', three books that concluded the Safehold series by David Weber and Paleden of Souls. In addition to these I read a number of Historical novels involving the Scott's plus the tracts I was given. It is safe to say that I read more books when I was in jail that I had in ten years, and that's saying a lot!

The configuration of this ward was different. On the West wall was the door, then the guards desk, a one piece of stainless steel that jutted out four feet into the room, behind which the guard sat and handed out papers or you could just get them yourself from a stack near the wall. Above the desk was a clock and further on was a computer, exercise bars and a small bookshelf. On the South wall was the quiet room, three telephones interspersed with windows, barred of course, and running up to a half wall. This wall contained a desk looking out over the parking lot, another telephone and two notice boards where official notes were posted or the TV guide Here the cells began and ran the rest of the wall. Halfway down the east wall contained three micro-waves, two fridges and the sink. In between these walls lay the common room with it's four small tables and three large tables. If you went round the corner you came to the washroom with it's three sinks, two toilets and two urinals. This room was peculiar in that it had no camera. Further on was the shower then around the bend came the washers and dryers. For almost the entire duration I was there only one of the washers worked. Finally at the end of the corridor opposite the cells were two more showers. In a little cub-by hole near the North wall was the janitorial room. Rows of cells filled the North wall until you came to a steel table upon which sat the coffee pot. More cells to the end of the ward.

This, then, was our world, forty souls all waiting for trial or serving a sentence of two years or less. Our cell had two beds stacked one on top of the other but separated a bit. The small table and it's equally hard stool looked out the North window. To the right of the desk were four shelves upon which inmates placed their possessions. In cell 129 the vent did not open so no fresh air. The TV was placed on the table and on the wall opposite the beds were two notice boards upon which you could place your pictures or any other personal possessions worth exhibiting. I usually put my rosary pamphlet and bulletins there. On the wall was a button which you had to press if you wanted to go to the bathroom. Once the guard opened your cell you could get out and go. This was only enforced at night or during lock downs. The toilets had one of the most powerful flushes you have ever seen. Only once have I seen them clogged.

The sociology of the place was like no other on earth. The "fours" tables had seniority and lorded it over those of us who ate at the "eights". Lord forbid that you should even sit at one of the fours, especially the table reserved for the SS ! They got a whole loaf of bread for the four of them while we had to make do with one loaf. Their stuff was piled on the table and only the foolhardy would be brave enough to take anything. I sat at the table nearest the " fours" for the entire six months I was on the ward. Usually the older inmates hung out there as trying to get into the mind set of some of these young people was really scary. Of course there were people who ate in their cells. Several people that I knew only ate there. It was one way of avoiding the merry go round that was meal time. To me it was fascinating!

My day had begun to take shape. Get up and have a muffin for breakfast. Read morning prayer,take a shower then lock down. I read or played cards until lock down before lunch. After lunch I would read or play crib, then it would be lock down again. Supper came early about 4:15 and would play crib or read until seven or eight when I retired to watch TV. Unlike the other inmates I watched the Learning channel, PBS or watched football or hockey, then it was lights out at 10:00 when I went to sleep and so the day began again. The only trouble was weekends. We were not allowed up until 10:15 when all of us were let out at once and began the mad dash for food and juice. I still got up at 7"30 or 8:00 much to the displeasure of my cell mates. I missed the quiet reading of my office or ordinary reading which covered so much of my stay there. On Sundays I longed for the companionship of my church. The jail had only two chaplains and one of them was away during the summer. As neither one was a Catholic it meant scrounging up a visit. I signed up for all of the chaplain's services but only got to go to one of them. The other inmates refused to go if I went. I told Kevin that I would not take their time away. There was one area that they excelled in. I had asked for books and they provided me with ample reading material. I must have read forty or fifty books during the time I was incarcerated.

Sunday and I read my office. Pancakes and sausages for breakfast so I spent the rest of the day observing the structure of the ward. I had another long visit from Roy and managed to sort out the finances. The next day my cell mate moved out and I grabbed the lower bunk. A long morning with french toast about ten clock and spaghetti for supper. A new cell mate was assigned and gave no trouble. Read and watched TV for most of the day. I had my priorities sorted out and wanted to phone Fr. Don. Had a good conversation and he promised to visit. For ten months he visited me every week. I don't know quite what I would have done without his guidance. He and Roy visited faithfully all throughout my imprisonment. You have to list the people that are allowed to visit you in the jail. For some reason, probably the jail screwed up, he did not get on the list. I submitted it again and this time everything went according to Hoyle. The motto of the jail is "Hurry up and wait"

July 3rd and French toast for breakfast so I read and observed. In the evening I got a new cell mate who was quiet so we got along well. Tuesday I broke my glasses on the way to the doctor. Fortunately he fixed them with tape. Once on the ward I was immediately given the name of Santa. My age, the out sized outfit I was wearing and my white hair made the resemblance impossible to resist. The other nick name I acquired was Colonel Saunders. Had a long chat with Roy and finally got my reading glasses, When I returned from the doctor I found the my clothes were missing. I had put them in the dryer with my room number on a piece of paper placed on the dryer. After a bit of a search I got them back but it was only the first of many trials that I went through on ward N. The only consolation was that some of the ward realized that the charges were not quite what they seemed. I started Bible readings with Eric who had been there two years ! He, at least, understood my predicament.

My new cell mate was French Canadian and came in with a long story of his own, how he was mistreated and misunderstood on his previous ward. The room mate he was with had put tacks in his bed. He was certainly messed up and was anxious to go somewhere, anywhere where he wouldn't be beaten upon. This did not last long. We had a number of good conversations before the rumour mill of the ward got him. Upon discovering I was accused of being a pedophile he turned on me. He became nasty, not even asking me about it. For the most part I ignored his tirade which was mixed with smatterings of incomprehensible French. One minute he would be friendly and talk to me like a human being and the next he was spouting curses. After a week of this I was getting very tired of all his mutterings. One night he woke me up at 2:00 in the morning to curse at me in his weird lexicon of speech. I ignored him. In the morning he started again as I was reading my office. I had had enough. In a loud chanting voice I began to sing the canticles. Every time he started his diatribe I began singing louder than before. When we were let out I told him that I would no longer tolerate his behaviour. I was a wreck. Two days earlier I had gone to health care where my blood pressure was elevated. I was hanging on by my fingernails. Afterwards I had a chat with Eric and we went to the guard and asked for him to be transferred. He also suggested that I get a medical for a second mattress. I did that and eagerly awaited its arrival. When the Frenchman left I noticed that my supply of six peanut butters had disappeared. Now I used this item as trading goods and was not happy about this turn of affairs. I had promised Eddy two of these and informed him at lunch time that I couldn't give him any as the Frenchman had stolen them. As he had considerably more clout than I had he retrieved all of the peanut butters. What is all this fuss over a few peanut butters. In times before this age of great affluence stealing was considered a great crime. To take from someone what little he has is abominable. Similarly here, where there is no chance of getting things from the outside, it becomes once more a serious offence.

Soon my second mattress arrived and I was once more able to sleep without having a pain in my side. It is the small things that make a difference when you are in jail. Another of my comforts was the possession of a second blanket. This kept me warm at night as I did not sleep with my clothes on. Eric gave me a pillow which helped considerably. At 2:20 I got to talk to Fr. Don and we spent an hour telling stories and generally laughing at the absurdity of things in the jail. I had been getting my medication in the drug lineup with fifteen other inmates crowded into the elevator. Except for a couple of them I was shunned. One day I went down and lo and behold I was give them in bubble packs to be taken on my own recognizance. That night I phoned Janice and we had a great conversation. In the meantime Eric and I had settled into a firm relationship. He talked and I listened. We began to study the bible and he helped me navigate the mores of this society. One day Eric gave me his copy of the King James version of the bible in large print. The next day I went to play some cards only to discover that they had been destroyed by putting jam in them, a parting gift from the Frenchman. On the plus side there was Marcell. He organized the native population at the eight table into a carefully organized symphony. They collected all their fruits and made fruit salad. He organized their meals, the days when they collected their dinners and then made a large pot of rice before adding sauces and other things to make a real meal. I will never forget what Marcell said to me when I was new on the ward. "Don't worry about the others. They are all here because they have committed some sex crime or another. No one has anything worse or somehow better than you. "He figured that he had spent nearly a third of his life in jail. When I asked him about what he did he freely admitted that he was a drug runner.

One day Bear came to me and said that he had heard that I had been a teacher and would I read the novel he was trying to put together. I said that I would be please to do so and he brought me the first instalment. I took his story into my cell and began reading. It blew me away. He had been born of a liaison between a Swedish man and his mother. As a half breed he was not well accepted into his native family. He was frequently beaten by his older brother and his mother. Periodically he was placed in a foster home but that usually didn't last long. He would run back to the only people that cared for him. It was some way of showing care! The one person the he could relate to was an uncle. In order to escape this violence he would creep into his trailer. There he found comfort and sex. I do not know at what age he was initiated into the fraternity of homosexuality but it was obviously consensual. His life had been one of being in on foster home after another. Eventually he ran away going to the only place that he knew as home. At thirteen he ran away for good and survived on the streets of Vancouver. Here he put his knowledge of homosexuality to work and landed a newspaper editor for a 'friend'. The gay man treated him well and he never lacked for clothes or food or shelter. Later he became involved with a con man who used his services to get into places he couldn't. How he became a youth leader and ran a homeless shelter is less clear. He was charged with sexual assault and spent three months in jail. When the trial came she refused to testify and he was released. How much of the story is true I do not know but it rings true. He once asked me if I was two spirited and I agreed.

SUNSHINE

The sun shines dappled through the bars,
Making pools of light on the concrete floor.
The inmates come in from recreation
All cheered by their hour of sunshine.

We wait inside while all is still,
The prosecutor stumbles over miles and miles
Of redacted material while I wait.
The cell door closes, locked in again.

From my window looking North,
The power line runs through the trees,
While a lone microwave tower stands tall,
Full sun upon the green clad firs, brightning.

My cell mate, wounded by misfortune,
Lies asleep upon the bed recovering.
The wail of sirens reaches me now fading
On it's journey to the hospital.

Alone among so many, my thoughts
Scrambled by the incessant chatter,
From the cell next door, mumbling
Incoherent thoughts from nothingness.

Once more I had a muffin for breakfast. One cup of coffee was allotted to each person out of the coffee given for the whole ward.

Coffee was an essential part of my diet. I was sent down to health care and waited forever through two code yellows. Code yellow occurs when there has been a fight in one of the wards and no one is allowed to move throughout the jail until it is resolved. Even the visitors to the jail are locked down! I discovered this after I was released. I spent the rest of the day reading before returning to my cell to watch two football games. At this time I got another cell mate, a native man named Jason. It became apparent that he was related to half the population of the ward.! The next day we arose late and had bacon and eggs. Once they were heated up the were acceptable. I looked longingly down the road where I knew my friends from church were going to the Crooked Goose for breakfast. During the lock down we had a marvellous conversation about cooking. Made me hungry. Eric arrived with two pillows which eased my head. Marcell arrived with a remote which was greatly appreciated. I watched Midsomers Murders then went to sleep.

During this first month I was constantly hoping to get out, but when I talked to my lawyers it appeared the the crown had produced masses of paper which which took a long time to file and an even longer time to sort out. Aug. the 10th was the day of my next hearing. I hoped to be out in time for my birthday. My hopes were dashed. Another wait until September the 12th. It was Saturday the 10th of August which was a prisoners day of remembrance. I gather that it was a day when the prisoners did not eat anything to remember the prisoners who had fought for so long to get them the privileges; micro-waves, fridges and TVs. I had just got a new cell mate who seemed like a nice guy. As he was just admitted he was hungry. At supper time I brought him a dinner. Bad mistake. I was accused of disloyalty and told that I had just made my stay in prison much harder. I ate my dinner about six clock when we were locked down. Chris had already scarfed one meal and now had another! When I finally broached the subject to the Rep. I was told that "It was merely voluntary. "So much for solidarity. The other prisoners who had canteen merely snacked away.

Writing has always been my way of releasing tensions. When I first came in I wrote three or four poems that helped me relieve the boredom. When I moved to N I was kept busy and as there was another person in the room my writing tapered off. Now I picked up my pen and began to write of all the things that had happened to me in this jail. By the time I got to the end some ten months later it was over sixty pages ! I wrote poetry about the view from my cell, about the birds that flew effortlessly and free and about my feelings. It was another coping mechanism.

Now I come to the tragic part of the story. Throughout the month that I had been on the ward Eric had been my staunchest ally. We had read the bible together and reminisced about my life. He had been there for me when I had trouble with the Frenchman and obtained my second mattress. About this time Tyler came to the ward. There must have been some arrangement between him and the rest of the ward. One night Eric was hauled away shouting at Tyler. "You bastard ! I'll get you for this.! "I presume that they had planted some noxious substance in his cell and that was the reason for his removal. With Eric gone I lost one of my best friends there. This was not the end of the story. A couple of weeks later I received a letter from him via the jailhouse mail. I didn't know about sending letters to another inmate until the letter arrived. It was full of concern for me and it touched me deeply. I wrote him a long letter telling him about the goings on in the ward and exhorting him to keep his faith. As we had studied the bible and I knew the he had only an imperfect view of the doctrine of the atonement I began by explaining it to him. He was sent to A block where all the people who are decent are sent. They also sent their worst customers there. We sent each other letters every two weeks or so and I hope that they eased his burden. I know he eased mine.

The pecking order in jail is quite distinct. First you have general population people who are in there for nothing worse than murder. Next comes the protective custody people. One day I was called down to wait for heath care with three other inmates. We had no sooner arrived than another 'customer' arrived. He was GP and wanted to know which ward we were from. We told him we were from N and he immediately wanted to know what we were in for. The other two mumbled something or other and I said that I was in for going to church. Then a second GP was let in and they both began a little speech that went like this. "If you were sensible you would beat up one of the members on N. Once you did that you would be welcomed with open arms in any other ward. "Fortunately I was taken out and put in a separate cell at this time. In protective custody there was also a hierarchy of crimes. Sexual crimes were the norm so it had to be more specific. On the bottom there was I.

PRISON

When through these burnt black portals
Pass I, with fear within my heart.
To Thee O God I turn in humble adoration.
To Thee my God, I put my trust, my faith.

Though the night be dark, sundering,
In all my paths walk I through death and darkness.
Be with me always, though the path be steep,
And the road about me strewn with snares.

Guide me through the lightness hours,
When pain and sorrow trammel all my hope.
Be near me when I traverse the paths of death,
And hold me close as with a little child,

At the table closest to the food were the four people I called the SS. They included the ward rep. and his cronies. Next came an assortment of tables that seated four, there were four of them. The three tables that seated eight were next. The native table was near the microwave. The other two took what they could get. For quite some time after the Frenchman left I was alone in my cell which suited me fine. Then Richard, into whose room the Frenchman had been dumped wanted to stay with me! He was only there for a couple of weeks before being released. He had the misfortune of being an exhibitionist. His acceptance on the ward was due to his ability to make liquor. When we had an inspection, which happened every month or so, he breathed a sigh of relief for he had only just gotten rid of the stuff. When he left I was alone in my cell. This suited me well. Into this cell I could retreat. One of the rules was no one in another cell except he had been invited. A couple of months later he was back having been caught with booze which was against his parole. He was in for a breech. I welcomed him back with open arms and began playing crib with him. As he was quite a good player the games were enjoyable. Alas all good things come to an end! As you can see the trading at mealtimes was classic. At the time I was trading various items with one of the fellows. I could invariably trade my dessert for a far more inviting main dish. He would trade his cookie for a meat pie! Extraordinary! The only trouble was that we only received the pies once a month. I had traded my cookie for his meal but when I came to get it it had disappeared. No inquiry could ascertain its whereabouts. Carl said that he had placed the meal on the table and no one would assume responsibility. At first Richard denied it. It soon became obvious that he was the culprit. The table shunned him. Eventually he was kicked off the table and went to another. I wasn't looking for restoration or anything but he refused to acknowledge that he had stolen my dinner. He left before I could offer him any sort of forgiveness. Such are the people that inhabit the jail.

ENDURING

I cannot state how much not having a cell mate means to one in prison. Most of the fights that occur in the jail are caused by this. A code yellow is generated and then everyone in the jail is locked down. Even the easiest person to get along with can have clashes upon occasion. There was no restriction upon changing cell mates and for good reason. The inmates sort themselves out according to likes and dislikes. The only constriction comes when one of the inmates has to have a lower bunk. This was my predicament. I was too old to scramble up the stool, climb onto the table then leap to the bed. Of the inmates there I was by far the oldest. In some ways I was well treated and my idiosyncrasies overlooked. There were people there like Marcel who respected the elders. For that I was grateful. Most of the inmates just hated my guts. The problem I had was that, of the handful of inmates compatible to me most of them were already on the bottom bunk. I was usually restricted to having a cell mate imposed upon me. For these reasons the two weeks without a cell mate were a godsend.

I sometimes got the paper but at other times it disappeared into a cell like the black hole of Calcutta. The SS always had the paper first and it is no wonder that I never got to see it. It became a sort of game to see who could get the paper. On the weekends I was usually up early and could then ask a guard for the paper. This meant an hour of reading to compensate for not getting out until 10:00. On Friday Aug. the thirteenth I received a visit from Father Alfredo. I had been in prison for seven weeks and just to be able to talk to someone and to hold his hand was balm for my soul. I received communion for the first time since I had been in prison. It was a magical moment which I will never forget. I was not forgotten by those whom I most esteemed. Back in my cell I watched two football games. The weekend was good for watching football, I had always been an avid fan. We had French toast for breakfast which comes with a long weekend. Finally talked to David and he said that I would be out in a couple of weeks. It ran through my mind and I had a poor sleep.

Visits were something to look forward to. On Sunday afternoons Roy visited. If you have never had to sit down with a phone and talk to someone who is with you but behind a window you aren't missing anything. The close proximity to one you love yet cannot reach to touch is palpable. The jail allowed one visitor a day five days of the week. To sit there and talk to Roy yet not be able to reach out and touch him was difficult. The person who visits first has to wait to get into the conversation room. Once there he is constrained to be there for one hour, no more or no less. Then you are brought in and the conversation can begin. Ever tried talking to a person for one hour when there is only the two of you in the room? Nevertheless we managed to fill the hour with conversation, me by telling of my experiences in the last week and he talking of things at home and bridge. Another visitor was Father Don. Like Roy he had to wait the be admitted to the cube with the telephone. Fr. Don and I do not go a long way back but our common ground was sufficient to generate conversation. We would laugh at the incongruities of life. For ten months these two kept me sane and hopeful. In addition to these two I received visits from Hans, my bridge partner and Janice, my liberator. I was incredibly lucky to have two such supportive and positive people to visit. Some of the inmates never had one visitor all the time they were there.

They were once more parcelling cell mates out. We had recently receive an older man on the ward who was due to be let out shortly. Why they had to bring him into protective custody I will never know. Shortly after his arrival the jail decided to rearrange the inmate situation. I guess they figured that they would put the two prisoners who gave the most trouble in the same cell, either that or it was put the two old guys in the same cell. Don was a fanatic about cleanliness. He had some peculiar ideas about personnel hygiene. For one thing he was firm believer in the drinking of bleach to cure all ailments. His concept for anal care was toothpaste. You could always cure whatever ailed you by the consumption of bleach and application of toothpaste. He did, however, keep the cell immaculately clean. From floor to ceiling he cleaned with virox and other cleaners till the cell shone like a bright beacon in the night. I tolerated his peculiarities and even let him sit on my bed to watch TV. This was cardinal no-no. I didn't care except that it had an unfortunate consequence. I'll get to that later for now we were two old men serving out their time. As he watched anything that was on TV he was remarkably easy to please and I was able to watch whatever I wanted. I tried to coax out of him what his life had been like. The only thing that I perceived was that he was raised a Catholic when the church was in its most extreme mode. His father died when he was about seven and his mother moved to Prince George. At one time he must have been in the army for he describes the making of the bedding. I think but I can't be sure that he got into trouble in the armed forces and was subsequently jailed. There was work of some sort in the logging camps and then the episode for which he received a long sentence. From what I can gather he beat a man then kicked him once he was down. This gave me clue to the nature of the assault. He had lost his temper completely and, as a result, badly injured or even killed another. That was as much as I could gather from him.

For a month or so we continued together and it was an up and down relationship. He kept talking about self medication when I wanted quietness to watch TV. One morning I had got up at 7:30 and turned on the light to read my office as there was not enough light coming into my cell. Don was in a rage and banged the light cover so hard it nearly broke it. If you've seen how sturdy the light covers are in jail you will know how hard he hit it. The guard came and agreed that 7:30 was a bit early for the weekend and made me turn it off. I was a bit flummoxed at this but realized why he was in jail and repeatedly. He had never controlled his anger. There is a reason that anger is one of the seven Deadly sins. In a moment of anger you can ruin a life or take one. I went on to try to calm him down and keep him calm. He was a lapsed Catholic and deserved the benefit of the doubt. He had the most bizarre schedule. At 3:00 in the morning I would be awakened by the sound of Don working out! Needless to say it was almost impossible for me to get back to sleep and nights began to have a disorienting pattern. Between that and the insistence on talking about his personal health care life was becoming uncomfortable. One other item of interest was this. One morning I found a condom on my bed. As I did know where it had come from I took it to the guard. He looked at me with a curious face. It was then that I twigged to the fact that I had been invited to share sexual intimacy with him. Of all the ways to make a proposal I can't imagine one more less likely to fail. Apparently my inviting him to share my bunk had convinced him that his offer would be accepted. He tried bushing up against me but no go. Eventually I had to get my friend Kim to have a chat with him. Things went from bad to worse and one night I returned and discovered all the goodies were missing from the bag. I have to explain what was in the bag for you to understand what went missing. At meals we got a certain amount of peanut butter, margarine, ketchup and mustard. If you didn't use them you got to keep them to trade or do with what you please. The loss of the whole bag was considerable. I lost my temper for the first time and kicked him off the bed before storming out.

It had now reached the breaking point. I know that he had stolen my reading glasses and apparently was going around heating things with my lens. His complete unwillingness to admit he was wrong reminded me of my father. Like a little child he would pout and say nothing. He was alternatively hot then cold. I suppose that one shouldn't expect any more from a psychotic personality. It was apparently fine for him to wake me so that he could have and early morning workout but it was not fine for me to read. In order to get away from the cell I began reading in the quiet room. The room was used by the officers and staff to interview inmates and was generally empty. One morning I reached my cell and Don was moving. I couldn't believe my luck. He got moved into Kim's room where he suffered the depredations I had suffered at his hands. Sic transit gloria more. Thus fades the glory of the day.

One other inmate was Martin the Mexican who was in for sexual assault of a female client. He admitted that he had a weakness for the female form. He was married but his wife and son were in Mexico. As he sat opposite me at the table we struck up a reasonable relationship. As he had a rather acute accent he was tough to understand sometimes but I persevered and we had good mealtime conversations. His method of facing his sentence was to write a novel. Now to write a novel in Spanish I could understand but to attempt the feat in English was more than I could fathom. I had a go at editing his novel but the number of mistakes in it made getting the meaning impossible. I suppose that as a method of keeping himself occupied during his incarceration it was good therapy. After three months he was gone and I lost another friend on the ward.

It became apparent that I was to be trusted with the stories inmates tell to only their closest friends. One man, I'll call him Bob, came to me with another strange tale. He was in for sending an image of some girl to another. Unknown to him he had sent it to a police officer. It was a sting. He had a limp and was using a crutch and as he had asked to see me we went into the quiet room. He was in foster care when he ran away and was picked up by some hippys who invited him into their motor home. Apparently they were enamoured of free love and showed him the tricks of the trade. He was gently lubed up before he had intercourse and remembers getting off on this experience. At one time he was bent over a log on some beach, lubed and had anal intercourse with several men. When he was a bit older he remembers going around asking for someone to suck him off. For him it was just sex and a good way to feel good.

It was about this item that Eric wrote to me from B block. He was in confinement with one other inmate. Life, he said, went on and he continued to read his bible. At least it was quiet there and there weren't forty other people bothering him. At one point his TV went down and he was staring at time without relief. He read his bible and what other materials he could obtain. I wrote to him and he was concerned that I would not be safe, Thus began our letter exchange that continued on for four months. Letters consisted of the news of the ward and some writing on scripture. I began exploring the doctrine of the atonement and it was some thing I had always wanted to do.

It was now time for a new cell mate. Josh was in for violating his bail. We had many conversations about his family and wife. For some reason their was some misunderstanding about religion. His wife wanted to go to church. At 33 years old he had to face the fact that crime was hurting his family. Whether he did anything about this I do not know but I pray that he finds the way. After a week he succumbed into moving in with Tyler. In exchange I got Justin. When Justin came tome I already knew about him as he ate at our table. He was famous for eating potatoes, his and anybody else. Now it is an odd thing that inmates would eat the powdered mashed potatoes but turned their noses up at baked potato. It was Nirvana for Justin! I have never seen anyone who could eat spuds like Justin. When he moved in with me he had been taken advantage of by Tyler. It was partly to stop this bullying that the guards moved him with me. Justin was functionally illiterate. Math was a foreign land and he showed little aptitude for English. His TV watching was at the cartoon level of the Simpsons. Nonetheless he was affectionate and enjoyed physical contact. You would think that a level of physical contact would be normal but it was quite the opposite. Sitting on the bottom bunk was considered a homosexual affectation. Nonetheless Justin would arm wrestle and reach down from his bunk to play. When he left he gave me a big hug. I did not expect to see him again.

Josh had begun to have second thoughts over his move. I never specifically found out for he was moved shortly thereafter. For some strange reason some of the inmates confided in me. Such was the case with Tyler. His mother had left his father when he was 3 and moved to Parksville. At aged ten or eleven his mother abandoned him. Either she couldn't handle him or she wouldn't try and he wound up with his father again. His father was a drunk. As plenty of booze was available Tyler began to be addicted. He moved on to drugs and by the age of sixteen he was trapped. He had a job yet continued to take money from his dad. When his dad asked him why the truth was out; a two thousand dollar a week drug habit.

Although I had appeared daily on ward B the standard of cleanliness expected on the ward was surprise. I was called out for not having showered so I showered, No good. The nearest shower took a long time to get warmed up and accounted for my many cold showers. It did not take me long to figure out that the showers tucked away in the back of what was euphemistically known as "Dave's" cell were better. In order to avoid clashes I established a new routine. Breakfast, office then a shower all accomplished by 8 AM. I even took a shit at this time and so moved that I did not have to encounter others. The kicker was the weekends. Not getting up till 10:00 AM proved frustrating. I solved this problem by showering during recreation time.

SUMMER

Summer slips away like dew in the morning sun.
Visions of trees now clad in the garb of green and dun,
Sway in the breeze, twisting, turning now yellow
In gentle rhythm to cool the forest floor below.

Alone within my cell a solitary voice cries out,
"Oh let them pass but not soon." it shouts.
Waft upon bitter trials of court dates wrangling,
The stern upholder bids me wait again, tantalizing.

I turn the the window, the hurrying cars rush on,
Unfettered, unchained, heedless of me a person,
They pass me by, a dim memory of forgotten years
While I look out upon summers fading tears.

GOD'S SERENITY

Alone yet not alone, for Thou art with me,
The solitude encompasses me, holds me as a oak tree.
In the silence of my mind, cool waters by,
And all my yesterdays have grown to fly.

Not the brashness of youth, now grown to maturity,
But the still, calm voice of God, serenity.
Grown in the fullness of God, upholding, uplifting,
Through the silent hours of the night, revealing.
Aug. 2017

Recreation occurred at at random times throughout the day ; sometimes occurring at 9:00 AM or not until 6:30 PM. Canteen was handed out on Saturdays and as nearly everyone went it was a great time to have a shower. The only problem was when I had canteen and had to go out to get it. During the summer it was marginally alright but as the days shortened it became miserable. If it was raining you had to stand in the rain, get your canteen then wait for the better part of an hour in the small gym. I began to avoid canteen. It was there that the boys loaded up on groceries at prices that were unbelievably high. Rice, noodles and chips were the main stock in trade and with them they supplemented the food that was provided.

Except for a few meals I thought that the food was good, especially for institutional food. There was plenty of fresh fruit be it only apples, oranges and occasionally a banana. Surprisingly c antelopes were sometimes available. Meals ranged from chicken to beef pot pie which was the best meal served. Breakfast consisted of porridge, cream of wheat or cold cereal; a muffin and bread which you could toast in the slowest toaster on earth. Lunch was a variety of sandwiches which varied from hot pizzas to tuna fish. Occasionally there was a change and you got hot roast beef, if you put it in the micro-wave, sausages or pyrogies. Dinner was invariably a hot meal. Chicken, noodles with meatballs, hamburger with a real baked potato, sometimes with sour cream and curried lentils were on the menu. Rice, potato and noodles were served with a variety of underdone vegetables. The dessert item were the hottest trading commodities. Trading a cookie for a meal or a revel for meat was standard fare. If you weren't fussy you could eat like a hog.

There were three microwaves and two toasters on our floor. I usually managed to have my meals so that they were hot at least. The fuss that was made over the microwaves was ridiculous! If, for example, someone put their drink into one you were not allowed to pull it out even if it's owner had left it. All alone it would sit there, unclaimed and no one else could use the oven. I got into hot water upon occasion for touching the precious cup. As I was at the bottom of the list I could easily be picked on. I soon avoided confrontation. It was mid morning on a Friday and everyone was out. Revelling in the silence I continued reading. The banging in the segregation cell under us and brought everyone to the window. The guard said we should pay attention as that is what happens when a guard was disobeyed. The beating inflicted was vicious. Later on I realized that the reason it was so quiet was that it was canteen day and I had missed it. There was no recourse. You had to be there to get your canteen. Presumably they shipped the goods back.

By this time I was playing crib with Rick on a regular basis. At first we began by scoring the match on paper, the usual crib board not being available to us. It helped to pass the time and Rick was the only person who would play continuously. The rest of the ward played one game then quit, short attention span. However it was Rick and I played until they shut us down to go to our cells. We began to play in the common room as it was a lot quieter. The ward had a room that could be shut away from the hurl-burly of everyday activity. It was used by teachers and staff for lessons or as an interview room. Most of the time it was empty so it was there that we retired to play. Every so often we would get booted so that someone could have a haircut or some staff wanted to run a lesson. Some of the inmates just worked around us and made no fuss. Others though had to make a great show of it and kicked us out on purpose. We were having too much fun in jail and that was not allowed. Rick was in there for some sexual assault on his girl friend. I never managed to get the low down but he was essentially barred from seeing her. He talked about Courtney and the life he lead as a child. As a young man he had gone to Calgary where he had married and fathered a child. On and on he went about how much he loved Laura and somehow he world arrange to get back together. At one point I suggested that he might try AA but he refused. He was happy as a drunk and would not relent, only looking forward to his eventual release and a booze up.

SUNRISE

A patch of pink across the horizon,
Illuminating the skyline silhouetted
In sharp contrast to the dark below,
While lights of different hues play on,
Twinking and winking in the shadows.

Through the bars, only half seen,
Lies the parking lot, cars and trucks
Go back and forth in seamless strain
Of motion, going onward, going forward,
Where I long to be, free and unencumbered.

The soft light falls upon the trees
And half hidden houses illuminating
In shades of pink and dappled Grey
The outline of the forest hid below.

In hollow dells the fog lies deep,
The power towers starkly stare
And the lone micro-wave stands
Sentinel, it's red light flashing.

And I within my cell look out,
Through horizontal bars to see
The geese fly by, a lonely gull,
Soaring free while my heart breaks.

    Kim was one of the most interesting people of the ward. Periodically he had seizures and we were hustled into our cells. Whether the beating he took from the police or from past misadventures caused the seizures I do not know. I had made friends with him although I'm not sure whether friendship was the right word. He took my peanut butters and any excess of food in exchange for protection. Sometimes he would give me a particular item that he had made or that he didn't want. On the street he was a drug enforcer, which meant that he went around shaving women's heads and assaulting men in order to collect the dug debt. By and large his charming nature obtained my support. When Don moved in with Kim the shoe was on the other foot. There must have been a fight or some interaction but one day they were both gone. In a couple of days Kim had returned.

REMEMBRANCE

Alone amid my thoughts, a quiet time of meditation,
The soft whisper of the breeze through my cell calms me.
I think of times past, of journeys long forgotten,
In the dim recesses of time my mind recalls, remembers,
The faint whisper of children playing amid the forest,
Deep silence hangs around the hill where I once played.

Alone a midst the towering cedars, in a glade,
Nestled among the bracken and fern I lie,
Arms folded in the sun dappled glory of summer.
I contemplate the stillness of the forest floor.
High above the clouds scud by, the birds chirp,
While I peacefully dream of times when I am free.

Ian was my next cell mate and for a while things were fine. He acknowledged my faith and were shared a common bond. For a while he went around the ward reading my bible in what was a pious fraud. Then one day, out of the blue, he came in and said. "You arrogant prick! "I presumed that he had talked to members of the ward most antipathetic to me. For a week it was bad. He stole from me and suddenly I was missing peanut butter and cereal. I did what I did to most people who turned on me, I shunned him. One day he packed up his things and went to court. He came back devastated. His lawyer hadn't even shown. As he was charged with assault on a homeless man I was not surprised. As he now had to stay he relented. All's well that ends well, was my response. We were cell mates for nearly a month. Never have I encountered anyone who could eat like he did. As his crime was preferable to the rest of the ward he obtained the wards excess. Sometimes there was so much of it that he shared it with me. Never have I encountered someone who gained weight in the prison. The diet was prescribed by a nutritionist for an average seventy year old. The young bucks who comprised most of the inmates were constantly looking for food. Most of their canteen money was spent on food. They worked out constantly doing push ups, chin ups or just walking endlessly around the ward. Solemn adoration of the body.

Exercise

Round and round the oval they go,
Two by two in unceasing parade.
Talking perpetually, inhuman chorus.
The exercise of the body laid out
In one gargantuan movement in space
Where only time counts as the days pass by.

Another peculiarity of the ward was the daily ritual of medications. Three time a day half the ward was sent off for methadone. I was placed in this line up until my medication arrive in bubble packs. This meant that I had no drugs that could be used for illicit purposes. Ten to fifteen people jammed into the elevator to take them to the bottom floor where we lined up for medication. Check was made of your mouth to ensure compliance. It was hell going down. The hatred in that elevator was palpable. There was the occasional snide comment thrown in for good measure. I once had to go down to take some potassium with a small newcomer who said "I ain't no badminton kid.' This apparently refereed to a newscast were I was accused of molesting my students. The news cast omitted to mention that any such behaviour had occurred some thirty five years ago. I was briefly tempted to turn around and squash him. At 8:00 PM the rest of the ward lined up for suboxone. This required a two phased affair; the giving out of the pills the after a time checking for compliance.

October the twenty- fifth and my hoped for release on bail. I went downstairs where I was refused my street clothes. Off the be shackled up the into the van. We took a detour to the Collwood court before hitting Victoria. There was some mix up but they started the hearing about eleven. The prosecutor laid out her case and took three hours! Most of which was either untrue or partly true. That left only an hour for my attorney. At the end the judge left his decision for Friday. Back to jail again. Friday I made the mistake of leaving my glasses taking only my reading ones. I was granted bail but it was surety bail of twenty five thousand dollars. I knew nothing about this type of bail. It appeared that I had to have someone besides myself post the bail. It appeared that I had to have someone besides myself who would post bail and vouch for me. I was returned to jail where another snag appeared. As I had received bail the jail assumed that I wouldn't be back and they had given my cell away. Not only that but Ian had moved down, stolen my glasses, and my copy of "the Lord of the Rings. It was a mess. Still I had only to phone my son to effect my release. With aid of Mr. Holiday I phoned Martin. He refused. I had given him thirty-five thousand to buy the house. Now he would not even sign my bail. I was devastated! For the rest of the week I made phone call after phone call with no result.

Memories

Once again I try to mend the fence,
Broken, shattered by deeds long past
Till only the facade of this remains
Deeply truncated by the lies now told.
Sundered by the shock, the impact
Of social media: half truths portrayed.

And I remember a day long past,
A baby born into this world, howling
Till the heavens wished for peace unfolding.
There was none to give, only the unending

Wail, sent up to the gods, implacable,
Forever rooted in the agony of birth.

Once again I see a child, angered by
The events of the year uncomprehending,
Till the tides of time softened his wrath.
A new beginning, a voice crying in
The wilderness, a song for Christ the King.
Follow the long lost path of re-newel.

And he grew in stature to sing for joy
The inexorable songs of Christ in a
Time of love, flowering to tenor proud.
And I too hailed the king inexorably proud,
Now dashed to pieces, bitter flagon
Of hemlock, drunk upon a prison cell.

Periodically the whole ward would be searched for contraband. A tribe of guards would descend on the ward and go through each cell while you were strip searched. This involved taking off all of your clothing while a guard inspected your intimate parts. You were then allowed to put your clothes on again and return to your cell. There you found that all of your extra blankets had been taken and your cell turned upside down. One search I had both my jackets taken. I was using one as a pillow and wondered how anyone could take both of them. It took me months to get it back again!

JAIL

A gentle fall of snow blanketing
the jail and all around, covering,
Yet not quite the trees and buildings
That stand as a monument to hate.

> Within these walls still struggle
> The inmates with their own demons
> Lust, hate yield to the gentleness love,
> Flowing from God to those who care.
>
> The sun shines weakly on the walls,
> Illuminating the snow, a blanketing
> Of loveliness on the symbol of hate,
> Long smouldering within these walls.

It was at this time that Rick reappeared having gone to Courntey for his trial. He was out of luck and was sentenced to a further four months in the forestry camp. Just before he left a new inmate appeared having been sentenced to a stint in the Ford institute. He had been sentenced for child abuse and was fearing the worst. Apart from someone jeering at him in the elevator they left him alone. Mike and I played crib and I discovered in him someone who could play. When Rick returned he had a short stay and then he was off to the forestry camp. As soon as he left I moved in with Mike. I had been in that cell for four months and Ian had begun to bug me with his constant getting up to go to the bathroom. Mike was a Christian although of a charismatic strain. His life had spun out of control and he was in misery. Having been booted out of the navy he sought comfort in marriage. When he was arrested his wife left him, and only his church stood by him. We were both in the same boat but only a few months separate. I had continued to say my office, morning prayer which is a combination of Lauds. and Terse, and offered to share it with him. He agreed and as it was the weekend when we were not allowed out until 10:00 AM I began, as usual, at eight o'clock. The chanting and canticles were strange to him but he was a great comfort to me. For the first time I had someone with whom I could share my faith. Not since Eric left had I had anyone. We had thought that he would be around for a month or so but it was not to be. Monday he was whisked off to the mainland. Before he left I gave him my copy of C.S. Lewis' 'Mere Christianity'. I had been given a copy by Fr. Alfredo on one of his visits and had read it twice. In such a short time we had bonded to the point of playing endless games of crib. Sic transi gloria mundi.

REMEMBRANCE

Alone amid my thoughts, a quiet time of meditation,
The soft whisper of the breeze through my cell calms me.
I think of times past, of journeys long forgotten,
In the dim recesses of time my mind recalls, remembers,
The faint whisper of children playing amid the forest,
Deep silence hangs around the hill where I once played.

Alone a midst the towering cedars, in a glade,
Nestled among the bracken and fern I lie,
Arms folded in the sun dappled glory of summer.
I contemplate the stillness of the forest floor.
High above the clouds scud by, the birds chirp,
While I peacefully dream of times when I am free.

Soon I had another cell mate, Alan. He had been transferred from F ward were they kept mentally unstable prisoners. Apart from a problem with psychiatrists he appeared to have few problems. His wife had left him in apparently messy divorce, I never quite got the handle on it. I don't know if he didn't have TV on his previous ward but here he watched TV from seven o'clock in the morning until I shut it down about ten o'clock! As I played crib or was out on the ward most of the daytime this did not concern me. I reserved the TV from seven o'clock till ten o'clock. We got along fine as we had little contact except when there were times of lock down. We kept referring to the other members of the ward as children. They spent endless hours trying to upset me but I kept right on going. At one point they had discovered that if you held a remote close to the exterior of the cell you could change the channel or do other nastier things. Alan soon got tired of this and placed a piece of tinfoil over the sensor. He referred to as "having foiled them." Things went along well until the day I came in late and decided to watch Jeopardy. The show was half over but I wanted to catch the end of it so I changed the channel. You never heard such a howl! He went on and on about how I couldn't change the show he was watching, as if he hadn't been watching all day. When I got him calmed down I expressed surprise at his predicament and assured him that if he felt so left out I would not change the channel except on the hour. Then he went on to say that he had been placed in my cell to keep me out of trouble! That was news to me considering that I had bent over backwards to accommodate him. Shortly thereafter he switched rooms and went to stay with Ian. I'm sure that he got to watch all the programs he wanted to.

About a week after Mike left Rick returned and I had my crib partner back again. It appeared that only workers were required and as he had been invalided out of the workplace he now refused to work. At this time we had an obnoxious character the ward. He began by flicking various objects at Rick and me before moving on to more sinister things. There were blinds put up on my windows which deteriorated to writing defamatory sayings. My door was constantly written upon until finally I had to speak to the ward Rep. to stop this. Shortly after this he was gone. I know had to await the arrival of a new cell mate. When Trevor came he acknowledged that he was not interested in what I was in for, he only wanted to serve his time. He was another like so many who was on suboxen. For a while this worked out well and he and I got along quite well. I had on hand two litres of eggnog and two Christmas squares, and after receiving canteen I had a block of cheese. I gave Treveor some of my eggnog and traded one square for egg sandwiches. The other litre of eggnog mysteriously disappeared. I still trusted Trevor and kept my cheese on the window. One night I was playing crib with Rick in the quiet room. Ty was heckling me and the guard was apparently oblivious. Unknown to me Treveor had moved. The first inkling I had was when Ty announced in a loud voice the my TV had broken and that I had a new cell mate. I returned to the cell to find a new cell mate who admitted to brushing the TV off the wall with the mattress. Now this was patently absurd. Whenever an inmate changed cells he took his bedding and left. There was no reason for the new man to be swinging his mattress. They had deliberately broken the TV.

SNOWFALL

Soft fluffy flakes falling from leaden sky's
Twist and turn in unending pattern of change.
Lights now winking and twinkling down,
Skyward halls to lie upon the twisted roof.

The trees now covered in a soft blanket,
A mantle thrown around by nature
To cover the outstretched arms and limbs.
Mother natures pure and pristine blanket.

Snow swirls down through the yard light,
Fireflies flickering and flashing, falling on
The roofs of the prison where I sit, alone.
Slowly the roof is covered with fluffy snow.

CHRIST-MASS LIGHTS

Through the bars of my cell,
Lights brightly shining clear
Through the frosted night air.
Twinkling their merry coloured
Skein of Christ-MASS cheer today.
Bright reds, muted yellows twinkling
In the darkness of this night.
Harbinger of Christ's nativity.

SNOWFALL IN JAIL

A gentle fall of snow, blanketing
The jail and all around, covering,
Yet not quite, the trees and buildings
That stand as a monument to hate.

Within these walls still struggle
The inmates with their own demons,
Lust, hate yield to the gentleness of love,
Flowing from God to those who care.

The sun shines weakly on the walls,
Illuminating the snow, a blanket
of loveliness on the symbol of hate,
Long smouldering within these walls.

That night the new cell mate grilled me about what I was in for. I told him what he wanted to know. As he was only twenty five himself I think that he believed me. The following night was better as we had a discussion on the bible. In the morning though he complained about my snoring. It was embarrassing but there was no way that I could explain my inability to control it. Justin came into our quiet room on the verge of tears. His cell mate had stolen his things and was mean to him. I took it upon myself to get him to bunk with me. The transfer was complete and though we had no TV we were immeasurably better off. On Christmas eve Mr Holliday came to see me and realized that the TV was missing. He took it upon himself to get us one. It was one of the kindest deeds done for me. The next day Eric had returned and all was well. I did not know it but it was the beginning of the end.

The next day Justin"s old cell mate was taken away in handcuffs. He had been caught making booze, a thing that the jail looks down on, and Justin was flagged with telling the guards. A rat is not a nice thing as the residents of the ward were supposed to look after each other. He was terrified! For three days I brought him his food and tried to comfort him.

At one point he attempted the commit suicide, slashing his wrist with the plastic knives only left deep marks but no other result. I was holding his hand in an attempt to calm him. That was a mistake. Justin was called to the sergeants office and I was called next. We were accused of having sex on the ward within view of everyone. I let the sergeant know in no uncertain terms that this was not true. I let him know that as Justin was functionally illiterate and that he had no method of coping with their call of being a rat. I had even had a conversation with Chas who was ward Rep. and assured him that Justin did not betray his cell mate. It was no use. Here was the final irony, that those who despised Justin for ratting were themselves culpable of inventing a lie to get us into trouble. The result was devastating. I was sent to my old cell and Ian, whom Justin feared most of all, was sent to mine. We were back in the old cell again and now Allan was outright hostile to me. Three days later Eric was swarmed by four guys with the kickboxing star in the forefront. They took Eric to the infirmary and took my ex cell mate off in handcuffs.

There were recriminations. The whole ward was locked down for four days. People were let out in shifts to exercise and our food was served to us in our cells. Allan had the TV on all day. At some point in the game Justin was taken out in handcuffs. Apparently he sexually assaulted Ian! If any charge was more ridiculous I have never seen it. Justin was five foot four and weighed one hundred and forty pounds while Ian was six foot two and over two hundred and fifty pounds. On New Years day weekend there were many changes with various people being reassigned. Monday Allan left to be with Ian again. I was alone in my cell again and revelling in the peace and quiet. We were locked down till noon on Tuesday at which point we were given a stern warning, no more shenanigans on this floor. The unit had been shaken up but not for the better. Ty and Josh left to do their time in the Penitentiary but Dave returned. On Sunday they brought in a new guy who had just recovered from an horrendous fall. He had been in a coma for two months. They booted me out into another ward where an older guy kept control of the remote. For once I didn't mind a he was a good guy and watched intelligent TV. I continued to spend my time out of the cell playing crib with Rick.

A RAY OF HOPE

At this time I received a letter from one of the children at church. For six months I had been in this place without having received any mail. Now a window opened and the light shone through. Tyler wrote a simple card with a Christmas tree on it. The front of the card said "Wishing you many blessings for 2018" On the inside was written, "Dear Harry. I hope you are keeping well and that you will be freed from prison soon. My parents and I are praying for you. God bless, Tyler. 'Out of the mouths of babes and sucklings thou hast perfected praise.' In it's simplicity and sincere faith he had touched me like no one else. I cried in my cell. For the remainder of the time this card was posted on whatever notice board I had, even to the extent of taping it on the wall in my last cell which had no notice board.

At five o'clock in the morning John left and I hoped that I would be left alone. Eric had gone swept up in the mass exodus and only Rick remained. I tried to talk Trevor into getting him to room with me but to no avail. Later that day I received a new cell mate. He was coming off a heroin high and for two days he slept. On the third day he came into our room after suboxen and placed three capsules on the table. One he ground up into a powder and snorted. The other two he planned to sell for five dollars a pop. How he managed to obtain these three pills I'll never know but I assume he had some way of concealing them when the mandatory mouth check was made. It was like the South Sea Bubble with no scruples involved. These men would do anything to get a 'hit'. Saturday he was gone to another room. My new cell mate was a real piece of work. He began by being semi friendly but that didn't last long. Again the ward was against me. It was not long before he began hollering at me to quit snoring. I tried all of his prescriptions but I figured that he only called out when he awoke. From that point on I breathed through my mouth. He got more abrasive resorting to a new tactic. He had asked me to wash my bedding as it smelled. I suspected a rat but I washed all of my clothing and my bedding. The next morning he got up and began to upbraid me for not washing my clothes. I had had enough! I hollered at him that I had washed my clothing and if he couldn't tell he must be crazy. He hollered back and I as was not about to stand down. He hit me. It was then that the guard game in. For six months I had been on that ward without a whisper of uncleanliness. Now he was going to oust me because he didn't like the way I smelled. I was moved back into my old room. I had to stay on the floor as John had the bottom bunk. Once again they tried to move me as I smelled. I was the only inmate who changed his clothing to sleep. The other thirty-nine slept fully clothed and I was the one who smelled! In spite of the guards insistence that he be out of the cell when I moved he remained. I took my remote for which I paid Chas a cookie. When I came back from playing cards the remote was gone and half a pack of cheese was missing. Still I thought I was well out of it.

Kim had returned and I once more had someone to turn to. He attempted to get my missing cheese back. Now I had no canteen left except some noodles that I had cooked up and only eaten half. Two days later all I had was a cleaned container. John had stolen it. I had taken to reading morning prayer in the quiet room right after breakfast. I was surprised to find Alan in the room reading of all things! He who always watched TV was now in my reading room so I quietly said my office at a table. Talk about dog in the manger! That Friday I received communion for the third time. I could see the writing on the wall. Various things began to go missing so I hid them away. Saturday John suggested that we get into a fight with the guards consent. Apparently he had been pressured to hurt me, although that wasn't going to happen, I was twice his size. Once more the guard complained about the smell so I took a bottle of virox to the room. If there was anything smelly about the room it had to be John. He slept with his clothes on and never washed them. It was strange. I had been on the ward for over six months and no one had complained. On Monday John jumped out of bed with his jacket on and headed out of the room. When I returned from my juice and coffee run there was no sugar pack. An inquiringly failed to turn it up and even though I told Kim to put pressure on John nothing could be done. Kim kindly gave me some sugar. The next morning I took my sugar pack first thing and hid it. After lunch John accused me of stealing his strawberry jam. Now I remembered that my noodles had disappeared. I knew who the culprit was. The only way he could have had extra strawberry jam was if he had stolen my pack. The argument got heated.

Now it is a strange thing that I didn't see what was coming. Numerous guards and a sergeant appeared. I was locked in my room. Half an hour later two guards arrived, handcuffed me and took me to segregation. I was stripped of all my clothes then given a jumpsuit which only covered half my stomach, and hung around my shoulders. About three hours later a guard came in and handed me a piece of paper with the charge; sexual assault. Well that was news to me. No one had interviewed me or asked for my opinion, it was just taken that John's word was law and they hauled me off. Having failed in every legal way they now trumped up this charge to get me off the ward. I hope that they are happy with their chicanery. It was good to give thanks to God and to be free of the shackles of humanity. Once more I was free to sing praises to our Lord who would surely look after me.

Segregation cells had no TV. There was a window that touched the top of my cell and looked out on the front of the building, the cell being mainly below ground. There was a toilet, sink and a double bunk. Only the top bunk had enough light to read by. The night went slowly by. My double mattress had gone and only a light blanket kept me warm. In the morning I phoned David and he arranged to see me. I perused the book items and selected C. S. Lewis' The Dawn Trader and some science fiction book then returned to my cell. I heaved the mattress onto the top bunk and began reading. About mid morning I was summoned to talk with the sergeant. He said that the warden's court would only decide that neither party could be ruled correct as it was his word against mine. Just as I figured the ward had decided. The remainder of the time in Seg., as it was known, passed quietly, well if you consider the racket kicked up by those in Seg. as quiet. There was at least no one else to interact with and I revelled in my solitude. The next day I attended wardens court and outlined my position. I was particularly peeved that the guards had not questioned me before hauling me off to Seg. The verdict was not guilty. Back to my cell for few more hours until I was re clothed and packed of to A.

After so long being with another person it was nice to be back in a cell alone. The TV didn't work but I was fine with that. My books had all been returned to me so I had plenty of reading material. My neighbour was a little noisy as he was obviously mentally disturbed. A pie for supper! Delicious! I read all the next day. Several cell mates who had been with me on N came to greet me. The next day I was transferred to ward B on the other side of the unit where they house difficult inmates and process those who are coming in. I was somewhat disturbed to find I was on the top bunk but as I had lost some weight during my stay getting up was not too difficult. My cell mate was an older transfer, just waiting to be placed in a federal facility. He went on and on about the joys of being in a federal system. We shared the TV but he referred to my watching the animal shows as "animal porn" On Monday morning he was moved out and I grabbed the mattress and headed down to more comfortable quarters. There was only one problem as the light shone on the bunk above, the bunks being placed directly on top of one another., making reading difficult. For the first time in ages I had the cell all to myself and revelled in it. I watched TV when I wanted and what shows I wanted, in the evenings I watched TLC, PBS or some particular program on the other channels. By ten o'clock I was completely worn out and went peacefully to sleep. It was a peaceful week. I read, sang and watched shows on TV. One of the first things I had done was to acquire another blanket and with that I was snug and warm. You do not know how cold the jail is. The doors are left open and the cold seeps into your bones.

For a week this continued on. Alas! It was to good to be true. Joey Smith, whom I knew from N ward arrived and I had to give up my double mattress. Eleven day's later one of the guards checked my file and found the double mattress order and I was once more comfortable. It was good to bunk with Joey as he referred to me a 'pepe'. We shared canteen and I got along well with him massaging my back. One of the things that you miss the most is the absence of any physical contact, besides it eased my aching back. Joey was a study in contradictions. He ran a drug ring and saw nothing wrong with that, except for the times he got caught. Again it was a common characteristic of the prison population. Prison was his home and he had spent a third of his life in prison. Scrapping and brawling down through the years had left what should have been a quiet, compassionate man an ogre, but a happy one. Ill equipped to survive in today's computer age and saddled with a criminal record he turned to drugs. Where else could he haul in the cash needed to survive in this day and age.

It did not take long to figure out that he function at a low level. TV programs that he espoused were a dead give away; cartoons. When he wasn't sleeping he watched the Simpsons, the Family Guy and Gold Rush. When I said we were watching a show like Morse he quickly lost interest and went to sleep. Another peculiarity was his inability to sleep without the background noise of the TV. He would have me turn on the idiot box at nine in the morning. Though I liked it quiet t would duly turn it on to the cooking channel. Thus mollified he would go back to sleep while I plugged away at my reading or writing. Eating and the search for food was something Joey yearned for. The day he got his first canteen he ate so much he threw up the lot. As he was diabetic I couldn't understand his eating habits. My wife was a diabetic and, though she took liberties with what she ate, would follow her guideline fairly well. He wouldn't eat egg sandwiches, which I loved, so he got my toast and cereal in exchange. Control and good diet was not his specialty. As soon as he arrived he was gunning for canteen. "Canteen day, Pepe, Canteen day. "he clamoured. It was like living with a child. In the evenings we shared the TV, I watched from seven til ten and he watched from then on. The only problem was his ability to sleep with the TV on. Frequently I awakened at two in the morning to find the television blazing. I got up and turned it off. The winter Olympics were on for two weeks in February and I revelled in the multiplicity of sport. Snow boarding, skiing, ski cross, curling, figure skating and hockey all presented at once. Once more I vicariously experienced the deeds of various athletes as they soared in a variety of twists and turns. The grace and form of the dancers to the more energetic rhythms of the pairs and singles held me spellbound. I even had Joey watching them! He admitted that he had not watched them since watching them with his mother twenty-five years ago.

Now I had been in solitary for nearly a month and had settled down to a rhythm. Instead of playing crib and being jolted by the encounters with the ward I read more and began writing. This came to an end with the arrival of Mair as guard. I had already had one encounter with this guard and it was not pleasant. It was he who put me in the cell with the heroin addict contrary to regulations. "A prisoner who is not sentenced is not to be placed in a cell with one who has" Besides this there was an empty cell next door which he could have put me in. He deliberately set me up to be punched out. He had a hate on for PC's of any stripe but saved his worst for me. All of the inmates could have had an encounter with someone like him. It was antipathy that fulled his hate. We were getting our trays of food from downstairs and I was just about to enter my room when Mair kicked me hard. Iw was all I could do to prevent dropping the tray. Now it was time to get retribution in full. The 24th of February started normally, when at seven PM Mair stormed into our cell accusing Joey of messing up the common room. It was not us who had messed it up but the GP group who was out after us. I endeavoured to add some statement to Joey's protest.

"Shut up Sadd. If I wanted to hear from you I would have said so." He shot back.

The end result was that he took Joey's job away from him. The next day at supper I had just picked up my food tray and was carrying it into my cell. Mair shoved me in the back. A few hours later he ordered me to move. I thought that he was going to put me in the cell without TV but we continued on to the main floor. I had to carry my mattress and then go back for my clothes. Little did he know that he had improved my lot. Once again I was completely free of other people. His petty vindictiveness did not end there; when he left at ten o'clock he shut the power to my TV off. It would take me until noon to get it back on. Two days later his sidekick in these matters banged on my cell on the way out then shut the power off. As I didn't watch daytime TV it didn't bother me. The following morning Mair let us all out for a break at 6:45. Just a bit early! The following Saturday my tray arrived without it's sandwich. I protested and guard threw it on the bed. For some reason Mair was on all sixteen hours.

ASSAULT

Sunday the 4th of March and I went for a visit. Roy could not come but Janice came instead. We had a great visit and I was boy up when I returned. I saw Mair through the window and he went off to the yard. Thinking nothing about it I entered. As soon as the door buzzed. I knew that something was wrong. Through my peripheral vision I saw the inmate who had repeatedly threatened me coming at me. I ran for my cell. It was no use. He was on me beating my head and punching my ribs. With blows raining down on me I fell to the floor. Still he continued to punch me in the chest. It was only a short time but I was shattered. I lay on the floor then crawled up to my bunk. Eventually health came came to take me away to be examined. My head had been pummelled but the greatest damage done was to my chest. As there was nothing to be done about broken ribs I was returned to my cell.

The next morning I phoned my lawyer and he agreed to come out that afternoon. I phoned Roy and told him about this beating. Mair came to me protesting the things I said, which was strange as I hadn't spoken to anyone. Portraying himself as the hero and saying that he had put his body in front of the inmates was not the right one to take. I could have accepted that he had made a mistake but to flog it off as one act of heroism on his part made no sense. If you believed that line I've got a bridge I want to sell you. The first assailant had reached me as soon as the door opened. How else could the inmates know that the door was opening or that I was on the other side ? The other guard, Parmer, was conveniently missing. Through the next couple of days I managed to piece the scenario together. As soon as I left for my visit he had let the others out for their recreation time. As this occurs only twice in twenty-four hours the timing was suspicious. He had to have informed them that I was on a visit and would be back shortly. He had the one other guard that was similarly minded on at the time and was conveniently absent at the time. Also the sergeant had to have been involved as I got down to health care and he said that the camera showed nothing. After a while I figured it out. Mair let the GPs out some time after I had gone for my visit. He then instructed the person who was to assault me only to punch me in places where it wouldn't show. Mair had gone to the enclosure well before I came and could easily have closed the door. For these reasons I knew for certain that he had set it up on purpose.

Monday afternoon I told David my tale. Tuesday I was assured that the problem would be solved. I subsequently heard that Mair was on administrative duty and not available for duty on the ward. I had no more contact with Mair until two days before my release but his sidekick remained. For four days I slept very uncomfortably as it was hard to breathe and every time I rolled over it hurt. Thursday I was shackled up and taken to the hospital. The guard was very nice and I was as comfortable as one could be all shackled up. It was at least a trip out of the prison. One cannot run or even walk with any alacrity so I was bundled up into a wheelchair. Into the hospital we went with me in my reds and the guard pushing the wheel chair. We went to the nurses station then waited to be called. I had brought a book but the guard was chatting amiably to another so I listened in. Eventually we were called and headed off to wait some more. I was wheeled into the clinic and asked to get onto the table. This proved a problem, shackled as I was. With some difficulty I managed to get up onto the bed but when I went to lay down I came up hard upon the lock. Eventually he decided to take of the handcuffs. With the procedure finished I was put back into cuffs, placed in my wheelchair and taken back to the car. Jail cars are different from ordinary cars. There is no seat so you just slide over until you are up against the far door. On the way traffic had been bad so the guard took another route back to the jail. To date I have had no further contact with Mair. Upon returning to my cell it had become obvious that my lower back was bruised. The ribs that were sore were just beginning to heal and now I was sore from having lain on the shackle! At least my meds had arrived and I had Ibuprofen to take. For about a week afterwards it was still sore.

This morning there was prisoner banging on the door. Now an ordinary door makes quite a racket but these heavy doors positively shake the building. This was followed by loud noises of protest and I thought that the world had ended. It was not common for us to be distracted by excessive noise but this was an exception even to these. At least we didn't have a chorus of hate pouring from the people in the cells. On the whole it was quiet and I was able to write. Although Joey and I were separated we still go out together on our twice a day sojourns. Twice a day for an hour we were allowed out of our cells and into the common area. I was usually let out early which suited me just fine. I could the make a pot of coffee and heat up my muffin. Except at dinner, and sometimes even then, meals arrived cold, not the most appetizing. We still traded food Joey and I. I took his eggs in exchange for cheese and we swapped marmalade for grape jelly or strawberry jam and I took his egg sandwiches which were part of his diabetic diet. I didn't want the cereal or toast that came with breakfast so I gave it away to Chris. In the sugar packs we got peanut butter which I also gave away.

As I mentioned before cleanliness was very important. You were expected to wash your hands after going to the bathroom. It was just and indicator of how low I was on the totem pole the the Rep. didn't bother to greet me upon my arrival. Consequently I floundered around for some time before I got the rules squared off. Some of the rules, like the washing of hands made sense. I have been here two hundred and fifty seven days and have not be ill once. Mind you, no self respecting germ would be caught dead here! Showers and the washing of clothes were also important. Except for a few days a ward of forty people had to make do with only one washing machine. You were not guaranteed that you would get your clothes back. I once had my entire laundry purloined, the residents having ascertained that it was mine did not return it to the marked place. Rick also had this problem. It was different on ward B. There all of the clothing was provided and all you had to do was exchange a soiled garment for a new one. When I was there in June they had a washer and dryer. These things are now gone along with the bookshelf and the little bit of grass. One thing that made no sense was the making of all the windows opaque. There was to be no contact with the outside world except your two hours of break, the only glimpse from my cell was the obscured view from the grill. At least that opened which it doesn't do on several cells. Being shut up with a fellow traveller was hard enough but to also deprive them of any fresh air was positively barbarous! The odour of stale flatulence in my cell with Joey was disgusting, I know it's jail but some semblance of humanity must prevail. It's not even like that in Seg.

On Wednesday I was taken to the hospital again and this time the guard was not at all friendly. He took my book away so I was unable to read while we waited. He got confused about where we were going so instead of the North tower he took us up the South tower. When we finally arrived we were put in a waiting room where I looked out across the straights at the snow covered Olympic mountains. In the sunlight they look magnificent. Soon we were wheeled into the room for an EKG. Half an hour later we were finished and we wended our wordless way back to the jail.

I tried to put on the compression stockings but it was no good. At the end of the day my feet were swollen up worse than when I used the jail's socks. My only conclusion was that my heart was not pumping hard enough to adequately service my feet. I was tired for the next couple of days as the rigmarole of changing clothes and being shackled took it's toll. I had a good visit with Fr. Don. Thank God! These visits renew my strength and enabled me to carry on. We are now headed towards ten months and while the current situation has it's drawbacks it is better that any I have had so far. They lock me up and leave me in peace to read, write and watch what I want on TV. For the most part the TV remains on the weather channel where the only access to the time of day is posted.

COMFORTER

> Yellow heads on purple stalks,
> Writhing and turning in the sun.
> Dandelions, the first fruits of spring
> While the wind makes the flowers run.

Run far away to that other land,
Where once I knew peace in company
With those whose shared values kept
Me alive in times of harmony.

For eight long months, bitter trial kept,
Me on the doorstep of frozen hell.
While the rats kept gnawing my soul,
Till the bright son held me well.

Into thy arms, keeper bold,
I come bleeding from the wounds of pride,
Deep into the comfort of thy bosom,
Only resting place, thy wounded side.

Sunday; its Palm Sunday and I will miss the service. I will try as far as I can to have a holy week of prayer and song. The latter caused some excitement when my door was suddenly thrust open. Parvenir stepped into the cell and shouted at me, "Stop the whistling! I told you before to shut up! "I looked up in astonishment as no one had told me I couldn't sing or whistle in my cell. I toned it down as he seemed to consider my singing constituted a mark of disrespect. Both guards were most indignant and locked us down after only half an hour out. I see that their pets who are only in for assault are now out for a full hour. It doesn't matter that the four of us are deprived, we are only three lost souls and me. There appears to be a chess match going on this ward. I put my name down for the meal, once a month the jail allows us to buy a restaurant meal, when lo and behold it was scratched out. I couldn't understand why my order of Chinese food and not materialized. Now it became clear. Little things amuse little minds and I didn't need the food anyway so no harm was done. This behaviour is manifested when Parmer is on duty. It boggles the mind how petty things can get.

Here I sit at my desk in my cell. The "window" is before me but as the glass is clouded there is no view. It does, however, open and through the grate I get what small view of the world that is offered to me. I can see the dandelions now blooming, now seeding then passing to nakedness. Assorted grasses are on view though their nature evades me. At least the fresh air pours in though the winter wind comes through as well. On the ledge I keep the food I may need at a future date; a small stack of peanut butter cups, a bowl filled with marmalade, ketchup and mustard a tray filled with margarine, sugar and salt plus my cheese. In addition to these things I keep my coffee cups, two of them, a glass of juice, some wrapped bread and my plastic eating utensils. Underneath the coffee cups are a couple of paper towels while peeping out from under the bowl are my religious pamphlets. To the right of the window is my bed. Over this is my light that glows blue during the night, just like the night lights provided for children who are afraid of the dark. I've long since ceased to let it bother me. On the bed are two sheets tied to keep them on my mattress. My aches and pains garnered me two mattresses and over these are two blankets one folded double which keep me warm. My jacket with my clothes wrapped up in it make an adequate pillow. Further on, in sort of cubby hole is the sink, it's taps reduced to buttons where I can summon hot and cold water. Mostly I use cold as it takes too long to to get hot. Under the sink is the hot air vent. Next to the sink is a solid steel toilet, presumably so that one cannot smash it. There is no seat so one has to use it as is. I remember as a child squatting down to defecate over something more fragrant. At least there is toilet paper which is a vast improvement on the leaves we used in times long ago. Over the sink is what passes for a mirror, a chunk of polished steel.

The North wall contains the door with it's narrow window looking out on the recreation room. This door, apart from being solid steel, has another portal in it so that the guards can slide in your food tray and thereby have no contact with you at all. Mine didn't work well and they invariably opened the door. Sometimes we are even invited to get our own meals, what a treat! The feeding holes are there to prevent the guards from being bitten! The East wall contains an emergency switch like the ones we used on N to get the guards attention. A television of the most primitive style is anchored securely in the middle of the wall. It is encased in steel with a sheet of indestructible glass in front of it and you have to manipulate a pencil through five holes in order to turn it on, change channel or increase volume. After a while you get used to the routine. Better to have complete control of the idiot box than to share it with one whose programs you abhor. Above the TV is the remains of a notice board, Here it had been stripped to bare wall. Once more we come around to the South wall with its' three hangers underneath the bookshelf. To the left of the window is an outlet used for some purpose now long abandoned. In the three shelves are my possessions. On the top shelf are two pair of socks, my canteen, a couple of books and my rice cooker. On the second shelf are my health requirements; a pair of clippers, tooth brush and paste, pens, and medication, they allow me to self medicate. In the middle of all this I keep my notes. The bottom shelf holds my personal books, a box of crackers, other books including a bible, hymn book and a package of Worthers. Being in this room has liberated me. My world has been stripped down to one cell eight feet by six feet. My dwelling place and possessions have shrunk. I am reduced to the level of a monk so a monk I will be. I spend my days reading, writing and singing Gods praises. It's not so bad for one who waits.

The population of the jail is 80 to 90 percent drug users, as I found out when I arrived. Towards the end of my stay on N ward I had a cell mate who was in jail for theft. He had got high on heroin and subsequently robbed an ATM. When he arrived he was higher than kite and it took three days for him to come down. This story in various manifestations is repeated over and over again. Once down off the drugs they are decent people, most of them at any rate. We hear how big the drug problem is in society, how many of these people are dying of an overdose. We are spending millions on programs to prevent drug overdoses. I'm afraid that the only way to stop this deadly symptom is to separate those who use, and not in a jail, in a hospital or retreat facility. There the treatment must include job reorientation along with methods for stopping, not merely ceasing, the use of drugs. A conviction for someone high on drugs needs to contain a compulsory treatment course.

On to the food story. As far as institutional food goes it's not bad; a long way from bread and water. The rotation goes through a full month with only minor repetitions. Breakfast contains juice, milk, a muffin, cereal and coffee. Mondays, Wednesdays and Fridays were oatmeal or cream of wheat while on Tuesday and Thursday we received corn flakes or raisin bran. On the weekend we had to wait until ten AM before getting brunch, bacon and eggs on Saturday and sausages and pancakes on Sunday. Lunch was more varied ranging from cold potato salad and sandwich to potato and vegetables; today we had sloppy Joes. Celery, carrots, they preserved our sight so that we could join the night fighters, or a salad completed these meals. One phenomenon of jail food were it's fresh fruit not a lot of variety, usually an apple or an orange. It was a great mystery to me how one could obtain a perfectly crisp delicious apple when those in the stores were invariably soft and unappetizing. I suspect that proper storage was the solution. Supper was at 4:30 and was always a hot meal, Sometimes it was chicken, stew, meat patty, hamburger, meatballs or a lentil curry served with a variety of vegetables. My favourite meal which only came about once a month was a fabulous meat pie; simply delicious! It was served with a large cookie which could be traded for another pie! Sometimes you got mashed powdered potatoes, noodles or rice and sometimes a real baked potato. A curious occurrence with the potato was that, although it was real, it was treated with disdain. More of these potatoes were thrown away than any other item on the menu. Occasionally we would have roast turkey or, one of my favourites, ham with scalloped potatoes in a pineapple sauce.

Health care again. I have written them to complain about my swelling feet. They wrote a nasty note back saying ' to use your compression stockings. I can't seem to get through that the stockings just make it worse. Once more I'll try again. I sleep with my socks on as my feet get frozen without them.

Keeping up with the religious holidays is one way to help the day along. Holy week and I do my best to keep it. Mauday Thursday arrives and I read my office with readings from the passage for the feast day. The institution of the mass is clear in the flowing words' take, eat, this is my body given for you. Drink this, all of you, for this is my blood which is shed for you. Do this in remembrance of me.' Down through the ages comes this injunction. Good Friday we remember the crucifixion, the price in blood paid for our sins. A day of deep devotion before a glorious morning. He is risen! Alleluia!

MAUNDY THURSDAY

The altar is now prepared, exultant,
Candles lit, ablaze of glory, shining
In the night foreshadowing His death
Yet first this one expectant moment.
Take, eat for this is my body, broken.
Drink you all of this, my blood on Calvary,
Poured out for all of us, redemption.

EASTER MONDAY

At this time and place I awake.
Early morning sun streams in through
Frosted glass, unheeding of mans
Attempt to fool the strained senses.

At last I'm out, free for a while
To walk the yard, sun streaming
Down, illuminating the wall
Half down to where I stroll, basking.

Rays from the sun now heat me up,
I begin to sing a song for the Lord,
Who made us all in his image,
Alleluia to the God of Gods.

> The grass is gone, obliterated
> By concrete, barren and sterile.
> I stand, sun streaming around me
> As I sing of the glories of God.

It is now 75 days since I left N and only the fact that I am locked up 22 hours of the day mars my time. In the sixty days I have been in solitary I have grown into a routine. Breakfast is at six forty five, after which I read my office. We are usually let out for a time in the early morning so I go onto the ward and make coffee. I share this with whomever is up. One hour and back to my cell to read the paper or my religious book. I watch the cooking show for an hour before lunch at 11:00. Usually I have a nap as all that food makes me drowsy. After that I write for a while, read some more then it's time for supper. From about five o'clock on I read my science fiction novel before turning on the TV about seven o'clock. I watch the sports and the hockey is on so that I have plenty to watch and apart from that I watch The Learning Channel. At ten or ten thirty I am bagged and go to bed. As long as the cell next door to me turns their TV off I'm out like a light til five thirty or six o'clock at which point I start over again.

Joey is at home in jail. He in invariably cheerful and upbeat. Soon after the fiasco with Mair he got the job of cleaning the ward. We split goodies ; my orange, creamers and strawberry jam for his marmalade and egg sandwiches. We shared coffee and sometimes I gave him a slice of my cheese. There is not a broken bone his body as he shares his foodstuff with everyone, particularly those who need it. It is like I am his father and he my son in this wacky world of jail. The one thing we agree on is that B is quieter than any other ward. For over a month we had been cell mates and though his TV watching habits were deplorable he was a very good cell mate. We had been separated for about a month when Joey's time came. He was transferred to N. I talked to him and knew that he was going to be among friends.

GEESE

Two geese stroll along the fence,
A gander and a goose, waddling
Along, pecking and the solid ground,
Food gathering an endless search.

Clad in grey, a long black neck held high.
Perched upon these their tiny heads
A slash of white from ear to ear,
Outlining their graceful form.

They wander across the green grass.
Heads bobbing in their constant search.
Strolling the yard where I gaze at
Them longingly; free, unencumbered.

The paper saga continues. On ward N I saw the paper infrequently and it would disappear into a cell and not come out again. Occasional I got the weekend paper by being first up in the morning. This involved setting the buzzer to go to the bathroom. Once out you had a chance at reading one of only two papers. As I was an early riser I frequently had the paper and read it before the rest of the ward was even up. In block B it was different. If I was out early I got the paper and could spend and hour or so reading it from cover to cover. I'm sure that I was the only one person in the whole jail who read the paper in it's entirety. Some of the inmates took the Sudoku, some the comics but most of them flicked through the headlines. In B I had a problem. One of guards positively hated me and would give the paper to one of the GP people. One day the paper had disappeared into cell 121 and had not reappeared. This guard was fond of Kenny, a poor soul who stammered his way through life not knowing which side was up. He new that he had given it to the inmate in 121 so went to retrieve it. The conversation went like this.

"I need the paper now John. I need it for Kenny."
"I don't have the paper." The inmate replied.
"Come on John I know that you have it so please just give it to me."
"Ha. Ha. Ha. You can't have it. I'll send it down the toilet."
"Come on now. I don't want to have to come into your cell."
"Oh no ! It just flushed down the toilet. Ha. Ha. Ha."

All the time this was going on I was killing myself laughing. The stupid sod had given it to an inmate whom he knew didn't give the paper up and now was trying to get it back! He never did get the paper back though a new paper arrived at the cell and I got to read it as soon as Kenny had gone through it which lasted about two minutes. The other item of interest involved my visits. One day we were out about noon which would normally involve our getting out again about five o'clock. I went for my visit at three o'clock and returned about four thirty. During that time my group was let out and my time when I returned was non-existent. It appeared that I was to have only a visit or a second break but not both. It was rather amusing to see the pettiness of this guard and I made a weak protest then gathered up my things and went into my cell.

Last night I had a dream in which I was lying on the bottom bunk with someone over top of me. As the boy climbed out of his bunk he didn't come the usual way, rather he came through the side where there was only a little room. At last he reached my bunk and snuggled down close to me, I felt pyjamas close to me. We merged, his body lean and supple and I held onto the dream but it was fading. I was left alone in my cell. For twenty eight years I have been unable to consummate my dreams, they are fled in the holocaust of the past. A voice came to me then and said, "To err is human, to love divine." These dreams are but the combined memories of the past, come to us on gossamer wings. I have been unable to complete these dreams though they do not come often in my old age. I pondered the massage that was sent by this dream.

I got a shock when I arose for breakfast; Mair was there. Fortunately he was accompanied by Mr. McNabb, who was one of the better guards. He let me out at seven thirty and I stayed out until nine thirty. When my meds were delivered. Mr. Holiday was there and I breathed a sigh of relief. I plunged through this abyss until I could work this out. It would appear that Mair was being chaperoned. The population of the ward had shrunk to four from twelve. Once over my surprise I decided that I could not bear a grudge. O how hard it is to forgive someone when the other party still regards you as vermin.

Easter time and the glory and majesty of the risen Lord. At this time I received a second letter from Tyler. He wrote, "I sent you a letter of Happy Easter on April2 but it was sent back because the colouring on it got smudged and they thought I used crayons. So now I will say Happy Easter again as it is still Easter for 50 days! … I hope you are well. It is tough being in prison but God brings good out of everything for those who love Him and I know you do. Your Friend in Christ, Tyler Joseph. "There were other things in this letter but the sentiments expressed were much more sophisticated than any I had thought to come from a child who was born with downs syndrome. May God grant him peace. I cried once again.

Shortly after I received this letter I had a visit with Janice and she said that she would bail me out. It had been three hundred and five days since I entered this jail and I hugged this knowledge like my best friend. I sang in the courtyard and told Kevin that I would be getting out, maybe as soon as Friday. Even the reappearance of Mair could not stop the elation in my heart. Mr. McNab was on duty when the order finally came after dinner Friday. I was able to thank him for his humane treatment of me during my stay. Then it was off to the changing rooms where I put on my own clothing for the first time. They did not even inspect the folder that I was carrying. I was off! I was free! Roy picked me up and at last I was home.

WASP

Crawling over the grate of my cell,
In a vain attempt to get in.
The small holes of the screen impede
Our intrepid wasp now buzzing here.

Now flying, now crawling, probing near,
While his buzzing brings to mind memories
Of dim past scenes of other critters,
Etched on my mind, wasps upon window.

No! No! You can't get into my cell,
Though you try all access is barred,
Till you fly away, gone instantly,
To wander the jail in search of a home.

In prison you would think that being segregated for long periods of time would engender homosexual relationships. Quite the opposite is the reality. Not only does the jail frown upon such conduct, it goes out of the way to stamp out any and all physical contact. The best example of this was my attempt to calm Justin. Oh! He's touching him! He must be having sex with him. Naughty! Naughty! A few homosexuals are in jail but they are on the outside looking in. Ninety percent of the inmates are heterosexual and violently opposed to anything other than straight sex. This means that those who have committed crimes against women are on the lower end of the scale. There was nothing I missed more than the close contact with others. For ten months I have been locked up and no punishment is a cruel as the lack of physical contact. When I was on N there was some contact but by and large the inmates shunned it, with a few exceptions. Justin when he was placed in my room the first time would hand wrestle and when he left he gave me a big hug. Rick would often precipitate contact by tapping me on the shoulder. The only other contact came from Joey. When I was on N ward he would rub my back which felt inordinately good! On B he continued rubbing my back and frequently initiated contact. Since he left there was no one with whom to have contact.

As human beings, except for a small minority, we are programmed to share contact. We shake hands, kiss our loved ones and cuddle our children. In many cultures and hug or kiss is a common form of greeting for two males or females. Not in this society. In our age and culture it has become common for the female to accuse the male, particularly one of high status, of sexual assault even though the event took place 25 to 40 years ago. How can you possibly judge this event in this time and place? The press is guilty of spreading this malaise and are all over the event, and are allowed to print anything prejudicial to a trial. Sex sells newspapers. Once you are accused you are hung out to dry without the bother of a trial. Certainly eases the policeman's job. You are guilty until proven innocent. How wrong is this in a society that is supposed to be compassionate.

I read in the paper that another man had bitten the dust for sex he had committed thirty-five years ago. When will this persecution stop. Nearly all of the men are homosexual and to deride one for an act committed under different circumstances then to sentence him as a murderer makes no sense. We are all guilty of lust but we are all endowed by love. Can the consensual relationship of two men be pried apart thirty-five years later? A young man has little to offer except his body. If it is freely given how can it be condemned some thirty-five years later? The relationship of a youth to someone older is complicated. On the one hand the youth desires all of the benefits that an older man can give. You say, "But he or she is too young." Consent implies consent and at least in a number of these cases consent is what happened. At what age do you draw the line? It was fourteen and has recently been raised to sixteen. Somewhere in this mad rush to condemn those in a relationship there must be some compassion.

It has become too easy today to dig up sexual relationships now long passed. As soon as a sexual assault charge is laid the first thing the police do is publish what THEY KNOW, weather it is true or just blown smoke. Now the next item brought up by the police is "we will believe you." That opens up a Pandora's box of confessions, some of which are even legitimate. The accuser's family is now tarred with the same brush and is ostracized. Most marriages break down under the stress. All this has happened before the legitimacy of the charge is even tested in court. Everyone who ever knew you has been scattered and taken away except for the church. The church, in it's wisdom, although condemning the the act does not condemn the sinner. Throughout the ages it is not the flesh that is considered primogenitor of sins but rather of pride. All feel pride in that they are not like this man but the sin of pride makes the other sins, including adultery, pale in comparison. ' Let him that is without sin cast the first stone.' In their pride of righteousness they had condemned the woman caught in adultery, and Christ's answer is the same today as it was two thousand years ago. Will we two thousand years later cast the first stone?

AFTERWARDS

In late April I was released from prison after ten months. I must say that they were the most interesting ten months of my life. Here I was considering just playing bridge and going to church until I slowly faded away into the sunset. The last of the blossom trees were in bloom and just driving around with Roy made me feel alive again. When we reached home the lilac was in bloom and the fragrance was overpowering, the sweet scented smell of spring. On my rockery there was a violet bloom that covered a part of it and added a splash of colour to the stones. In the back yard the blackberries from the neighbours yard had taken control. I could see that there would be some work for me to do. The house was still the same but my son and daughter in law had taken over the whole house and there would have to be some space made for me to fit in. I agreed to bar-b-cuing my meat outside on the grill so that no odour of meat should permeate this vegan house hold. My bedroom was as I remembered it though rather a lot of additional stuff had been stored there. The living room was just as I left it with the Eastern half being filled with the chesterfields that provided room for plenty of guests. In the Western half my chair was there with the books lining the shelves and two other recliners spaced so that three could sit at ease. The hall was cluttered with cats toys and all the paraphernalia that comes with the four cats that the kids had acquired. The bathroom was a mess with a large hole in the ceiling where the repairman had fixed the leak in the pipes. There were things left over from Val and I had to sort out what was useful from what wasn't. The hallway was cluttered with assorted cat toys and cages that made getting to the bathroom quite difficult. The kitchen had been rearranged so that the freezer blocked the broom cupboard and the cat dishes were clustered around it in an L shape. On to the dining room and I found the recycling boxes fully full and ready to go out to the curb. Out on the deck my hot tub was perking away and I eagerly looked forward to the evening when I would plunge in.

The basement was not changed but tires and other objects had been put in my shop. My den was unchanged. The computer screen stared at me inviting me to transcribe the contents of my folder which I had laboured on for ten months. Same TV, video recorder and tape recorder still waiting for me to become reacquainted. All around me the tools of my trade and the memories of a lifetime filled the room. I was home. That night I watched my own TV though I don't remember whether I watched a video or not. By ten o'clock I was tired and headed off to the hot tub. Blessed relief! For an hour I sat in the jets moving hot water over me. I could lie out there under the stars and watch the planes go by. And, as I usually did, sang my songs to my creator. Then it was off to the bathroom where my electric toothbrush awaited me. One doesn't think too much about these things until you don't have them; then you realize what you are missing when you have a measly little brush to use. I was lucky or, as I believe, protected from any kind of toothache. I knew many residents who had bad teeth and I can only imagine what that was like. With a thankful prayer I retired to my own bed and slept the night away.

I had agreed to eat vegetarian while I was at home and to cook any meat over the barbecue. Now eating vegan after months of prison food was a bit of a come down but I stuck to my diet eating eggs, almond milk and vegetables. I had always eaten a muffin for breakfast and this time I cooked my own muffins. They came fresh out of the oven and I put tons of real butter on them. Eggs and cheese for lunch and whatever they chose to cook for supper. Real potatoes that could be baked, mashed or scalloped and then fried up again for breakfast. Meals were simple pleasures that were made bountiful by the company, to eat with other people instead of alone or in the presence of those who hated me. Above all was the music. My eclectic collection of CDs now came fully into play and the music of Motsarc, Brahms and Handel rang throughout the house. I heard once again the voices of Johnny Cash, the Everly brothers, the Rankins and more. The ecstatic sound of Kings College in the Deus Misereri echoed through the house and through my consciousness. Once more I heard my son's voice come clear to me, not through a veil of mistrust, as he sang with that glorious voice that only God can give. I was content.

For the first three weeks I was busy typing my poems and notes that I made in prison. I stayed at home and was driven to my appointments by Roy. These became increasingly difficult as his schedule and mine failed to coalesce. It culminated in my walking home from downtown as I had another appointment. I was exhausted! I was just too old to make that kind of journey. When they went to Vancouver on the weekend I insured my car and installed a battery so that I was no longer dependent on them for transportation. Once again I went to breakfast at the Crooked Goose which I had longed to do when I was looking out the prison window. It was a small crowd and I don't know quite how they took this. I was home but it was different. I talked with another couple who had a bi-polar son so the meal went well. It was great to be able to drive to my favourite park and walk again under the rhododendron with it's mass of blooms soaring twenty feet into the air. Once again I watched the water as it poured out of the basin making a rapid out of the narrows. In a quiet backwater stood a heron as it eyed the waters for fish. Again I went to the Crooked Goose and this time Fr. Don was there with his wife Virginia and we had a merry conversation.

I had by now finished my writing and had taken a breather from these activities which had taken a toll on me. Now, at last I was free to move on to other pursuits. It was good to get back into a routine without the interference of a jail cell. I shopped for the clothing that I would need for my trial. Getting my car ready was a priority and I went about the process of getting a new battery and insurance. I t seemed that the company who sold me the insurance had made a mistake and should not have give me their policy for an accident that my son had in 2013. Oh well! We just went back to the old ICBC policy. It was cheaper than the enhanced policy I had taken. Now gassed up and ready to go it was pleasant to be able to go to the places that I had haunted before. One doesn't realize the difference that driving makes until you don't have a car! Just to be able to drive to the park, to see the blossoms on the rhododendron, the water rushing over the rapids and the utter tranquility of the scene made it all worthwhile. In the shallows there was a heron wading and catching fish. His mate was at the other end of the park sitting on a post in the water. There are benches along the walk way and it is there I rest my tired bones and look at the incredible scenery. I pet the innumerable dogs that go by and talk to their owners which gives me a window into their lives. In the Japanese garden I take my last rest and gaze at the innumerable plants that blossom there. The lilies cover one bank while the water flows down into one pool after another until it reaches the larger pool with it's lily pads with flowers that bloom out of the water.

Now we sit at a crossroad. I do not know whether my case will turn out well or not but of this I'm sure, whatever God has planned for me will come to pass. I have lived for seventy-two years and have lived a life that would make a fairy tale in the real world. I have no regrets for to have them only amplifies them and no matter what course my life takes from here I will stand by it. Would it have turned out differently if I had been diagnosed with bi-polar in Riverview? Would I have stood by my first love had the circumstances been different, I do not know? Life is full of choices and I made those choices and take full responsibility for them. Perhaps it is my father's nature coming out in me but I have always stood apart from the rest of society and made up my own mind on matters. What I do know is that this society is playing with fire when it accepts the word of the accuser when the time is some thirty-five to fifty years in the past. In the end it doesn't matter as only God will judge for He alone knows the heart of what I have done.

Harry Sadd, 1st Canadian serial rights, May 9 2018

www.ingramcontent.com/pod-product-compliance
Lightning Source LLC
Chambersburg PA
CBHW030308080526
44584CB00012B/489